An Introduction to
Nineteenth-Century French Literature

NEW READINGS
**Introductions to European Literature and Culture**
Series Editor: Nicholas Hammond

*Retelling the Tale:*
*An Introduction to French Medieval Literature*
Simon Gaunt

*Creative Tensions:*
*An Introduction to Seventeenth-Century French Literature*
Nicholas Hammond

*The Search for Enlightenment:*
*An Introduction to Eighteenth-Century French Writing*
John Leigh

*An Introduction to Nineteenth-Century French Literature*
Tim Farrant

*An Introduction to Twentieth-Century French Literature*
Victoria Best

*French Cinema Since 1950: Personal Histories*
Emma Wilson

*The Challenges of Uncertainty:*
*An Introduction to Seventeenth-Century Spanish Literature*
Jeremy Robbins

*An Introduction to Twentieth-Century Italian Literature:*
*A Difficult Modernity*
Robert S.C. Gordon

# An Introduction to Nineteenth-Century French Literature

### Tim Farrant

Bristol Classical Press

**Published by Bristol Classical Press 2012**

Bristol Classical Press, an imprint of Bloomsbury Publishing Plc

Bloomsbury Publishing Plc
50 Bedford Square
London WC1B 3DP
www.bloomsburyacademic.com

Copyright © Tim Farrant 2007

First published by Gerald Duckworth & Co. Ltd. 2007

The author has asserted his rights under the Copyright, Designs and
Patents Act 1988 to be identified as the author of this work.

ISBN: 978 0 715 62907 9

A CIP catalogue record for this book is available from the British Library

Typeset by e-type, Liverpool

Printed and bound by CPI Group (UK) Ltd, Croydon, CR0 4YY

*Photo credits*: p. 24 Gemäldegalerie, Dresden;
p. 126: Réunion des Musées Nationaux.

# Contents

Acknowledgements     7
Author's Note     8
Preface     9
Chronology     11

**1. Histories**     13
    1.1. Napoleon: myth and impact     13
    1.2. *Désenchantement* and *arrivisme*     16
    1.3. Representing the contemporary: histories and novels     23
**2. Stories**     33
    2.1. Confessional narratives     33
    2.2. Memoirs and autobiographies     37
    2.3. Short stories     45
**3. Poetry**     52
    3.1. From Classicism to iconoclasm     53
    3.2. Lyricism and vision     56
      3.2.1. Lyricism: Lamartine and Desbordes-Valmore     56
      3.2.2. Vision: Hugo and Baudelaire     60
    3.3. Things and effects     66
      3.3.1. *L'Art pour l'art* and Parnassianism: Gautier and
          Leconte de Lisle     66
      3.3.2. Verlaine     69
      3.3.3. Rimbaud     71
      3.3.4. Mallarmé     78
**4. Drama**     86
    4.1. Public and private, political and personal     86
    4.2. Dramas of money and morals     93
    4.3. The farce of objects: Labiche and Feydeau     96
      4.3.1. Labiche: *Un Chapeau de paille d'Italie*     96

4.3.2. Feydeau: *Le Dindon*                                      99
4.3.3. Becque: *Les Corbeaux*                                   101
4.4. Dramas of interiority: Maeterlinck, *Pelléas et Mélisande*
    and *Intérieur*                          103

**5. Novels**                                                  109
5.1. From Gothic to modern                                     110
5.2. Fiction: a women's genre?                                 116
5.3. Serialisation and seriousness: the *roman-feuilleton*     120
5.4. Reality and Realism                                       123
5.5. Objectivity and vision                                    125
5.6. Naturalism and the novel                                  129

**6. Modernities**                                             135
6.1. Science, subjectivity and fiction                         135
6.2. Dreams, prose poetry, subjectivity and the
    Unconscious                             146
6.2.1. Dreams: Nerval                                          146
6.2.2. Prose poetry: Baudelaire, Lautréamont                   149
6.2.3. Subjectivity and the Unconscious: Laforgue              154
6.3. Modernity and experiment in theatre                       157

**7. Margins, Peripheries and Centres**                        168
7.1. Space, place and perspective                              168
7.1.1. Paris and the provinces                                 169
7.2. Artists and bourgeois, bohemians and dandies              172
7.3. Gender and sexuality                                      176
7.4. Travel, the exotic and race                               180
7.4.1. Travel and the exotic                                   180
7.4.2. Race                                                    183
7.4.3. Anti-Semitism and the Dreyfus affair                    186
7.5. Coda: two telling texts                                   188

Glossary of Literary Figures                                   195
Index                                                          211

*Illustrations (on pages 24 and 126)*

G. Courbet, *Les Casseurs de pierres* (1850), formerly Dresden, Gemäldegalerie; E. Manet, *Le Déjeuner sur l'herbe* (1863), Paris, Musée d'Orsay.

# Acknowledgements

Sincere thanks are owed to Nick Hammond, and to Martin Rynja and Deborah Blake of Duckworth, for their tact and patience in seeing this project to fruition. I am particularly grateful to Adrianne Tooke for her meticulous reading of, and invaluable comments on, the final draft, and to Simon Thomson for indispensable technical support. The librarians of the Taylor Institution, Oxford were, as always, unfailingly helpful. I am greatly indebted to the University of Oxford and to Pembroke College for generous sabbatical assistance, and to the many scholars whose work may have informed these pages but who, in this footnote-free environment, must remain otherwise unrecognised. Finally, I must thank my wife, Juliet, for her astute advice and unstinting interest in the whole enterprise. Under its initial title, *Romantic Realities*, it is appreciatively dedicated to her.

# Author's Note

For ease of reading, detailed bibliographical references have been kept to a minimum. References to novels, poetry collections and plays are given in the form I.1, 1.22 (Book/Volume/Act I, Chapter/poem/scene 1, line 22). Versification is notated conventionally, e.g. 6.6 = alexandrine line, two hemistichs of six syllables. Suggestions for further reading are made at the end of each chapter; unless otherwise indicated, works cited are published in Paris. Translations of passages quoted are my own.

# Preface

The nineteenth century is arguably the defining century of French literature. It produced some of the world's greatest novelists – Hugo, Balzac, Flaubert, Zola, Dumas, Verne – and, in Mérimée and Maupassant, some of its greatest storytellers, too. They continue to delight all kinds of readers, just as dramas like *Hernani*, or *Lorenzaccio*, or *Cyrano de Bergerac*, or the farces of Labiche and Feydeau, still engage both on the stage and on the page. Its poets – Hugo, Baudelaire, Rimbaud, Mallarmé – have lost none of their power to move, enlighten, challenge, or suggest. There is, in fact, no genre in which the literature of nineteenth-century France is not outstanding.

The overall shape of this book is chronological. But within that broadly chronological frame, I shall be combining exploration of themes, genres, authors and texts. History is the raw material of the past, story, its particular narrative formulation. So Chapter 1 will explore the historical context of the beginning of the century, through a defining figure, Napoleon, and a defining moment, Waterloo, before looking at the particular responses to history in the historical novels of Balzac, Stendhal and Mérimée. Chapter 2 looks at the apparent opposite of this broad narrative fresco, first-person narrative and autobiography, and at a form that is both a cultural constant yet also the litmus test of social circumstance, the short story. Chapters 3, 4 and 5 deal respectively with poetry, drama and novels, each in essentially chronological order. Building on this chronology, Chapter 6 looks at various forms of modernity in the novel, poetry and drama – ways in which the nineteenth century anticipates its successors. Chapter 7 closes by looking at marginal themes and texts which, paradoxically, illuminate some central issues, ending with two, *Cyrano de Bergerac* and *Le Journal d'une femme de chambre*, which both express key tensions of their era, yet have had a peculiar fascination for our own. Throughout, my aim has been to map the great authors, movements, texts, but also to make some new connections, to expose the unfamiliar, and see the familiar afresh. The nineteenth century is two hundred years distant. But with each new reader, it can still speak powerfully today.

# Chronology

1789 *Assemblée des États-Généraux*; storming of the Bastille (14 July); march on Versailles; *Déclaration des droits de l'homme et du citoyen*

1792 Fall of the Monarchy; declaration of the Republic

1793 Execution of Louis XVI (21 January)

1797-9 Directory

1799 Consulate; Napoleon's *coup d'état* of *18 brumaire* (9-10 November)

1800 Creation of *Banque de France*

1802 Promulgation of *Concordat* with the Papacy

1804 Empire; Napoleon crowned Emperor; *Code civil*

1814 Napoleon abdicates; First Restoration; *Charte constitutionnel* of Louis XVIII; Congress of Vienna (September 1814-June 1815)

1815 Napoleon seizes power during the Hundred Days (20 March-28 June); Waterloo (18 June); Second Restoration (July)

1816 *Charte* promising rights to individuals

1824 Accession of Charles X

1830 July Revolution (28-30 July); abdication of Charles X; accession of Louis-Philippe; 1830-47 conquest of Algeria

1848 Revolution; abdication of Louis-Philippe (23-24 February); Constitution of Second Republic (4 November)

1851 *Coup d'état* of Louis-Napoléon Bonaparte (2 December)

1852 Proclamation of Second Empire (1 December)

1853 Haussmann's reconstruction of Paris begins

1859-93 French quest for control of Indochina

1870 Franco-Prussian war; France defeated; Napoleon III captured at Sedan (2 September); Third Republic proclaimed (4 September); Siege of Paris

1871 Paris Commune (28 March-28 May), ended by Versaillais march on Paris (21 May); Armistice; Government of Thiers; evacuation of five departments by Prussians; National Assembly in Bordeaux

1873 Resignation of Thiers (May); end of German occupation (September); Constitution of Third Republic

1879 National Assembly returns to Paris

1881 Tunis becomes French protectorate

1882 *Loi Ferry* establishing free primary education

1886 Boulanger Minister of War

1887 Indochinese union; Cochin-China, Annam, Cambodia and Tonkin under French rule

1889 Boulanger elected in Paris (January); flees capital (April); Republican election victory (September)

1894 Dreyfus found guilty of spying

1898 Zola, *J'accuse* (January); Formation of *Comité de l'Action Française*

1899 Dreyfus retried, found guilty of high treason with extenuating circumstances

1904 Anglo-French *Entente Cordiale* (April)

1905 Establishment of *Parti Socialiste*; separation of Church and State (December)

1906 Dreyfus pardoned

1908 *L'Action Française* becomes a daily paper

1940 France defeated and occupied; constitution of Third Republic suspended

# 1

# Histories

## 1.1. Napoleon: myth and impact

Centuries have a way of starting late: the nineteenth is no exception. Napoleon's 1815 defeat at Waterloo drew a line under France's Enlightenment adventure, definitively establishing the Restoration, a flashback to the *ancien régime*. Napoleon, embodiment of eighteenth-century rationalism in his 1799 self-proclamation as First Consul, had proved to be a tyrant, exiling or executing opponents, taking all power unto himself. A tactically brilliant solider, unrivalled in snatching great victories – Ulm, Austerlitz, Jena, Eylau, Wagram – from the jaws of defeat, he was also a ruthless adventurer, sending millions to their deaths in ultimately fruitless wars. A titanic, mesmeric leader, he had turned France into Europe, and Europe into France, ranging her Empire to Africa, to the Balkans, to the Baltic, and to Russia, with forty-four million subjects in his sway. A dictator of genius, he endowed her with institutions that serve her to this day: the *Banque de France*, centralised administration, specialised schools for her military and political elites and, in the *Code civil*, a unified legal system. The first great soldier to exploit the new mobility of armies, with light guns and fast horses on straight, smooth roads, he became the very emblem of social mobility, creating a new nobility; yet this supposed guarantor of revolutionary freedoms, in attempting to turn the Church and nobles to his ends, entrenched some of the old regime's most reactionary features, surrounding himself with courtiers, appointing relations and favourites to top posts (or thrones). Barrès dubbed him a 'professeur d'énergie'. He was a visionary, but a knave.

Napoleon is the century's founding political fact. Both supporters and opponents would define themselves against him. Those to whom he had opened the way, and which the Restoration would apparently convert or cast out, would, throughout the Restoration and July Monarchy, offer a persistent political alternative, eventually realised with the *coup d'état* of his nephew, Louis-Napoléon Bonaparte, on 2 December 1851. Not even the defeat of the Emperor Napoleon III, as he became the following year, and of France at Sedan in September 1870, would finally expunge Napoleon's legend, which persists in the French liking for strong unifying rulers – Boulanger, Pétain, De Gaulle – in the face of political diversity and dissent.

But Napoleon is also a founding literary fact. His sheer momentousness provokes starkly polarised reactions – sometimes in the same writer. Chateaubriand's *De Buonaparte et des Bourbons*, written in 1814, the year of the first Restoration, is an invective against a fraudulent tyrant; his *Vie de Napoléon* (*Mémoires d'outre-tombe*, books 19-24, completed 1840, ed. M. Fumaroli, 1999) is very different: a memoir of an exceptional destiny, and a lament for a significant Other reflecting the statesman poet Chateaubriand himself:

> … après Napoléon, néant: on ne voit venir ni empire, ni religion, ni barbares. La civilisation est montée à son plus haut point, mais civilisation matérielle, inféconde, qui ne peut rien produire, car on ne saurait donner la vie que par la morale; on n'arrive à la création des peuples que par les routes du ciel: les chemins de fer nous conduisent seulement avec plus de rapidité à l'abîme.... (*Mémoires d'outre-tombe*, XXIX.12)

> (… after Napoleon, oblivion: we see the arrival neither of empire, nor religion, nor barbarians. Civilisation has reached its highest point, but an infertile material civilisation, which can produce nothing, for it is not possible to give life save through morality. Peoples can only be created via the paths of the sky: railways merely lead us more rapidly to the abyss....)

Napoleon's very brilliance has destroyed everything in its wake; for the Royalist Chateaubriand, Napoleon's very rationalism has created a materialism he laments. The Republican Béranger's most famous song, *Le Roi d'Yvetot* (1815), is anti-Napoleonic, yet amused Napoleon; but his anti-clerical, anti-Royalist pieces contributed significantly to the Restoration's downfall, and during the July Monarchy helped to keep the Emperor's legend alive. Stendhal's journals and two lives of Napoleon (1817, 1836) display an ambivalence towards the Emperor developed in his novels. In *Le Rouge et le noir* (1830), Julien Sorel makes Napoleon's memoir, the *Mémorial de Saint-Hélène*, his Bible, interiorising Imperial discipline and duty in both his life and loves. In *La Chartreuse de Parme* (1839), the hero, Fabrice, reflects a different aspect of the Emperor – the adventurer. Victor Hugo, son of a Republican, and later Napoleonic, General, first a Royalist, later a Republican, and always abreast of his times, provides various views of Napoleon during his long career. But they can be summarised by one line from very early on:

Tu domines notre âge; ange ou démon, qu'importe? ('Lui', *Les Orientales*, 40, 1.79, 1828)

(You dominate our age; angel or demon, does it matter?)

For Hugo, as for Chateaubriand, Napoleon is an almost Miltonic figure, an amoral fallen angel, a sublime of evil and of good, an incontrovertible absolute, 'Lui', 'Him', against which all else is measured. When, 25 years later, Hugo, in exile from Napoleon III's dictatorial regime, measures the gulf between Napoleon I and his nephew, he sets the epic against the petty and the noble against the base:

Te voilà, nain immonde, accroupi sur ce nom. ('Napoléon III', *Les Châtiments*, VI.1, 1.2)

(You've arrived, you odious dwarf, squatting on this name.)

Hier la grande armée, et maintenant troupeau. ('L'Expiation', *Les Châtiments*, V.13, l.8)

(Yesterday the Grand Army, today a mere flock.)

Hugo and Napoleon III invoke the Emperor's legend, but to opposite ends, Napoleon III to bolster his regime, Hugo to destroy it. Such paradoxes also inform political responses, illustrating how Bonaparte, or Bonapartist leaders like Napoleon III or Boulanger, can appear both as exceptional individuals yet also as embodiments of the people. Napoleon's paradoxes reflect the paradoxes of his age, perhaps indeed of France: its need to contain and channel dynamism and diversity within unity. But more tellingly, these differing, sometimes diametrically opposite reactions can help to alert us to the subjectivity of response itself. As Barrès observed, Napoleon is 'capable de servir de centre, de point de contact aux imaginations françaises, aux plus simples comme aux plus civilisés' ('capable of serving as a centre, a point of contact for French imaginations, for the simplest and most civilised alike'). His personality and purposes provoke interpretative problems, raising questions about where truth really lies.

Napoleon raises moral problems, too – about the validity of means and ends, about how applicable the Napoleonic example may be to the individual – problems, given Napoleon's meritocracies, with wide appeal, explored in the Romantic *arriviste* (or careerist) novel, as we shall see. Napoleon combines these problems with a powerful aesthetic appeal – that of a sublimely energetic yet perhaps also sublimely amoral personality, composed of contradictory, almost conflictual and schizophrenic qualities that spoke powerfully to a turbulent, tormented age. Napoleon, more than a man, is an idea – an idea of the sublime.

### 1.2. *Désenchantement* and *arrivisme*

Napoleon's defeat left not only a political void, but also an existential void. Writers of the next generation lamented the loss of an epic grandeur, which, they imagined, their fathers had enjoyed. The July Monarchy – that of Louis-Philippe, the *roi bourgeois*, the reign of money and the rising bourgeoisie – seemed to close down opportunities for heroism and imagination, in deference to the rule of grocers, the emblematically boring, repressive, bean-counters of their day, and what Balzac calls 'l'omnipotence de l'argent' ('the omnipotence of money'). Nowhere is this disenchantment, or *mal du siècle*, more poignantly expressed than in the second chapter of Musset's *La Confession d'un enfant du siècle* (1836):

> Alors s'assit sur un monde en ruines une jeunesse soucieuse. Tous ces enfants étaient des gouttes d'un sang brûlant qui avait inondé la terre; ils étaient nés au sein de la guerre, pour la guerre. (...) Ils n'étaient pas sortis de leurs villes, mais on leur avait dit que, par chaque barrière de ces villes, on allait à une capitale d'Europe. Ils avaient dans la tête tout un monde; ils regardaient la terre, le ciel, les rues et les chemins; tout cela était vide, et les cloches de leurs paroisses résonnaient dans le lointain.

> (Then troubled youth sat down on a world in ruins. All these children were drops of a burning blood that had flooded the earth; they had been born in the bosom of war, for war. [...] They had not left their towns, but they had been told that, by each gate of those towns, you went to one of Europe's capitals. They had a whole world in their heads; they cast their gaze at the earth, the sky, the roads and the paths; all that they saw was empty, and the bells of their parishes rang out in the distance.)

Musset makes the political personal. The disruption of history is offered as an explanation for the protagonist, Octave's, personal disruption; for the restlessness that makes him permanently dissatisfied, and a trusting, enduring relationship or successful career impossible. His story challenges us to decide whether the explanation is merely an excuse. The first-person narrative offers unrivalled opportunities for special pleading, and this text has long suffered from being seen merely as a self-indulgent transposition of its author's affair with George Sand. Yet it presents itself as a confession, with the implicit hope of repentance and amendment; and as the confession of an *enfant du siècle* – a 'child of the century', with an explicitly representative status. Musset's *Confession*, as it is generally known (rather than as its protagonist's, Octave's), can be seen not just as the personal memoir of either of them, but also as a narrative about the displacement and frustration of desire, a lament at the impossibility of achieving fulfilment in the contemporary world. It is no accident that Octave's only, albeit temporarily, successful relationship should be with Brigitte, a woman he meets after the death of his father and who acts towards him like a mother, symbolising Octave's inability to grow up and move forward in the world. His love affair with a mother figure compensates for the absent fathers described in Chapter 2; he remains, in the most absolute sense, an *enfant*. Chateaubriand, and his fictional analogue, *René*, engage in intensely emotional, quasi-incestuous relationships with their sister, in Chateaubriand's case for lack of a real lover in the external world, and as a result of love withheld, or unfelt, by Chateaubriand's father. And in Flaubert's *L'Éducation sentimentale* (published in 1869, and thus written under the reign of Napoleon's nephew, Napoleon III), the hero Frédéric Moreau, the literary offspring of Octave and René, like them disenchanted with the contemporary, pursues a novel-long affair with the maternal Mme Arnoux (whom Flaubert originally called Mme Moreau), passing up his final chance to seduce her for fear of committing a kind of incest. In each case, the refusal, or inability, to consummate mature sexual relationships with another betrays the disappointment of more overarching hopes and desires. It symbolises an inability to move on.

Musset, or rather, Octave, then, retreats from a contemporary reality he cannot master, interiorising desires he cannot realise outside. Julien Sorel, in *Le Rouge et le noir*, makes the personal political, exploiting, rather than regretting, the Napoleonic model, and applying it to his own internal life. Napoleon's example as an outsider triumphantly conquering French society is used by Julien, a peasant, as a way of making his own way through its ranks. He applies Napoleonic energy and method to his career in the Church, which, in the Restoration, has replaced the army as the principal means of ascent. And Napoleonic principles, apparently unworkable in Restoration society, are internalised in his personal life, Napoleonic duty becoming a pretext for prosecuting love affairs like military campaigns. He sets himself tasks like battlefield objectives, determining that he must kiss his employer's wife's, Mme de Rênal's, hand before the clock strikes ten, or seduce the aristocratic Mathilde de la Mole simply because she is his social superior, 'née dans le camp ennemi' ('born in the enemy camp'). Balzac's Rastignac, in *Le Père Goriot*, pursues a similarly Napoleonic objective in his conquest of Parisian high society. It is a Napoleonic Paris that Rastignac surveys at the novel's end, in a Napoleonic posture:

> Il lança sur cette ruche bourdonnante un regard qui semblait par avance en pomper le miel, et dit ces mots grandioses: 'A nous deux maintenant!'
>
> Et pour premier acte du défi qu'il portait à la Société, Rastignac alla dîner chez Mme de Nucingen.
>
> (He cast on this buzzing hive a gaze that seemed to suck out its honey in advance, and said these grandiose words: "It's down to the two of us now!" // And, for the first act in the challenge he was making to society, Rastignac went to dine with Mme de Nucingen.)

Yet that his heroic act should be merely going to dine at his lover's table is enough to tell us that heroism is no longer possible in the modern age, that mere personal ambition and selfishness are all that can stand in for the Emperor's Grand Design. To apply a political, or ideological, or indeed any extraneous model to the personal, without at least trying it for size, is to err profoundly indeed: neither Rastignac nor Sorel does so without profoundly compromising his integrity. Rastignac resists the criminal Vautrin's blandishments, but, like the trusting old man Goriot's profitably married daughters,

is seduced by the lure of high society away from his initial innocence and altruistic devotion to Goriot himself. Julien betrays Mme
de Rênal in favour of the more socially advantageous Mathilde
before seeing the light, rejecting the pseudo-aristocratic alias ('M. le
Chevalier de la Vernaye') he had adopted for social advancement
and, significantly, acknowledging his own true identity as a peasant
who has risen up against his lowly fortune when he is tried for
attempting to kill her. Only in prison does he realise that public
success is at the expense of private truth to the self: 'Je suis hypocrite
comme s'il y avait là quelqu'un pour m'écouter' ('I am being as
hypocritical as if someone were there listening to me'); 'J'oublie de
vivre et d'aimer, quand il me reste si peu de jours a vivre' ('I am
forgetting to live and love when I have so few days left to live') (*Le
Rouge et le noir*, II.44). These men gain the whole world, but lose
their true selves.

Rastignac and Sorel are *arrivistes*, careerists who ruthlessly pursue
their own objectives to make their way in the world, part of the
generation born with the century that came from the provinces to
Paris in the years around 1820, writers like Balzac and Dumas, but
also the lawyer-historians and politicians Mignet and Thiers,
bearers of bourgeois liberal ideas that would triumph in the July
Revolution – of the alliance of youth, the people and ideals marvel-
lously realised in the painting by Delacroix (another member of this
generation), *La Liberté guidant le peuple* (1830). In its combination of
the real (the pistol-bearing boy, the barricades, the gun smoke) and
the ideal, Delacroix's painting expresses many of the contradictions
inherent in nineteenth-century French writing – between self and
society, the individual and history, the real and the romantic.
Indeed, Romanticism, the century's determinant literary, artistic,
and cultural movement, is at root a form of Realism, the kind of art
most capable of speaking to present generations (Stendhal, *Racine et
Shakespeare*, 1823, 1825, 3) and according to Hugo, 'le libéralisme
dans l'art' ('liberalism in art') (*Cromwell*, Preface, 1827). For
Baudelaire, Romanticism was 'dans la manière de sentir' ('in the
manner in which one feels') (*Salon de 1846*). The last two remarks

stress the importance of freedom (from aesthetic, but also political, rules), and of subjectivity – the pre-eminence of the individual's own world view, progenitor of the individualism that marks the modern western mindset. From them flow Romanticism's many secondary manifestations: the adulation of nature, especially of nature as embodying God; salvation through art as a surrogate religion; the suffering individual, adrift in a world that is out of joint; the specificities of the exotic and local colour; escape in time and place, often via stimulants and dream. Implicit in all these, however, is a paradoxical relation between subjective and objective, between the 'romantic' and the 'real'. The one cannot exist without the other, the romantic without a reality to kick against. Rastignac and Sorel are both 'romantic' and 'real', individuals yet also types, fictional representatives of real, wider social phenomena, as well as being fictional individualists, striving for self-fulfilment. The type is a central concept in Realist fiction, embodying in the particular more general social relations, mirroring the real historical forces of the time.

Yet the relationship between history and story, between raw events and the narratives that are made of them, can be significantly more displaced than the straightforward parallel between fictional characters and their real counterparts might suggest. The story of Julien Sorel, for example, can be seen as effectively mapping the post-revolutionary history of France. Julien denies his own authentic identity, his very paternity, assuming the aristocratic alias M. le Chevalier de la Vernaye, and swapping his secretary's black coat for a noble's blue one, in order to become socially acceptable when he becomes M. de la Mole's secretary and is to marry his daughter Mathilde. Julien's story parallels the cover-up in the official history of France, in which the Restoration king Louis XVIII was presented as the heir of a line of *ancien régime* monarchs unbroken since Saint Louis, whereas in fact he was the brother of Louis XVI, who had been guillotined in 1793. (Louis XVI's son, the titular Louis XVII, had died as a boy in 1795.) Similarly, Rastignac's devotion to 'Père Goriot' ('father Goriot'), can be seen as a fictionalised version of the French national quest, during the Restoration, to find a father figure

in the king – a role that, in *Le Père Goriot,* the infernal criminal
Vautrin also appears, for a while, to fill. As Vautrin tells Lucien de
Rubempré in *Illusions perdues* (1837-43):

> Il y a deux Histoires: l'Histoire officielle, menteuse, qu'on enseigne
> (...) et puis l'Histoire secrète, où sont les véritables causes des événe-
> ments, une Histoire honteuse.

> (There are two kinds of History: the official, mendacious History that
> is taught [...] and then secret History, wherein lie the real causes of
> events, a History of shame.)

In Flaubert's 1869 novel *L'Éducation sentimentale,* it is *arrivisme* itself,
and the novels that portray it, that has become the myth. Its 'hero',
Frédéric Moreau, is a promising young man, trying to make his way
in Paris 'comme Rastignac dans *La Comédie humaine*', as his sidekick
Deslauriers tells him. But the very pairing of dreamer hero and plod-
ding friend goes back to Cervantes's seminal *Don Quixote* (1605-15),
reflected in later pairings like Wilhelm and Werner in Goethe's
*Wilhelm Meister* (1796-1829). Even *L'Éducation sentimentale*'s main
female characters reflect fictional stereotypes the hero can exploit in
his attempted social ascent: Mme Arnoux the angelic woman, the
prostitute Rosanette, Mme Dambreuse the *femme-marchepied* (literally,
'stepping-stone'), Louise Roque the heiress. The 'angel'/'whore'
opposition (here Mme Arnoux/Rosanette) echoes the contrast
between Brigitte and Octave's first unfaithful mistress in Musset's
*Confession*; the *femme-marchepied,* Rastignac's mentor, Mme de
Beauséant, in *Le Père Goriot*; the heiress, Eugénie Grandet, in Balzac's
eponymous novel. We are left to decide whether these female stereotypes mirror social realities, or are mere products of the (writer's,
reader's, protagonists') misogynistic imaginings. That they might be
the latter, pieces of sadistic wish-fulfilment, is suggested in the recon-
ciling of these opposites in the figure of Marguerite, the courtesan
redeemed by love in Dumas *fils*'s *La Dame aux camélias* (1848), and in
France's *Thaïs* (1890), the story of a courtesan turned saint.

The problem of the reality, or otherwise, of female stereotypes can be a litmus test for the larger, and more metaphysical, problem of the authenticity of both the individual's acts and socio-political reality. In *L'Éducation sentimentale*, Frédéric's actions are guided by, but parody, his famous *arriviste* precursors: instead of journeying up to Paris, he begins by travelling away from it; instead of making a brilliant *début*, he spectacularly flunks his exams; he inherits a fortune, but squanders it, as he does the chance to begin a ministerial career. Where the Napoleonic *arriviste* impacts decisively on the larger world, Frédéric is so absorbed by his internal one that he is incapable of acting decisively at all. Political 'reality' itself is subsumed by the individual's preoccupations, and by imitation: the 1848 Revolution passes scarcely noticed by Frédéric, his mind set on sleeping with Rosanette, while the members of the *Club de l'intelligence*, whose name deliberately recalls the great revolutionary clubs of 1789, can only parrot clichés and applaud a speech in Spanish, a language they do not understand. Both language and experience have become detached from reality; authenticity, spontaneity, fall prey to cliché; reality becomes a matter of fiction. This 'histoire morale des hommes de ma génération' as Flaubert put it ('moral' or 'psychological history of the men of my generation') shows both history, and the moral, to be a matter of psychology, its sentimental education revealing only that in politics, as in the personal, progress is impossible, reality a matter of perception.

## 1.3. Representing the contemporary: histories and novels

These novels by Balzac and Stendhal can be described as early Realist novels – novels that attempt to provide an objective account of contemporary social reality. Realism did not crystallise as an artistic and literary phenomenon until 1855, when the painter Courbet, with the support of his writer friend Champfleury, set up his own exhibition, 'Le Réalisme', in opposition to the official art establishment that had been scandalised by canvasses such as *Les Casseurs de pierres* (*The Stone Breakers*, 1850) foregrounding, but monumentalising, the vulgar and the unwashed – a literally gritty Realism.

Gustave Courbet, *Les Casseurs de pierres* (1850),
formerly Dresden, Gemäldegalerie.

But the word *réalisme* is first recorded with an aesthetic rather than philosophical sense in the *Mercure français du XIXe siècle* in 1826, and was applied in 1835 to Hugo's poetry, as a criticism of its excessively material, visual qualities; these allegedly neglected the spirituality which, in the view of this conservative critic and of the establishment he represented, should be the very essence of poetry. In 1855, Courbet and Champfleury thus appropriate what had hitherto been a term of abuse, making the term *réalisme* their vehicle, much as, in our own day, gay people have validated the word 'queer'. (We will be dealing with Realism in more detail in Chapter 5.)

Yet Realism, in essence if not yet in name, underpins the work of earlier writers like Stendhal and Balzac. What we now call the French Realist novel grew from the historical novel, the dominant novel genre in 1820s France, its popularity in turn deriving from France's anxiety about its present, expressed through an obsession with its past. The 1820s and 1830s saw the appearance of major histories, notably by Barante, Thierry and Michelet. The century was to be one of great historians – Michelet, but also Tocqueville and Quinet, memorable variously as colourful, poetic storytellers (Thierry, Michelet, Quinet), political actors, theorists or provocateurs (Michelet, Tocqueville, Quinet), or detached, appraising scholars (Fustel de Coulanges; the *Revue historique,* the senior French academic history journal, was founded in 1876).

The paradox of the historical novel is essentially the paradox of history. On the one hand, its authority and authenticity depended on its veracity – on its supposed use of documentary evidence or archival research. On the other, like Romantic history itself, it was a work not just of the intellect, but also of the imagination, whose concerns were governed not just by the past or its materials, but by the preoccupations of the present. (Thierry, indeed, believed that history should be constantly retold from the perspective of the present.) It was the present that determined the tastes both of writers and of readers for the past. So the great Romantic historical novels were those that spoke most closely, if sometimes covertly, to that present. The greatest French success of Sir Walter Scott, whose works launched the vogue for the genre in France, was his novel *Quentin Durward* (1823), which appealed because of its continental setting, telling the story of the fight for the creation of France that appealed particularly to a nation questioning its own identity. Vigny's *Cinq-Mars* (1825) and Mérimée's *Chronique du règne de Charles IX* (1829) do something similar, the conflicts between Reformation and Counter-reformation paralleling the struggle between Revolution and Reaction. Balzac's *Les Chouans, ou la Bretagne en 1800* (1829; originally *Le Dernier Chouan*) mimics both Fenimore Cooper's *The Last of the Mohicans* (1826) and Scott's *Waverley, or 'Tis Sixty Years Since* (1814). Like both these novels, it deals with a dynamic conflict between the forces of progress and reaction, in the case of *Les Chouans* between Republican forces and those of the Royalist reaction in western France. Such conflicts were later treated by Barbey d'Aurevilly in *L'Ensorcelée* (1854) and *Le*

*Chevalier des Touches* (1864), and most memorably by Victor Hugo in his last novel, *Quatrevingt-treize* (1874).

In many ways, then, historical novels are actually about the present, something revealed by a fascination, yet impatience, with the paraphernalia of the past. Even one of Scott's greatest admirers, Balzac, sees the genre as formulaic, and in *Illusions perdues* (1837-43, but set in the 1820s) gives the formula: dialogues, description, action. Mérimée's *Chronique* sends up this model, refusing to give the reader the thing historical novel readers most expect – a description of the protagonist's face and dress – sending him instead to see his bust in the *Musée d'Angoulême* (today's Louvre: *Chronique du règne de Charles IX*, 8). In refusing description, Mérimée attacks the foundation of the historical novel – the supposed evidence that the writer has done some research, the guarantee of a straightforward, factual relationship between language and reality. Mérimée's refusal throws the reader back on himself, apparently inviting him to do his own research, but actually referring him to the only verifiable source of truth – his own judgement and imagination.

Mérimée's novel, however, hardly killed off description entirely: in Hugo's *Notre-Dame de Paris* (1831), for example, it is both the guarantor of veracity and the agent of the imaginative evocation of the past. In Balzac, who effectively applies Scott's historical novel technique to the present, it supposedly attests the fiction's factual reality, and gives access to the truth about a character and his milieu – or rather, a social milieu and its characters. In many of Balzac's novels (*Eugénie Grandet*, 1833, *La Recherche de l'Absolu*, 1834, *Le Père Goriot*) we penetrate the often-forbidding exterior of a building to discover its inhabitants; his miser Gobseck, in the eponymous story (1830), appears in an environment embodying his avarice. However, both Balzac and Stendhal explode the allegedly direct and unproblematic relationship between writing and reality on which the historical novel is based. Although, for Stendhal, 'un roman est un miroir qui se promène sur une grande route' ('a novel is a mirror carried along a high road') (*Le Rouge et le noir*, II.19), what is shown is a matter of choice, aesthetic and political: 'Tantôt il reflète à vos yeux l'azur des cieux, tantôt la fange des bourbiers de la route. Et l'homme qui porte le miroir sera par vous accusé d'être immoral! Son miroir montre la fange, et vous accusez le miroir! Accusez bien plutôt le grand chemin où est le bourbier, et plus encore l'inspecteur des routes qui laisse l'eau croupir et le bourbier se former' ('Now it reflects to your eyes the blue of the sky, now the mud of the quagmires on the road. And you call the man carrying the mirror immoral! His mirror shows the mire, and you blame the mirror. Blame rather the high road where lies the quagmire, and even more the highway inspector who allows the water to stagnate and the quagmire to form') (*Le Rouge et le noir*, II.19).

The choice is the writer's, and the reader's. The supposedly objective depiction of reality is in fact a matter of subjectivity, of the reader's imagination, too. So although *Le Rouge et le noir*'s subtitles (*Chronique de 1830, Chronique du XIXe siècle*) parallel famous historical novels (Mérimée's *Chronique*, Hugo's *Notre-Dame de Paris*, subtitled '1482'), Stendhal's novel is anything but a chronicle, recounting little of the historical chronology or major events or figures of the period (despite revealing much about its social and political realities). Even its precise time span is unclear: unlike in Scott's novels, or Balzac's, or Mérimée's *Chronique*, or Hugo's *Notre-Dame de Paris*, we don't know exactly in calendar terms when it begins or finishes, or even where it happens. Although its initial setting, 'la petite ville de Verrières' (a *verrière* is a glass window, roof, or wall) has a name connoting transparency (and actually resembles Dole, in the Jura), the narrative's relationship to reality is anything but straightforward: in a final footnote, the narrator tells us that he has placed it in Besançon, 'where he has never been'.

The net effect of all this is to question any straightforward relationship between language and reality, to query the narrator's authority, upon which history and (by aspiration) the novel is based – and ultimately, authority itself. *Le Rouge et le noir* is scattered with epigraphs that supposedly lend authority to the text. But these epigraphs are both apocryphal and obscure. The one ascribed to Hobbes ('Put thousands together/Less bad,/But the cage less gay', I.1), smacks more of Stendhal's idiosyncratic English than of the author of *Leviathan*. The very first, ostensibly derived from Danton, is even more problematic, since Danton never wrote down his speeches – what we know of them derives merely from others' transcriptions. Even transcription, however, gets a poor press in *Le Rouge*: Julien makes a noblewoman, Mme de Fervaques, fall in love with him simply by copying some Russian letters acquired second hand (despite failing to replace 'Moscow' and 'St Petersburg' with more appropriate French names); just as in Stendhal's other great novel, *La Chartreuse de Parme*, a draper's daughter, Anetta Marini, falls for Fabrice, when his words are really aimed at the heroine Clélia (II.27). These are hardly good advertisements for authenticity. And, in the wider realm of social meaning, as in the more narrowly linguistic one, signs and words do not mean the things they seem to. Julien can recite the Bible by heart, but for social advancement not religious faith; the bishop of Agde, supposedly the representative of unvarnished truth, is more concerned by manipulating his appearance. In Balzac's *Illusions perdues*, books succeed or fail, reputations are made or broken not on the basis of real merit, but of what is written and said about them. Writing, in other words, does not designate reality: it creates it. No wonder *Illusions perdues* begins with an account of the printing process, for it is concerned with the manufacturing of reality. *Paraître* has replaced *être*, the sign which it supposedly signifies.

But what may be a practical weakness – the historical novel's questionable objectivity, its sometimes uncertain foundation in fact – is actually an aesthetic strength. What the historical novel lacks in precise reference or factual accuracy it makes up in imagination, in its challenge to the reader. *Le Rouge et le noir*'s title designates nothing with certainty, yet can suggest almost anything: the red of the solider's uniform, or of passion; the black of the cassock, or of death. The novel may not be a chronicle; but the subtitle *Chronique* invites the reader to view his own age with the critical detachment he would apply to the past. On one level, the title *Illusions perdues* describes accurately the experience both of its protagonists, who lose their innocence, and of the reader, who loses the illusion of a straightforward imitation of reality. Yet, on another, a different sort of illusion is created, whereby we set aside our awareness of fiction's artifice, and engage in a creative imagining of the characters. Stendhal, like Mérimée, appeals to the imagination by describing emotional reactions more than physical appearance, enabling us to 'read in' things for ourselves, verifying his fiction with our experience, our reality. And he makes it impossible for us to second-guess his real opinion of his characters by voicing conflicting views on their conduct, allowing them to act, apparently, completely erratically, in ways absolutely at odds with those of conventional novelistic leads. When Julien is about to seduce Mathilde, the narrator comments: 'il entreprenait de juger de la vie avec son imagination. Cette erreur est d'un homme supérieur' ('he undertook to judge life by his imagination. This is the error of a superior man') (II.19). Balzac, in contrast, gives very precise accounts both of his characters' appearance and of its meaning, of the physical and the figurative, abetted by striking symbolism and contemporary scientific theories – phrenology, physiognomy and mesmerism. In *Illusions perdues*, the hero Lucien's sexually ambiguous appearance, his 'young girl's skin' and 'hips shaped like a woman's' indicate both bisexuality and amorality: for the right price, he is anyone's. In *Le Père Goriot*, the police informer Mlle Michonneau's treachery is signalled by the medical student Bianchon's phrenological diagnosis of her 'Judas protrusions'. The notation is both scientific and symbolic: evidence firing the imagination.

Drawing on the historical novel, Stendhal and Balzac create imaginary but emblematic characters – unlike Vigny's Cinq-Mars or Mérimée's Charles IX, who are supposedly real figures sanctioned by history, but which have the potential double drawback of being both imaginative recreations, and thus exceeding strict historical fidelity, yet also by being supposedly bound by fidelity to that same supposed historical fact. Although Balzac's *Avant-propos*, the general preface to *La Comédie humaine*, alleges subservience to history ('La Société française allait être l'historien, je ne devais être que le secrétaire', 'French society would be the historian, I was to be but the secretary'), in fact his work has a very far from straightforwardly transcriptive relationship to history. More than four thousand characters, many recurring, appear in its ninety-five fictions, in some as protagonists, elsewhere as mere extras, creating a virtual multiplicity of perspective, in which the order of reading of the narratives, and what fills the imaginative gaps between them, are left to the reader: 'Il n'y a rien qui soit d'un seul bloc dans ce monde', writes Balzac in the preface to *Une Fille d'Eve* (1839), 'tout y est mosaïque' ('Nothing in this world is a monolithic block, everything is a mosaic').

And so although Balzac's narrator often appears categorical in his presentation of his characters, his ultimate reference is to the reader. Via frequent appeals to our knowledge, in formulations like: 'C'était un de ces hommes qui ...' ('He was one of those men who ...'), it is our experience that he draws on. And although Stendhal's narrator can seem dogmatic in his opinions of events and characters, the most intense emotional moments are left blank for the reader to fill: Julien feels most strongly (both love and hate) for Mme de Rênal when he cannot have her and tries to shoot her, Fabrice for Gina or for Clélia when furthest from them, in prison, or a pulpit. For Balzac, it is the reader who 'makes' the writer ('Lire, c'est créer peut-être à deux', 'Reading is creating, maybe for two', *Physiologie du mariage*, 1829); for Stendhal, 'un roman est comme un archet, la caisse du violon *qui rend les sons* c'est l'âme du lecteur' ('A novel is like a bow, the violin box *that renders the sounds* is the reader's soul'). Both writers transcend the alleged objectivity of history with their own subjectivity and the reader's, showing that history is but a story, 'reality' a sham cramping the imagination, authority an imposition on the potential and freedom of desire.

## Selected reading

*General (in French)*
Daniel Oster (ed.), *Dictionnaire des littératures de langue française. XIXᵉ siècle* (Paris: Albin Michel, 1998). Wide-ranging entries on writers, political and philosophical figures, movements and themes.
Alain Vaillant, Jean-Paul Bertrand and Philippe Régnier, *Histoire de la littérature française du XIXᵉ siècle* (Paris: Nathan, 1998). Stimulating, well contextualised, comprehensive account of topics, authors and themes.

*General (in English)*
John Cruickshank (ed.), *French Literature and its Background. 4: The Early Nineteenth Century. 5: The Late Nineteenth Century* (Oxford: Oxford University Press, 1969). Sound, in some ways dated, essays on major subjects.
F.W.J. Hemmings, *Culture and Society in France, 1848-1898* (London: B.T. Batsford, 1971). *1789-1848* (Leicester: Leicester University Press, 1987). Invaluable, accessible illustrated cultural history of movements, associations and ideologies in literature, music and the visual arts.
Martin Evans and Emmanuel Godin, *France 1815-2003. Modern History for Modern Languages* (London: Edward Arnold, 2004). Wide-ranging and accessible account of literary, social, cultural phenomena in the period.

*Napoleon: myth and impact*
Sudhir Hazareesingh, *The Legend of Napoleon* (London: Granta, 2004). Masterly social, political and cultural history.

*Désenchantement and arrivisme*
Paul Bénichou, *L'École du désenchantement. Sainte-Beuve, Nodier, Musset, Nerval, Gautier* (Paris: Gallimard, 1992). The definitive scholarly study, psychologically and historically assured.
Raymond Giraud, *The Unheroic Hero in the Novels of Stendhal, Balzac, and Flaubert* (New York: Octagon Books, 1969 [1957]). Solid exploration of the challenges for heroes in the bourgeois age.

*Representing the contemporary: histories and novels*
Claudie Bernard, *Le Passé recomposé. Le Roman historique français du dix-
neuvième siècle* (Paris: Hachette, 1996). Intelligent, well rationalised
overview.
Sandy Petrey, *Realism and Revolution. Balzac, Stendhal, Zola and the
Performances of History* (Ithaca, NY: Cornell, 1988). Challenging essays on
literature as product and producer of history.

# 2

# Stories

## 2.1. Confessional narratives

There are no more individual treatments of history than confessional narratives or autobiographies. We will begin by looking at these two genres, before exploring short stories as peculiarly immediate responses to the real.

Confessional narratives (first-person fictions recounting the protagonist's emotional experience, often a displacement of the real-life author's) present the most extreme example of the polarising of the individual and society, History writ large, versus 'histoire', his or her personal story. The word *individualisme* is first recorded in French in 1826: readers were developing a sense of themselves as individuals, as well as citizens, with rights, not just responsibilities, and a growing conviction that happiness lay not in society, but in the self, in that shared narcissism that was love. Enlightenment ideals, still catastrophically collapsing when Chateaubriand's *René* appeared in 1802, stood as the ruins of reason by the time of Sainte-Beuve's *Volupté* or Musset's *Confession* (1834, 1836), casting long shadows over the will o' the wisp whims of their heroes. They, like their readers, had been sensitised to their egos and made sceptical of social constraint by Goethe's *Die Leiden des jungen Werthers* (*The Sorrows of Young Werther*), first published in Germany in 1774, and rapidly translated. The story of Werther's unhappy love for Charlotte, married to the prosaic Albert, spoke to the spirit of the age. 'All felt it', wrote the Scottish historian Carlyle; 'he alone could give it voice'. The letter form Werther uses to record his torment and quest for solace in nature perfectly embodies the

central conflict between the individual and society. And the tragic
ending, when Werther shoots himself, spawned a wave of copycat
suicides. Werther was the mouthpiece and the model of an age, the
product of theologically sceptical Germany, whose conscious self-
scrutiny was a central factor in the growth of individual
self-awareness that marked the Romantic sensibility.

Werther's tragedy is that society is not big-hearted enough to take
his otherness, his illicit love for Charlotte. It is reflected in *René*, in
Senancour's *Obermann* (1804), in Constant's *Adolphe* (1816), in
Musset's *Confession*, and in later heroes, like Frédéric Moreau, in
Flaubert's *L'Éducation sentimentale*, who imagine themselves to be
like René. (Frédéric's companion, the prosaic Deslauriers, seems to
echo Desgenais, Octave's cynical lawyer friend in Musset's
*Confession*, whose name sounds solidly corporeal, a virtual homophone of *déjeuner*.) And the tragedy is heightened by the narrative
form of these French successors. The heroes of *René*, *Adolphe* and
Musset's *Confession* are set against society by emotion: Amélie's
incestuous feeling for her brother René, Adolphe's relationship with
Ellénore, the debauched Octave's serially unhappy affairs. What
marks these stories is their lack of consummation, sexual or otherwise. All their heroes are left adrift: René questioning his values,
Adolphe wandering, Obermann and *Volupté*'s Amaury retreating
respectively into nature and religion in despair, Octave alone. Their
tortuous relationships with others are mirrored by tangential narrative perspectives, putting first-person narrative in a third-person
frame, opposing the protagonist's and society's view, giving social
norms for judging the hero. René's story is countered by two
differing angles on his conduct: the natural, represented by the
native American, Chactas (*René* takes place in Louisiana), versus
Christian social orthodoxy, embodied by Père Souël. A foreword
precedes Adolphe's story, explaining its discovery and publication;
two letters follow, one arguing its moral utility, the other its status as
a document of 'la misère du coeur humain' ('the wretchedness of the
human heart'). Musset's *Confession* opens by distancing the author
from the story. 'Pour écrire l'histoire de sa vie, il faut d'abord avoir

vécu; aussi n'est-ce pas la mienne que j'écris' ('To write one's life-story, one must first have lived; thus it is not mine that I write') (I.1) and closes by panning out, with a final-paragraph switch from first to third-person narrative (V.7), revealing that the narrator's adored partner Brigitte has all along really cared for another. The fact that the other lover is, emblematically, called Smith, adds to the general value of the story. And *Volupté* is recounted by an apparently repentant narrator, who has renounced profane love for sacred, and become a bishop.

Such contrasts raise ethical dilemmas: where does the moral high ground lie? With the individual, or society? The protagonist, or others? Our answers to those questions depend on more fundamental interpretative issues: who to believe? – the first-person narrator, or society's spokespeople? What to believe? – not just morally, but in terms of basic fact. For we are crucially dependent on that narrator for our knowledge of his motives, actions and effects, and his lover's character. Only through these men can we know their lovers – a measure of these men's egotism, and, with few exceptions, of the general weakness of women's voices. Some of the most important female-authored confessional narratives have remained unavailable in French paperback until our day: d'Agoult's *Nélida* (1845), Colet's *Lui* (1860 – a corrective, from Sand's viewpoint, to Musset's *Confession*, but also a transposition of her own affair with Flaubert), and Judith Gautier's autobiography *Le Collier des jours* (1902-5).

These canonical male first-person narratives, and their contrasting perspectives, have a second consequence: an emphasis on the past, on reconstructing motivation and causation. The various frames and narrators problematise perspective not just spatially, as it were, in terms of their relationship to each other in the present, but also in terms of their relationship to the past, in terms of wider social history, as in Musset's *Confession*, or of their supposed textual status as a discovered manuscript, as in *Adolphe*; presenting the narrative as a manuscript literally turns it into an object for analysis. Such devices encourage us to try and establish what made their heroes act as they did. They stress the gap between the first-person narrator's present, as he is relating the story, and the past in which the events supposedly took place. In Musset's *Confession*, Octave's relationship with his first, unnamed, unfaithful mistress is coloured by the retrospective nature of the narrative, but had he been keeping a journal at the time he was in love with her, his account would no doubt have been as effusive as is his treatment of his later affair with Brigitte.

The inherently retrospective nature of first-person narrative tends to turn it into a threnody, a lament for lost love, increasing sympathy for the hero, clouding our moral judgement, with the effect of suggesting that neither individual nor society can be happy, that right is with neither, or both. This poignant, melancholic quality is concentrated in Fromentin's *Dominique*, published in 1862, some six decades after *René*. *Dominique*, like *Adolphe* and *Volupté* (but unlike the other narratives discussed) appears as a reaction against the overblown outcast Romantic ego, an 'I' who has overcome his youthful passion for a married woman and fitted in (or sold out to) society, married, become a father, and mayor of his provincial town. Yet from his very first words, we are led to doubt the truth of his recovery. Dominique's opening gambit ('Certainement, je n'ai pas à me plaindre', 'Of course, I have nothing to complain about') is hardly a ringing endorsement of his present situation, and as we advance through the narrative, numerous other features – the fact that he tells his story in a tower whose walls are marked with inscriptions and mementoes of his lost love, that the narrative follows a circular path between his home, Paris, and back again, its predominantly autumnal tone – all suggest that Dominique has not recovered at all, that his past is still his present. Although his friend, the doctor (embodiment of bourgeois reason) declares 'Tout homme porte en lui un ou plusieurs morts' ('Every man carries one or more dead men within him'), that Dominique should recount his love at all suggests that the dead are still very much alive. And although *Dominique*, like other confessional narratives, contains a character, Augustin, representing the Romantic hero's stolid, bourgeois side-kick (or alter ego: the very name Augustin evokes the archetypal

repentant confessional sinner, Saint Augustine, and Fromentin's
Augustin plays the role of Desgenais in Musset's *Confession*, echoed
by Deslauriers in *L'Éducation sentimentale*), the contrast between
Augustin and Dominique is far less clear than it is in other confessional narratives, as is the purpose of confession – repentance –
itself. *Volupté*'s preface, too, doubts its power to correct 'un penchant
[...], une passion [...], un vice' ('an inclination [...], a passion [...], a
vice'); but Dominique is half-repentant and half-regretful of his
earlier, exciting past, and the presence of his friend, Olivier, whose
letter attests his own similar Romantic experience, suggests perhaps
how typical that experience was. Where earlier first-person narratives embody the contrast between the individual and society, in
*Dominique* it is the protagonist who feels the conflict in himself. As
Flaubert observes, 'Chaque notaire porte en soi les débris d'un
poète' ('Every notary carries within him the remains of a poet')
(*Madame Bovary*, III.6). Nineteenth-century first-person narrative
laments the impossibility of really achieving our desires.

## 2.2. Memoirs and autobiographies

The nineteenth century, a period of turbulent history, was an age of
great memoirs and autobiographies. Nearly all its major figures left
memoirs, from Napoleon (*Mémorial de Sainte-Hélène*, 1822-3,
dictated to his secretary, Las Cases) and Talleyrand, to the
Revolution's chief executioner, Sanson (whose memoirs were
published, partly ghosted by Balzac, in 1830) or Vidocq, the arch-
supergrass of his time, or the condemned murderer Pierre-François
Lacenaire (1836), to writers like Dumas. Memoirs, significant
people's accounts of their own experience and their role in history
writ large, raise the expectation of chronological narrative that we
have already seen evoked, but subverted, in Mérimée's *Chronique* or
*Le Rouge et le noir*. Autobiography, in contrast – initiated by St
Augustine's *Confessions* (397-401), established by Rousseau's
*Confessions* (1761-8), but not recorded as a dictionary term in French
until 1842 – is self-life-writing, with the acts of self-transcription,

recollection and representation taking precedence over objective chronology. Where first-person narrative is often a ventriloquised *cri de coeur*, a transposition and exploration of the author's real experience in fictional terms, autobiography promises a truthful account of the development of the author's personality, and of the past from the standpoint of the present. Rousseau's *Confessions* begin with a daring claim: 'Je veux montrer à mes semblables un homme dans toute la vérité de la nature; et cet homme ce sera moi' ('I wish to show my peers a man in the whole truth of his nature; and that man will be me'). As we shall see, it is a promise hard to keep, and tempting to break.

Chateaubriand's *Mémoires de ma vie* (1803-32) and Stendhal's *Vie de Henry Brulard* (1835-6) are important examples of the flexible relationship between life and writing, history and story. Chateaubriand, the greatest of French Romantic Memorialists, moves life-writing on from Rousseau's extravagant claim of total truth. His *Mémoires de ma vie* (1809-17), corresponding to books I-III of the monumental *Mémoires d'outre-tombe* (1847), reveal much that the later text alters or conceals. The short *Vie*, begun when he was still relatively young, can be a way into the *Mémoires d'outre-tombe*, for where the *vie* covers the author's childhood and youth up to his leaving home for the sea, and is very much work in progress (its first two books were written under the Empire, the last under the Restoration), the *Mémoires d'outre-tombe* are in many ways a memorial, presenting the great man's image to posterity, integrating his personal story within the larger history in which it played a very significant role. The *Mémoires de ma vie* are simpler, more spontaneous and less sonorous (and much shorter) than the *Mémoires d'outre-tombe*; where the *Mémoires d'outre-tombe* are explicitly monumental – described by Chateaubriand as 'un temple de la mort élevé à la clarté de mes souvenirs' ('a temple of death raised to the light of my memories') – the *Mémoires de ma vie* are more exploratory, tentative and intimate. The following remarks concentrate mainly on the shorter and more accessible *Vie*, as an encouragement to read the magnificent *Mémoires d'outre-tombe*.

The tension between public and private, between ambition and an awareness of its vanity, is at the centre of both these *Mémoires*. The *Mémoires de ma vie* begin as an intimate enterprise – they existed only in a manuscript copy until published in 1874, long after the author's death – and much of their charm resides in the vivid evocation of private episodes from his youth: raiding a magpie's nest, schoolboy capers, the Gothic arrangements at home, the Château de Combourg, his father's ghost-like appearances, the author's bedroom in an owl-haunted tower. 'J'écris principalement pour rendre compte de moi à moi-même' ('I write principally to give an account of myself to myself') (*Mémoires de ma vie*, I). Yet the competing perspectives and distancing ironies of past and present, private and public, make this personal stocktaking a quest for identity in an altogether more absolute sense. Seeing the great man as a hapless schoolboy deflates him, yet also makes him more immediate and endearing. But seeing the schoolboy as a great man may be harder for those who knew him in his youth:

> Je sais qu'ils ont douté longtemps que l'homme dont ils entendaient parler fût le petit chevalier qu'ils avaient connu. (...) Ces dignes gens qui ne mêlent à mon image aucune idée étrangère, qui me voient tel que j'étais dans mon enfance et dans ma jeunesse me reconnaîtraient-ils aujourd'hui à travers le temps et l'adversité? Je serais peut-être obligé de leur dire mon nom, avant qu'ils voulussent me presser dans leurs bras.
>
> (I know that for a long time they doubted that the man they heard talk of was the little knight they had known.[...] These good people who mix no alien ideas with my picture, who see me such as I was in my childhood and in my youth, would they recognise me today through time and through adversity? I would perhaps be obliged to tell them my name, before they would wish to take me in their arms.)

There are undermining ambiguities here. These people might not recognise the author because of the passage of time; or he might not be recognised because of the very different, perhaps not entirely truthful, account he gives of himself here; or they might acknowledge him when he gives his name because it is the great man of the present whom they wish to recognise, rather than the *polisson* ('little rascal') they knew in the past. Does time, or its telling, change the man?

Irony, then, leavens the fundamental solemnity of the enterprise, and makes clear its real nature: that autobiography cannot be a matter of simply telling the truth, but is inextricable from the dual, and thus inherently ironic, perspective of public and private, past and present, identification and detachment. So the sometimes shocking accounts of Chateaubriand's extraordinary upbringing are tempered by comments explaining how hard routines toughened him, enabling his greatness; a remark on his outstanding prowess in a given area (in maths, for example) will be taken as evidence of no particular merit in their owner. The result is to present the writer as both extraordinary, yet of no account; exceptional, yet also typical. Chateaubriand, in his *Mémoires*, becomes emblematically singular; like the protagonists of his (or other) first-person narratives, *René* or *Adolphe*, he becomes a means by which ordinary readers, nobodies, can identify with a great man, by which failures can understand the emptiness of success. The ironies are carefully controlled, by both attentive (re-)writing (as the *Mémoires de ma vie* became the *Mémoires d'outre-tombe*), and by the way in which potentially negative points (admissions of inadequacy) are balanced by accompanying virtues, giving an impression of integrity that it is hard to doubt.

Yet, like any writer, Chateaubriand could not totally control the reception of his work, and his distress when the *Mémoires d'outre-tombe* were published without his permission shows how much they, like *Mémoires de ma vie*, spring from the fundamental motive of all autobiography – a sincere doubt about one's identity, and a sincere need to explore it, rather than a more public ambition to expose it. The tensions spring from Chateaubriand's ambivalence about himself; about the need to play a social role, and the contrary need for solitude. His writing stems from an essential doubt about, and conflict within, the self; from a frustration and displacement of desire. Failing to understand his adolescent urges, and, *faute de mieux*, creating for himself an imaginary ideal woman (as children create imaginary companions), it is only at the suggestion of his sister Lucile (another surrogate love-object) that he begins to work out this desire through writing, history through story: 'Écrire, c'est vivre'. Writing becomes a moral as well as a libidinal imperative, bringing the author face-to-face with the consequences of his writing and his life, in an anticipated literary Last Judgement. 'I made history, and I could write it', he declares at the end of the *Mémoires d'outre-tombe*: 'the old world is ending, and the new one beginning. I can see the glints of a dawn whose sun I shall not see rise. It remains for me only to sit on the edge of my grave; after which I shall descend boldly, crucifix in hand, to eternity'. Chateaubriand reveals life-writing's fundamental nature: one does not write about one's life, one writes it. Autobiography is less self-recording than self-creation, for the reader has no access to any reality other than that of the words on the page.

Stendhal's *Vie de Henry Brulard* (1835), the summit of his autobiographical work, explores this idea to the full. Its beginning reflects the end of Chateaubriand's *Mémoires*, but with a full, not a rising, sun. And where Chateaubriand has a quest, Stendhal has questions ('Qu'ai-je été, que suis-je, en vérité, je serais bien embarrassé de le dire', 'What I have been, what I am, in truth, I would be very hard put to say'), and no firm answers. Where Chateaubriand holds himself to account before his superego ('rendre compte de moi à moi-même'), marshalling memories, stressing his acts, their cause and consequence, Stendhal lets the ego roam, seemingly random, uncertain recollections juggling past and present, self and other, sketching a seemingly more authentic inner man than Chateaubriand's full-length portrait. Stendhal's 177 cryptic diagrams suggest what really matters: private emotional experience, relationships with family, with lovers, geometrically rendered, bareness of expression rendering (as in his novels) intensity of feeling. Shaky dates, stark notation, show that it is what happened, more than when, which is important; the fact, or rather, its emotional impact; private, not public, time.

But this does not mean that Stendhal does not care about the public: he is obsessed with the book's reception, but in a very radical way. The conventional methods of autobiographies become precisely the obstacle to reception, standing between the writer and the reader. If '*Je et moi*' would be 'comme M. de Chateaubriand, ce roi des *égotistes*' ('*I* and *me* [...] like M. de Chateaubriand, that king of *egotists*'), then writing in the third person raises the problem of how to account for 'les mouvements intérieurs de l'âme' ('the soul's inner movements') (ch. 1). And writing, with its inevitable activities of self-criticism and self-correction, is inherently disingenuous: how many precautions, asks Stendhal, does it take not to lie? Stendhal's awareness of the unavoidable artifices of self-writing leads him to be upfront about them, to exploit the ambiguities of a genre which, in the guise of self-recording, is also self-creation, inevitably containing (like Stendhal's response to life) an element of self-fictionalisation. Like autobiography itself, the pseudonym Henry Brulard is both a mask, or a lie (like Stendhal itself, not the author's real name), and the truth: it is an obliteration of his own detested father, and a substitution of a new identity of the writer's own; a lie paradoxically revealing the writer's true feelings, yet in a way accessible, at the time of writing, only to the author – a secrecy that guarantees sincerity. As when Julien is in prison, or Fabrice preaching apparently to all, but in reality only for Clélia (*Le Rouge et le Noir*, II.44; *La Chartreuse de Parme*, II.27), the moments of greatest truth are the most private.

It is for this reason that Stendhal is suspicious of absolutes – of Chateaubriand's confidence descending to the grave, of language purporting to give us the thing itself. Detesting Chateaubriand's *style diamanté* (diamond-studded style) burdened with striking images and stylistic tics, Stendhal relies only on the truth of feeling, expressed in the simplest possible terms:

Tout fut sensations exquises et poignantes de bonheur dans ce voyage, sur lequel je pourrais écrire vingt pages de superlatifs. (ch. 13)

(All was exquisite and poignant sensations of happiness in this journey, on which I could write twenty pages of superlatives.)

He has a different kind of faith in language – not as a sort of transubstantiation of emotion, but as a pointer to it, whose power resides ultimately with the reader. Where Chateaubriand positions himself, in the *Mémoires d'outre-tombe*, vis-à-vis a posterity that is almost a person, Stendhal concerns himself only with discourse: of Ingres and Gros he chooses 'those who will still be talked of in 1935' and mocks Chateaubriand's absolutes: 'Ce qui serait un blasphème à dire aujourd'hui de M. de Chateaubriand sera un *truism* [sic] en 1880' ('What it would be blasphemous to say today of M. de Chateaubriand will be a *truism* in 1880') (ch. 1).

This relativity of viewpoint, this dependence on reception, is both Stendhal's Achilles' heel and his greatest strength. His seeming neglect of style made his work unreadable for contemporaries fed on grandiloquence. But for posterity (Stendhal's primary target) he seems spontaneous and open, as serendipitous as the links made by thought itself. The end of Stendhal's *Vie* makes Chateaubriand look contrived. Stendhal's sun does not suffuse his eminent person – it simply blinds an emblematic 'on' – both 'I' and 'you':

On ne peut pas apercevoir trop distinctement la partie du ciel trop voisine du soleil, par un effet semblable j'aurai grand peine à faire une narration raisonnable de mon amour pour Angela Pietragrua. Comment faire un récit un peu raisonnable de tant de folies? Par où commencer? Comment rendre cela un peu intelligible? (...)

En me réduisant aux formes raisonnables je ferais trop d'injustice à ce que je veux raconter. (...)

Quel parti prendre? Comment peindre le bonheur fou?

Le lecteur a-t-il jamais été amoureux fou? A-t-il jamais eu la fortune de passer une nuit avec cette maîtresse qu'il a le plus aimé en sa vie?

Ma foi, je ne puis continuer, le sujet surpasse le disant. (Stendhal, *Vie de Henry Brulard*, ch. 47)

(One cannot see too distinctly the part of the sky nearest the sun, for similar reasons I shall have great trouble giving a reasonable account of my love for Angela Pietragrua. How can one make a vaguely reasonable narrative of so many excesses? Where to begin? How to make it even slightly intelligible? [...] // By reducing myself to reasonable forms of speech I would do too much injustice to what I wish to recount [...] // What course to take? How to paint mad happiness? // Has the reader ever been madly in love? Has he ever had the good fortune to spend a night with that mistress he has loved most in his life? // By Jove, I cannot continue, the subject surpasses the sayer.)

Where Chateaubriand's rising sun symbolises the divine, Stendhal's speechlessness before his feelings for Angela may look like an artistic failure, but is a literary and human triumph. Eschewing Chateaubriand's eloquence, Stendhal's 'on', in the quotation above, is both personal and interpersonal, putting the emphasis on the reader, inviting us to imagine her, invoking an image that is at once tangential and central, his sun illuminating just how vital Angela was without telling us explicitly anything at all. In contrast to Chateaubriand's religious universals, Stendhal creates his own meaning by alluding to the sun and the sky. Stendhal's ineffably light touch shows that creating meaning in life-writing, as in life, is a matter of making one's own connections, exploiting the objective to transcend it.

Although the nineteenth century produced many other remarkable journals and autobiographies by Amiel, Renan, Quinet or Sand, Stendhal's quest for meaning in the self on his own terms, not God's or anyone else's, makes him more completely our contemporary. Stendhal anticipated his first readers in 1880, and it is the *fin de siècle* that most completely realises the potential unlocked by Stendhal's autobiography; the genre itself moves from being a business of self-recording, of sincerity, to self-confection and solipsism. Redon's autobiography *A soi-même, Journal* (1867-1915, 1922), is a compelling collage of recollection and aesthetic reflection. Amiel's massive, multivolume *Journal*, kept over more than three decades, is a real paradox: perhaps the largest gathering ever of incisive comments on life, delivered as an in-extenso lament on its author's supposed inability to make anything of his, all in a mysteriously compelling way that makes his aberrant mindset seem completely rational. And Schwob reaches a pinnacle of irony and paradox, composing fictional biographies which, in their wilful (re)creation of the past, are in some ways the very opposite of Stendhal's: imaginings of the lives of real others (great figures like Empedocles, Lucretius, the painter Uccello), but also forgotten nobodies (Katherine the lacemaker, Alan the soldier), and semi-mythical figures (princess Pocahontas) rather than attempts to recover the realities of a fictionalised self. His *Vies imaginaires* (1896, preface) makes plain that, in concentrating on history, or the history of individuals, on the writing, thought, or acts of great men, biographers have deprived us of the particularities that were most interesting about them – that Aristotle wore on his stomach a bag of hot oil, that Hobbes was maddened by flies on his bald head. Such peculiarities are common to everyone, famous or insignificant, remembered or forgotten: what fascinates is their humanity. In concentrating on the anecdotal, the interest of singularity, in seeing real experience as a trigger for the imaginary, the *Vies imaginaires* attest that all life-writing, whether bio- or autobiographical, is a matter of stories as much as history, foreshadowing twentieth-century fictionalised biographical or autobiographical writings, Gide's *Si le grain le meurt*, Proust's *A la recherche du temps perdu*, where fiction, displacement, and the fragmentary play more overt roles in the search for the truth of the self.

### 2.3. Short stories

The short story, a specifically Anglophone term coined in 1884, embraces various French generic labels such as *conte* (tale), *nouvelle* (novella) and *récit* (narrative), designating brief, self-contained, tightly constructed works, often organised around a single dramatic event or dominant symbol. Short stories have often been downgraded because of the popularity, brevity and target market of the most widely-read examples (didactic fairy and moral tales, aimed at

women and children, undoubtedly second-rate citizens in nineteenth-century France: see Section 5.2 in Chapter 5, this volume).
But these very factors, the purposiveness, popularity and pointful-
ness of stories, along with their often rapid production and eager
consumption by their readers, make many peculiarly vivid
responses to their era, and enticing challenges to our own.

Of several important stories about historical turmoil, such as
Nodier's *Inès de Las Sierras* (1837) or Balzac's *Un Épisode sous la terreur*
(1829), Balzac's *Le Colonel Chabert* (1832) is one of the most telling.
Beginning in 1819, *Le Colonel Chabert* opens with what is virtually a
rewriting of history: the lawyer Derville's clerks are copying, and
mocking, the Restoration edict restituting property to aristocratic
émigrés deprived of it by the Revolution and Empire. Into the
chamber comes a dishevelled stranger claiming to be Chabert, a
colonel in Napoleon's defeated army, to have been left for dead and
buried under a pile of corpses at the battle of Eylau (1807), and to
have walked back to Paris to seek his wife and family. No one
believes his tall story: times have moved on, Chabert has been
assumed dead, his wife has inherited his property and remarried,
and does not want to know him. The tale is largely concerned with
Derville's attempts to discover and reclaim Chabert's identity and
his wife. But Chabert ends in an asylum, denying his identity,
answering only to a number.

*Le Colonel Chabert* underlines an evident but important truth: that
a narrative is only ever one version, or one person's version, of
events. This is particularly apparent in short stories, whose generic
names in various languages – *conte, racconto, Erzählung,* tale – often
point to the business of giving an account: *contes* are *contés,* tales are
told. 'History', conversely, disguises this, being ostensibly objective
or transparent. In Balzac's story, Chabert and Derville's accounts
are pitted against the Restoration's official (hi)stories, its legal
discourse, and his ex-wife's lawyer's, making History, 'reality' a
competition of rival stories, won by the party with the best lawyer
or the most power: the current Establishment, the Restoration. In
being about, but also exploiting, different stories, *Le Colonel Chabert*

also demonstrates a key feature of short fiction: a striking mirroring of form and content. Where novels are generally concerned with process, with how things happen more than simply what happened, stories often focus on a single event or nexus of events, and on a dominant symbol or symbols that crystallise the narrative's meaning. In *Le Colonel Chabert*, there are several, all pointing to the same fact. The clerks' opening legal drafting symbolises Chabert's deletion from the past; his burial under corpses is a literal burial by history, showing how, at the bottom at the pecking order, although alive, he might as well be dead. And his asylum incarceration demonstrates that those who do not fit society's moulds can readily be presented as mad, or even made mad by other people's refusals to acknowledge them.

Stories like Chabert's make us question the real: one of the main story-genres of nineteenth-century France is the *conte fantastique* (fantastic tale). *Contes fantastiques* disrupt a seemingly stable reality by the sudden intrusion of rationally inexplicable phenomena, lead us from the real to the unreal or supernatural or vice-versa. In Gautier's *La Cafetière* (1831), or *Le Pied de Momie* (1840), two of many tales emulating the German Romantic E.T.A. Hoffmann, seemingly supernatural events turn out to have rational explanations: *Le Pied de Momie* is explicitly presented as a dream, yet some of its events remain inexplicable. But in Mérimée's *La Vénus d'Ille* (1837), the archaeologist Peyrehorade, who presents the eponymous statue of Venus, the precision of description, the sceptical narrator's detachment, form the perfect foil for the incredible events that follow, culminating in its crushing of the bridegroom, Alphonse, to death. So convincingly are the circumstances described, so obsessive is Peyrehorade, that it is 'reality' that comes to seem fantastic, uncanny, as the mind struggles to reconcile seemingly incompatible phenomena – a statue apparently endowed with motion and volition, related by a narrator who is undeniably down-to-earth. The events are so rationally inexplicable that we are compelled to seek explanations elsewhere.

One source of such explanations is the supernatural or the symbolic, the realm of absolute, mythic meanings and connections

of which the real is only a sign. *La Vénus d'Ille* can be read variously
as an allegory of male fears about women, of castration and confinement (Alphonse's crushing suggesting consumption by the *vagina
dentata*); as a symbolic opposition of the sensual and the spiritual,
the pagan and the Christian (after its dreadful exploit, the statue is
melted down into a church bell – an act of revenge?), or of reason
and imagination. When Balzac's Chabert turns up in Derville's
chambers, he removes his wig to reveal a scar across his skull,
symbolising the loss of the memory on which the self depends, yet
recalling also the Gothic monster or spectre returned from the dead.
Such instances lie on the cusp of fantasy and reality as both hard
facts and pointful symbols, giving short stories a suggestiveness akin
to poetry's – a mysterious, emblematic, dramatic quality transcending the narrative itself, endowing their protagonists with
resonance and life beyond their bounds.

   *La Vénus d'Ille* and *Le Colonel Chabert*, like other famous French
short stories such as Mérimée's *Carmen* (1847) and Maupassant's
*Boule de Suif* (1880), are more precisely *nouvelles* (novellas) – stories
that lay less overt stress than *contes* on narration or event, and more
on their emotional implications. As in the founding French novella-
cycle, Marguerite de Navarre's *Heptaméron* (1558), most of whose
stories are about relationships between the sexes and their difficulties, relational difficulties of one sort or another are the subject of
many nineteenth-century *nouvelles*: Chabert tries to retrieve his wife
from another, Alphonse is caught between his bride and the statue,
José between love and Carmen, Maupassant's prostitute-protagonist
Boule de Suif between her honour and selling herself to Prussian
soldiers to save her self-righteous bourgeois companions. Where the
*Heptaméron*, like its inspiration, Boccaccio's *Decameron* (1348-53),
contains overt discussion of morals, French nineteenth-century
examples rely on action, serious emotional content and revelatory
surprise to raise moral questions more than answer them: it is our
astonishment that Boule de Suif should be the heroine, or that the
whores should be more humane than the local worthies who visit
them in *La Maison Tellier* (1881), that makes the moral point.

A cursory reading of Maupassant's stories could suggest that he had set out chiefly to subvert what had gone before. Many of his most famous – *La Parure* (1884), *Mon oncle Jules* (1883), *Le Gueux* (1884) – seem merely to play jokes on the reader, to lead us into a situation before revealing that it was not as we thought by means of a snappy punch-line at the end. In *La Parure*, Mme Loisel's decade spent working to replace a borrowed but lost diamond necklace is nullified when it turns out to have been fake. In *Mon Oncle Jules*, the uncle, thought to be making his fortune in the U.S., is encountered on the ferry to Jersey, working as a humble seaman, and ignored by the relations who had been so ready to welcome the millionaire. The starving tramp in *Le Gueux*, locked up for begging in a village, is found dead the following morning: 'Quelle surprise!' snorts the story's final line.

Yet these 'jokes' are very practical. *La Parure* leads us to question Mme Loisel's vanity in wanting to borrow the necklace, and to wonder whether, if she could not tell whether it was made of diamonds or paste, there is really any difference between them. *Mon Oncle Jules* raises a different question about value, and about the sincerity of human emotion; *Le Gueux* leads us to consider whether we ought indeed to be surprised by the fact that a pauper has been left to die. But none of this is done explicitly – there is hardly ever narratorial commentary to guide us on our way. We are presented instead with problems with little hint on how to solve them, situations whose very extremity shocks and forces us to think.

Maupassant is far from being the only writer with this skill: story-tellers such as Alphonse Allais, or Villiers de l'Isle-Adam, can also challenge us in this way. Villiers's *L'Appareil pour l'analyse chimique du dernier soupir*, or *L'Affichage céleste*, from his *Contes cruels* (1880), raise the literal to the pitch of the fantastic, sampling the dying man's last breath to discover the composition of his soul, projecting advertisements and wanted notices for criminals in the sky to exploit every last inch of space – satirical fantasies now at risk of becoming fact. The fantastic thus acts as a mode of social protest, a way of questioning objective reality, and whether there is only one way that things can be. Maupassant's seemingly straightforward tales are invariably open to at least two, not necessarily incompatible, readings – as in his apparently xenophobic Franco-Prussian war tales. *Mademoiselle Fifi* (1882) is indeed about a cowardly baby-faced Prussian solider, but the girl who betrays him also acts dishonourably. The protagonist of *L'Aventure de Walter Schnaffs* (1883) is certainly pusillanimous, but the French soliders who trumpet their valour in capturing him thereby make themselves absurd. *La Peur* proposes a fantastic reading to deflate it; *Sur l'eau* does quite the reverse. The ghost outside turns out to be a dog; but among the strange beings a boatman whimsically imagines on the river appears a corpse. Maupassant's most powerful fantastic stories query our perceptions, cause us to wonder where the boundary between the real and the imagined really lies. In *Qui sait* (1890), the narrator returns from a night out to be passed by his furniture, which is subsequently mysteriously returned; how this has happened is never explained. In *Le Horla* (1887), perhaps Maupassant's greatest story, the narrator's mind is taken over by a mysterious being, the Horla, which has come off a ship at Rouen. Does it really exist, or has he just imagined it? Is the Horla *au dehors*, in external reality, or *là-dedans*, in his mind? It is for us to judge. Like poetry or drama, more than like the novel, short stories challenge us with events and their resonance, incident and symbol, to use our imagination to make sense of the real.

## Selected reading

Richard A. Bales, *Persuasion in the French Personal Novel: Studies of Chateaubriand, Constant, Balzac, Nerval, and Fromentin* (Birmingham, AL: Summa Publications Inc., 1997). Clear and accessible study, focusing on techniques and their effects.

Pierre-Georges Castex, *Le Conte fantastique en France de Nodier à Maupassant* (Paris: Corti, 1987 [1951]). The classic work on the subject.

Peter Cogman, *Narration in French Nineteenth-Century Short Fiction: Mérimée to Schwob* (Durham: Durham University Press, 2002). The clearest recent overview, on a key aspect of the genre.

Beatrice Didier, *Stendhal autobiographe* (Paris: Presses Universitaires de France, 1983). Far-reaching exploration of the methods and motivations of Stendhal's life-writing.

Florence Goyet, *La Nouvelle 1870-1925: Description d'un genre à son apogée* (Paris: Presses Universitaires de France, 1993). An unusually cogent account.

Daniel Grojnowski, *Lire la nouvelle* (Ivry sur Seine: Armand Colin, 1993, reprinted 2005). Comparative literary study, useful on both theory and practice; contains analysis of Maupassant's *La Nuit. Cauchemar* (1887).

Bernard Masson, *Lectures de l'imaginaire* (Paris: Presses Universitaires de France, 1993). Revealing essay on Musset's *Confession,* as well as on his drama, Flaubert, Labiche and Sand.

Michael Sheringham, *French Autobiography from Rousseau to Perec: Devices and Desires* (Oxford: Clarendon Press, 1993, reprinted 2001). Authoritative, wide-ranging overview; includes treatments of Chateaubriand and Stendhal.

Margaret A. Waller, *The Male Malady: Fictions of Impotence in the Male Romantic Novel* (Piscataway, NJ: Rutgers University Press, 1993). Persuasive study of male weakness in the Romantic (not exclusively first-person) novel.

Damien Zanone, *L'Autobiographie* (Paris: Ellipses, 1996). Historical and theoretical overview, covering writers from St Augustine to the present.

# 3

# Poetry

La poésie, c'est tout ce qu'il y a d'intime dans tout. (Hugo, Preface to *Odes et ballades*, 1826)

(Poetry is all that is intimate in everything.)

Peindre non la chose, mais l'effet qu'elle produit. (Mallarmé, Letter to Cazalis, October 1864)

(Paint not the thing, but the effect it produces.)

These two statements, by the nineteenth-century's emblematically contrasting poets (one public, one private; one accessible, one hermetic), symbolise poetry's journey from the intimate to the inward, from what can be said through words to what words can say for themselves. Poetry, a word derived from the Greek *poieein*, to make, may be defined as language exploited not instrumentally, but creatively. 'Elle vous manque' ('You miss her') is a simple piece of information. But the first great French Romantic poet's, Lamartine's, line: 'Un seul être vous manque, et tout est dépeuplé' ('You miss a sole creature, and all is unpeopled') ('L'Isolement', *Méditations poétiques et religieuses*, 1820, l.28), for all that it is as over-familiar in French as Wordsworth's 'I wandered lonely as a cloud' in English, posits a different order of experience, and a link between the individual and the absolute, an existential truth. Poetry is inherently a convergence, sometimes a compromise, of subjective and objective, of the poet's individual experience and the public expression that mediates it. Great poetry is anything but cliché; yet it is the paradox of great poetry that repetition and dissemination can often make it so.

### 3.1. From Classicism to iconoclasm

In the nineteenth century, the tension between private and public, between individual feeling and its expression, was peculiarly acute. At the century's outset there was apparently no tension at all; but in reality, the link had become so strained that it had all but snapped, leaving poetry and innovative self-expression in virtually separate domains. The private part of poetry, feeling, was most definitely kept private, Romantic stirrings voiced only timidly (by, say, Millevoye) in conventional Classical form. Its public elements, in contrast, undoubtedly got the upper hand, in epics and odes celebrating Imperial achievements, or verse dissertations on improving themes (by Lemercier, Chênedollé or Legouvé). Poetry was made a matter not of originality or feeling, but of imitation, craft and thought; of subservience to the Classicism of the elevated genre of verse tragedy – Corneille, Racine, Voltaire – prized as the very embodiment of the pre-eminent rationalism of the national art of France. In literature and art, as in politics, the measure of value was obedience to this ideal. Poetry was defined as rhetoric and versification, of composition along set lines: the 12-syllable alexandrine line, periphrases (circumlocutions) and euphemisms, a fixed repertory of tropes and subjects, if not epic, then tritely-precious moments, amorous dalliance, taking tea, expressed with portentous platitude by Parny and Delille.

This was a 'materialism' in Imperial literature deplored by Lamartine (*Méditations*, preface), a rigidity of form and poverty of expression definitively supplanted from the Restoration in landmark collections that broke Classicism's back: Hugo's *Odes* (1820), which became *Odes et ballades* in 1826, and Musset's *Contes d'Espagne et d'Italie* (1830). They combine foreign influences – Teutonic, nostalgia for the medieval past in Hugo; Spanish, Italian and English (Shakespeare, Byron) in Musset's tales of passionate love –

with radical re-workings of verse form, breaking the alexandrine, stretching it over successive lines or even over stanzas, using wrong-footing combinations of irregular line length and teasing images well out of Classical order. The greatest assault was on language, whose Imperial and Classical power to designate, command, describe, was countered by a Romantic need to express, enjoy and play: Hugo's tripping rhythms in the *Ballades* were followed by wilder excesses in *Les Orientales* (1829) and, again, in Musset's *Contes*. Hugo's 'Les Djinns' (*Les Orientales*, 28) mirrors its action (jinn, spirits, in Muslim belief, swarming down on a town), swelling in eight-line verses of successively two, three, four, five, six, seven and eight syllables to a central 10-syllable climax, then diminishing via the same pattern in reverse, something scarcely surpassed by Verlaine's irregular experiments decades later (*Romances sans paroles*, 1874). 'Sara la baigneuse' uses a different kind of mirroring, visual and verbal, of rhythm, rhyme and assonance:

> Sara, belle d'indolence,
>> Se balance
> Dans un hamac, au-dessus
>> Du bassin d'une fontaine
> Toute pleine
> D'eau puisée à l'Illyssus;
>
> Et la frêle escarpolette
>> Se reflète
> Dans le transparent miroir,
> Avec la baigneuse blanche
>> Qui se penche,
> Qui se penche pour se voir.
>
> (*Les Orientales*, 19, l.1-12)

(Sara, lovely with lazing,/Swaying/In a hammock, over/The bowl of a fountain/Brim-full/With water from the Illyssus; // And the frail swing/Glints/In its clear glass/With the white bathing-lass/Leaning over,/Leaning over to see herself in the glass.)

Verse is the message and the medium, something plastic, malleable, its capacity to designate reality underpinned, or undercut, by artful play with words: in 'Les Djinns', the breath of the night 'brame/Comme une âme' – literally 'brays like a soul', *âme* ('soul') coming where we would expect *âne* ('donkey'). Language draws attention to itself as well as describing something else, showing that the links between expression and experience are not fixed, delighting in a vibrant, many-coloured reordering of reality, challenging order itself. In Musset's playful lines

> C'était, dans la nuit brune,
> Sur le clocher jauni,
>     La lune,
> Comme un point sur un i.
>     (*Contes d'Espagne et d'Italie*, 'Ballade à la lune', l.1-4)

(It was, in the night maroon,/On the yellowed steeple in the sky,/The moon,/Like a dot on an i.)

the picture of steeple, night and moon dissolves before our eyes into mere letters on a page, making reality something as much mocked as made. Musset explores the freestanding value of language for and in itself, some fifty years ahead of Mallarmé (see Section 3.4 in Chapter 3, this volume). Here is a freedom of expression and association amply justifying Romantic poetry's dream of being a universal way of making meaning.

Yet verse innovation is far from being the whole story. What is expressed changes fundamentally as well. Two pairs of poets, Lamartine and Desbordes-Valmore, and Hugo and Baudelaire, can particularly pinpoint poetry's dichotomy of private and public, lyricism and vision, in the century's first six decades, map its move from the Romantic to the modern, before we look at the objective, objects and their opposite, things and effects, in the century's second half.

## 3.2. Lyricism and vision

### *3.2.1. Lyricism: Lamartine and Desbordes-Valmore*

A lyric is a song, a poem expressing personal emotion. Lamartine's *Méditations poétiques* (1820) is the century's first major expression of such feeling – a cycle of elegies in all but name, prompted by real experiences of loneliness, transience and loss. How much that experience is doctored matters less than the poet's will to voice his authentic self, and the readers' will to hear him. Contemporaries certainly did: *Méditations* sold 20,000 copies in two years, prodigious then, unrivalled later in the century – a measure of the unquenched thirst for 'sincerity'. To modern readers, Lamartine can seem anything but sincere: theatrically self-conscious and technically conservative, retaining Classical octosyllables and alexandrines, periphrasis and vocabulary ('Aquilon' and 'Zéphyr' for the north and west wind, for example), posing, staging suffering:

> Ainsi, toujours poussées vers de nouveaux rivages,
> Dans la nuit éternelle emportées sans retour,
> Ne pourrons-nous jamais sur l'océan des âges
>     Jeter l'ancre un seul jour?
>
> O lac! l'année à peine a fini sa carrière,
> Et, près des flots chéris qu'elle devait revoir,
> Regarde! je viens seul m'asseoir sur cette pierre
>     Où tu la vis s'asseoir! (...)
>
> O temps! suspends ton vol; et vous, heures propices,
> Suspendez votre cours:
> Laissez-nous savourer les rapides délices
>     Des plus beau de nos jours!
>
>              ('Le Lac de B...', *Méditations*, 14, l.1-8, 21-4)

(Thus, forever driven towards new shores,/In eternal night swept off for evermore,/Can we never on the ocean of the ages/Cast the anchor a single day? // O lake! The year has scarcely finished its

career,/And, next the dear waves she would fain have seen
again/Behold! I come alone to settle on this stone/Where you saw
her sit alone.[...]// O time! Suspend thy flight; and you, propitious
hours!/Suspend your course!/Let us savour the fleeting joys and
ways/Of the brightest of our days.)

But it was precisely the marking of self-awareness, of
expressing pain hitherto unvoiced, which mattered to Lamartine
and his readers, as it can matter still to us. The sense of loss is
historical and universal as well as personal; the meditations can
be ours as well as his. If we look, and listen, carefully, his verse is
less conventional than it seems. Here, the 12.12.12.8-syllable
metre of the first five, and last seven, verses frames 12.6.12.6 in
the middle four, the variation mirroring the flux of feeling, the
waters and winds. And within these well-managed modulations,
Lamartine gently pushes aberration: if verse 1 is overwhelmingly
regular, the pauses after 'Ainsi' and at the ends of lines 1 and 2
mimic the halting drifting of human cargo that is ineluctably
swept on by the unbroken last two lines. Verse 2, in contrast,
abruptly slashes regularity with sudden exclamations ('O lac!',
'Regarde!'), making lines 2 and 4 uneven in the extreme (2.10,
3.3.6) as the poet attempts to stop the unstoppable, an effort
repeated with similar means in stanza 5; while later lines cry
heart-rendingly: 'O lac! Rochers muets! Grottes! Forêt obscure!'
(l.49; cf. 45-6). (Rimbaud's 'Le Bateau ivre' is hardly less emotive;
see Section 3.3 in Chapter 3, this volume.) Lamartine fears
neither rhythm nor repetition, signs of time-swept sincerity like
the in-mid-flow opening, startling if we read the poem on its own,
self-explanatory after its predecessor, 'La Retraite', as part of a
longer personal journey. Yet elsewhere, in 'Souvenir', for example
(*Méditations*, 9), a plangent regularity of rhyme, metre and assonance paints a state of unvarying plenitude. As its quasi-religious,
personal, title suggests, *Méditations* casts off from Classical
models, giving voice to what Lamartine's 1849 preface calls the
'chant intérieur de l'âme' ('the inner song of the soul'), turning

poetry once more to music, to the metre of experience, to the welling flow of thought. We can be lulled, but we should not be fooled: Lamartine's sense of security is always false.

We meet even greater immediacy in Marceline Desbordes-Valmore's *Élégies* (1819). This, the first volume of a compact output, despite its title's Classicism, offers something totally unique: a lyricism uncluttered by Classical remains or Romantic baggage, ahead of Lamartine by a year. Her work, drawn from her tragic life, gives a complete expression of that abnegation of the self that is the Romantic self's most whole expression, and was the lot of nineteenth-century woman. Her sex makes her an emblematic victim, but also an authoritative, accessible spokeswoman on themes of loss and aspiration common to all mankind. What distinguishes her from male contemporaries is a lack of affectation, and a transparency unshadowed by an intrusive ego, known biography, or doorstep prefaces. We seem to get straight to the person, speaking as freshly as if today:

> Son image, comme un songe,
> Partout s'attache à mon sort;
> Dans l'eau pure où je me plonge
> Elle me poursuit encor;
> Je me livre en vain, tremblante,
> A sa mobile fraîcheur,
> L'image toujours brûlante
> Se sauve au fond de mon cœur.
>
> ('Souvenir')

(His image, as if a dream,/Everywhere clings to my fate;/When I plunge in the purest stream/It still pursues me yet;/In vain I give myself, trembling/To its ceaselessly moving cool,/The ever-burning image/Rushes off to my heart as a pool.)

The 'I' of her poems is anonymous and thus universal and (usually) ungendered, with direct and wide appeal: indeed, in 'Souvenir', what matters is the other and the image, more than the 'I', or eye, that sees it. And, in contrast to Lamartine or Musset, there is no breast-beating lament of misfortune: that was simply a woman's lot. Instead, there are movingly vivid poems on timeless experiences ('Le Coucher d'un petit garcon'), and uncompromising lines on the brutally repressed riots of 1834, too honest to be published even thirty-five years later:

> La mort est un soldat qui vise et qui délivre
> Le témoin révolté qui parlerait demain....

> ('Dans la rue')

(Death is a soldier who takes aim and executes/The revolted witness who might talk tomorrow....)

It is telling that the witness is a woman: Valmore's writing is the verse analogue of Sand's fiction. Against religious pessimism she pits serene faith ('Au Christ'); her modesty is magnificent. Most remarkable are her developments of verse form, unflashy yet as radical as anything later attempted by Verlaine – who, with Rimbaud, discovered the irregular 11-syllable line in her verse, calling her line:

> ... J'ai semé ma joie au sommet d'un roseau!

> (... I have sown my joy on the tip of a reed!)

'perhaps the most extraordinary line in our language or any human language!' (*Le Figaro*, 8 August 1894).

Here too, unlike male counterparts, she engages in anything but gratuitous innovation: 'Souvenir' has unusual, seven-syllable lines, but we notice their restless effect, not the number of syllables. Expression matches feeling in her natural but magical touch; content and form converge in perfect integrity.

### 3.2.2. Vision: Hugo and Baudelaire

The visionary is the power of perceiving vivid mental images, of seeing, often prophesying, an absolute mystical truth. In the nineteenth century, poetry was an ideological battleground where poets were major campaigners. The Classical view that poetry could not simply sing, but must say something universally significant, issue a public declaration of belief, made visionary poetry, with its epic treatment of mythic or cosmic subjects, a major form. Vigny's *Poèmes antiques et modernes* (1826) and *Les Destinées* (1863), Lamartine's *Jocelyn* (1836), Hugo's *Les Contemplations* (1856) or *La Légende des siècles* (1850; 77, 83), all wrestle with the problem of man's place in the world, with quavering faith (Lamartine), providential fatalism (Vigny), unfailing wonder (Hugo), or hermetic pantheism (Nerval, 'Vers dorés', *Les Chimères*, 1854). All but the last are lengthy. But all consist of shorter fragments, with significant lyrical components: the vision cannot be seen without the seer.

No two collections focus the tension between lyricism and vision, public and private more sharply than Hugo's *Les Contemplations* (1856) and Baudelaire's *Les Fleurs du mal* (1857) (hereafter referenced as *Cont.* and *Fleurs* respectively). They seem to look both inwards and outwards, backwards and forwards, from the Romantic to the dawning modern. In both cases, the vision emerges from lyricism, the portentous from the personal. Hugo's daughter Léopoldine's death is the hinge of *Les Contemplations*, falling halfway through its two volumes ('Autrefois' and 'Aujourd'hui') and six books, its spiritual portent most crucially illuminated in the pivotal final poem of book III, 'Magnitudo parvi' ('The greatness of the small'). But Baudelaire's journey is far more anguished, oscillating between poles of intoxication and despair, transcendence and abjection, even from one poem or line to the next, opening with the poet's birth-ejection into 'ce monde ennuyé' ('this bored [but also troubled] world') ('Bénédiction', 1.2) and proceeding, via expository opposites of Spleen and Ideal, the 'Tableaux parisiens' exploring modern life, the illusory intoxications of wine, the central 'Fleurs du mal' themselves, as pivotal in Baudelaire's collection as book III of Hugo's, showing how beauty may be extracted from evil, and then via Revolt to Death.

There are deeper differences. Hugo composes his experience, seemingly guided by nature's seasons (but doctoring dates and sequences to this end); Baudelaire is thrown about by it. Hugo's *Contemplations* leads from sunny celebrations of the natural and love (I, II), via suffering (III) and acceptance (IV) to vision and revelation in the last two books. 'Les Mages' (VI.23) shows the poet's role as prophetic leader of humanity ('poet' now encompasses philosopher, priest and scientist) and visionary, spiritual guide, while the unnumbered closing poem, 'A celle qui est restée en France' transcends intellectual divisions in an eclectic and glimpsed vision of God: 'Tout est religion et rien n'est imposture' (l.329).

Paradoxically, the two collections' similarities reveal their differences. Both open by asserting a direct connection with the reader:

Hélas! quand je vous parle de moi, je vous parle de vous. (*Cont.*, Preface)

(Alas! When I speak of myself, I speak of you.)

– Hypocrite lecteur, – mon semblable – mon frère! (*Fleurs*, 'Au lecteur')

(Hypocritical reader, my brother, my like!)

The Poet is a kind of Universal Self, who is you and me, as well as himself. These are extraordinarily presumptuous mental violations of our space, very muscular bits of lyricism, but they lead to opposite insights: Hugo's to a vision of redemption, expressed in (among innumerable other places) an oppositional, awestruck, image of two worlds, found in 'Magnitudo parvi' and explained in its closing lines:

Vois donc, là-bas, où l'ombre aux flancs des coteaux rampe,
Ces feux jumeaux briller comme une double lampe (...)
– L'un est un feu de pâtre et l'autre est une étoile,
      Deux mondes, mon enfant!

C'est l'astre qui le prouve et l'esprit qui le voit;
      Une âme est plus grande qu'un monde.
      ('Magnitudo parvi', *Cont.*, III.30, l.37-8, 41-2, 788-9)

(See then, yonder, where the shadow creeps on the sides of the slopes,/Those twin flames shining like a double lamp[...]/– One is a shepherd's fire and the other is a star,/Two worlds, my child! // It is the star that proves it and the mind that sees;/A soul is greater than a world.)


    Arbres, roseaux, rochers, tout vit!
            Tout est plein d'âmes.
      ('Ce que dit la bouche d'ombre', *Cont.*, VI.26, l.48)

(Trees, reeds, rocks, all is alive!/Everything is full of souls.)


For Hugo, the great is within the small, the divine within the earthly. Baudelaire, too, conceives his world in terms of oppositions, but the oppositions hold each other in tension, betraying deep psychological conflict. Where Hugo abolishes hell ('Pas d'enfer eternel!', *Cont.*, VI.26, l.693), Baudelaire's man is doomed to evil and damnation: 'Nos péchés sont têtus, nos repentirs sont lâches' ('Our sins are stubborn, our repentances weak') ('Au lecteur', *Fleurs*, l.5); there is, blasphemously, no hope of religious redemption. Death, for Hugo, is a beginning ('Mourir, c'est connaître', 'To die is to know', *Cont.*, III.30, l.444; the angel in the final poem's last line cries 'Commencement!': 'Ce que dit la bouche d'ombre', *Cont.*, VI.26, l.786). But, for Baudelaire, it is merely the inevitable end. Man is earthbound, destined by the ennui of this spiritual void to be trapped in an earthly cycle of desire and consummation, where even the infinite is only imaginary or material, reached fleetingly through physical pleasure, triggered by some feature of his mistress – her hair ('La Chevelure', *Fleurs*, 23), her breasts, her arms, her legs ('Le Beau Navire', *Fleurs*, 52) or perfume (which can give the illusory pleasure of conquering time via memory: 'Le Flacon', *Fleurs*, 48), or wine ('Le Vin des amants', *Fleurs*, 108). Where Hugo's seekers of the sublime are great thinkers ('Pleurs dans la nuit', *Cont.*, VI.6, 1.625), Baudelaire's seekers of the infinite are lesbians, bursting sexual boundaries ('Femmes damnées', *Fleurs*, 111, 1.23). Woman is lauded for her beauty, creating sexual and aesthetic transcendence, but vilified for dooming man to damnation; yet, given the inevitability of that damnation, and the certainty of spiritual void, the only possible morality is amorality, the only relevant question is how to kill time before it kills you, how to fool your boredom – as the work's very last lines declare:

> Plonger au fond du gouffre, Enfer ou Ciel, qu'importe,
> Au fond de l'Inconnu pour trouver du *nouveau*!
>
> ('Le Voyage', *Fleurs*, 126, 1.142-4)

(Dive to the depths of the abyss, Heaven or Hell, who cares,/To the ends of the Unknown to find something *new*!)

Novelty replaces progress, for the only progress, for Baudelaire, would be an impossible 'diminution of the traces of Original Sin' (*Salon de 1846*).

Central to vision is, of course, the image. The imagery of both collections is oppositional; both are built on analogy, but use it to contrasting ends. Hugo's images (they are less images, than keywords that acquire an awesome resonance, words like 'noir', 'gouffre', 'abîme', 'ténèbres') suggest metaphysical mystery by dint of incantatory repetition, and because they express a clear spiritual belief, here, man's freedom to do good or evil, and ultimate redemption through good:

> L'homme est clémence et colère;
> Fonds vil du puits, plateau radieux de la tour (...)
> ('Ce que dit la bouche d'ombre', *Cont.*, VI.26, l.392-3)

(Man is clemency and anger;/Vile pit of the well, tower's radiant belvedere [...])

Baudelaire's function similarly, recurring throughout the collection, to a similar end: 'mer', 'métal', 'pierreries', 'parfum', 'vin', 'liqueur', and others, are, in their different ways, all suggestive of endurance and transcendence. But where Hugo's transcendence is in metaphysical earnest, vaulting from earth to heaven, Baudelaire's reveal a modern insight, the self-referentiality of language:

> La Nature est un temple où de vivants piliers
> Laissent parfois sortir de confuses paroles (...)
>
> Les parfums, les couleurs et les sons se répondent.
>
> Il est des parfums frais comme des chairs d'enfants,
> Doux comme les hautbois, verts comme les prairies,
> – Et d'autres, corrumpus, riches, et triomphants,
>
> Ayant l'expansion des choses infinies,
> Comme l'ambre, le musc, le benjoin et l'encens,
> Qui chantent les transports de l'esprit et des sens.
> ('Correspondances', *Fleurs*, 4, l.1-2, 8-14)

(Nature is a temple where living pillars/Sometimes let slip diffident words[...] // Perfumes, colours and sounds all correspond. // There are perfumes cool as children's skin,/Soft as oboes, green as fields,/– And others, corrupt, rich, and triumphant, // Having the expansion of infinite things,/Like amber, musk, benzoin and incense,/Which sing the transports of the mind and the sense.)

On one level, this closed system of synaesthesia, where the perception of one sense can be expressed in terms of another, evokes the thought of the eighteenth-century Swedish theosopher Emmanuel Swedenborg, who saw the visible earthly world as the mere analogue of an invisible heavenly one. But on another, the closed system is just that: one experience can only be expressed in terms of another, one word in terms of another, because there is nothing outside language, because art, as Hugo had already put it in the Preface to *Cromwell* (1830), cannot give the thing itself. So our visions of transcendence are just that – imaginings, figments of the imagination – and the poet's journeys are travels of the mind, precious precisely because we can never arrive: their power resides in their potential, in the imaginative tension the possibility of the journey can create:

> Mon enfant, ma sœur,
> Songe à la douceur
> D'aller là-bas vivre ensemble!
>> ('L'Invitation au voyage', *Fleurs*, 53, l.1-3)

(My child, my sister,/Think of the sweetness/Of going to live together down there!)

Here, as in other poems ('Le Chat', 'Le Beau navire', *Fleurs* 34 and 52 respectively), the swaying rhythm expresses, rather sexily, restrained energy. Yet it is also somewhat repetitive and circular, embodying enclosure, the productive limits of man's infinite. If transcendence is only language, this is both its greatest weakness and its strength. For there is, nonetheless, a kind of infinite in Baudelaire, reached through art, language, and the imagination, 'cette reine des facultés' ('that queen of the faculties') as he put in the *Salon de 1859*. If we are doomed to sin, then in his view sin we must completely, for it is through sin that we can reach a kind of absolute. And if we have no choice about committing evil, our greatest glory is awareness of that evil, 'Un phare ironique, infernal (...) – La conscience dans le Mal!' ('A beacon, ironic and infernal.[...] The awareness of our Evil!') ('L'Irrémédiable', *Fleurs*, 84, l. 37, 40). For Hugo, redemption comes through suffering; for Baudelaire, through our ability to express suffering to God through art, 'the best witness to our dignity',

> (...) cet ardent sanglot qui roule d'âge en âge
> Et vient mourir au bord de votre éternité!
>
> ('Les Phares', *Fleurs*, 6, l.41, 43-4)

([...] that ardent sob which rolls from age to age/And comes to die on the verge of your eternity.)

### 3.3. Things and effects

*3.3.1. L'Art pour l'art and Parnassianism: Gautier and Leconte de Lisle*

In his belief in art's redemptive power, Baudelaire is the last of the Romantics; but in his awareness of man's earthbound nature, of alienation, and of the illusions of love and transcendence, he is also the first truly modern poet of nineteenth-century France – a forerunner, as we shall see, of Rimbaud and Mallarmé, and among those, including Rimbaud, whom Verlaine had dubbed *poètes maudits* (cursed poets) in 1884. But *L'Art pour l'art*, the idea of art as a refuge from bourgeois ugliness, utilitarianism and ennui, the idea of art as an Ideal, had been crystallised by Baudelaire's friend and mentor Gautier in the preface to his novel *Mademoiselle de Maupin* (1835-6): utility is relative; what is useful to the cobbler is useless to the poet, and vice versa; the utility of human beings themselves remains to be discovered. 'Rien de ce qui est beau n'est indispensable à la vie. (...) Il n'y a de vraiment beau que ce qui ne peut servir à rien; tout ce qui est utile est laid, car c'est l'expression de quelque besoin, et ceux de l'homme sont ignobles et dégoûtants, comme sa pauvre et infirme nature' ('Nothing beautiful is indispensable to life.[...] The only truly beautiful things are those which are completely useless; everything useful is ugly, for it is the expression of some need, and those of man are base and disgusting, like his poor and infirm nature).

It is in poetry that this stress on the aesthetic is strongest.

Banville's *Cariatides* (1842) and *Stalactites* (1846), and, above all,
Gautier's *Émaux et Camées* (1852), emphasise the description,
marmoreal perfection and technical control that Heredia was to
give ultimate expression in *Les Trophées* (1893). In Gautier's 'A une
robe rose', the aesthetic, the dress, seems to matter more than the
wearer. Or rather, the wearer becomes the dress, the real the ideal,
the concrete the abstract, and vice versa. Banville's somewhat
bloodless preciousness is outstripped by Gautier's more vital sensuality, showing how imagination drives desire:

> D'où te vient cette robe étrange
> Qui semble faite de ta chair,
> Trame vivante qui mélange
> Avec ta peau son rose clair? (...)
>
> (...) l'étoffe est-elle teinte
> Dans les roses de ta pudeur?
> Non; vingt fois modelée et peinte,
> Ta forme connaît sa splendeur. (...)
>
> Et ces plis roses sont les lèvres
> De mes désirs inapaisés,
> Mettant au corps dont tu te sèvres
> Une tunique de baisers.
>> (Gautier, 'A une robe rose', l.13-16, 21-4, 29-32)

(Whence didst thou get that strange dress/Which seems to be made
from thy flesh,/Living weft which weaveth/Its pale pink with thy
skin?[...] // Is the fabric tinted/With the roses of thy chasteness?/No;
modelled twenty times and painted/Thy form well knows its greatness.[...] // And those pink folds are the lips/Of my desires
unsated/Dressing the body that thou quittest/With a tunic made of
kisses.)

And in 'Contralto', the poem's bisexual subject symbolises art's
transcendent power: the two voices, and sexes, fused in a single

superior being uniting the qualities of both. That the poem trans-
poses other art forms – a statue, and the music that inspired it –
makes art entirely self-contained, referring only to itself, rather than
to some external criterion of utility or reality, existing only to give
delight. In this absence of explicit moral imperative lie the seeds of
decadence.

Gautier's 'L'Art' encapsulates the distinctive trait of *L'Art pour l'art*
that Parnassianism was to develop: a stress on formal control:

> Oui, l'œuvre sort plus belle
> D'une forme au travail
>     Rebelle,
> Vers, marbre, onyx, émail.

('L'Art', l.1-4)

(Yes, the work emerges more gorgeous/From a form to chisel/
Resistant,/Verse, marble, onyx, enamel.)

This control (here, lines of 6, 6, 2 and 6 syllables) is anything but the
tousled freedom of Hugo's early work: form and content express the
difficult business of chipping away at recalcitrant material.
Parnassianism, a pivotal mid-century movement led by Leconte de
Lisle, and among younger poets by Catulle Mendès, takes the aspiration towards the highest forms of purity in art to a far conclusion.
Inspired, as its name suggests, by the highest ideals (Mount
Parnassus was sacred to Apollo and the muses in ancient Greece), it
avoids the anecdotal, favouring impassive description of ancient or
exotic (African, Indian or Oriental), animal rather than human
subjects, and silence, immobility or at most slow movement ('Le
Coeur de Hialmar', 'Les Éléphants'); if something rapid happens, it
is usually in a dream ('Le Rêve du Jaguar', 'Le Sommeil du
Condor'). Yet the impassiveness and tight verse control, exerted by
strict alexandrines in these pieces from *Poèmes barbares* (1871), but
also in Lisle's other works, constrain violence or absent reverie,
both symptoms of desires denied direct outlets; while the overt

control turns the poem into a very substantial thing in itself, a monument, or weighty ornament, but also risks emptying it of feeling, of turning it into precisely the kind of bourgeois object it sought to avoid. The emphasis on description and formal constraint might suggest the discipline of Napoleon III's regime, while Lisle's exoticism seems an implicit celebration of colonialism, complaisant towards the new regime, like Gautier's refusal politically to protest. In Lisle's most famous poem, 'Midi' (*Poèmes antiques*, 1852), God, man, any kind of explicit human viewer is absent; only vegetable and mineral and animal, in the shape of the cattle it describes, are there. The poem figures a void, impeccably versified and described. The words relate to objects, conveying experience that is coherent but disturbingly detached.

### 3.3.2. Verlaine

It is this sense of coherent experience that Verlaine, Rimbaud and Mallarmé begin to attack. Growing initially from Parnassianism, Verlaine's poems create a radical fragmentation of both feeling and form. The pentasyllabic (five-syllable) lines of 'Soleils couchants', so short as to be almost non-existent, suggest an emotion too painful or indeterminate to be expressed, while the irregular repetition of words and phrases almost empties them of meaning:

> Une aube affaiblie
> Verse par les champs
> La mélancolie
> Des soleils couchants.
> La mélancolie
> Berce de doux chants
> Mon cœur qui s'oublie
> Aux soleils couchants.
> Et d'étranges rêves,
> Comme des soleils
> Couchants sur les grèves,

Fantômes vermeils,
Défilent sans trêves,
Défilent pareils
A des grands soleils
Couchants sur les grèves.

(Verlaine, 'Soleils couchants', *Poèmes saturniens*, 1866)

(An enfeebled dawn/Pours over the fields/The melancholy/Of the setting suns./The melancholy/Cradles with soft songs/My heart which is lost/In the setting suns./And alien dreams/Like evening suns/Setting on the shores/Vermilion phantoms/Process without rest/Process resembling/Great evening suns/Setting on the shores.)

The external world is not so much absorbed into the self (as in Baudelaire, where it becomes the 'fodder' of the imagination: *Salon de 1859*), as the self is lost in the external world. In Verlaine's subsequent collections, emotion is explored through a variety of analogues that are surrogates for the self, screens for, sometimes from, experience. Where Baudelaire compares his mistress to a ship, her breasts to a wardrobe, her legs to witches, and her arms to boa constrictors ('Le Beau Navire', *Les Fleurs du mal*, 52), in Verlaine it is the poet's own self that is so unstable, self-questioning and insecure as to be played out in other roles or vaporised into the environment. 'Charleroi' (*Romances sans paroles*, 1873-4) is about Verlaine's arrival with his lover Rimbaud in Rimbaud's home town. But you would never know it: the poem is a disorientating collage of seemingly random images and sensations – Kobolds (subterranean spirits), railway stations, wind, a bush slapping the passer-by's eye. Who or what do the Kobolds represent? Rimbaud and Verlaine? Who wants to believe that the wind is weeping, but is not confident enough to do it? Who is so unsure as to ask: 'On sent donc quoi?' ('So what do we feel?'). The lines suggest the sensory aggression of arrival, yet project it entirely onto the environment, leaving no hint of who might be feeling what. The soul is fused with its context. Verlaine must be the only poet to have compared his lover to the pivot of a railway-wheel (*La Bonne chanson*, 1870, 7, l.13-16), or to have been so divided as to have written a pastiche of himself ('A la manière de Paul Verlaine', *Parallèlement*, 1889, 'Lunes', 2).

Yet there is a constant running through Verlaine's verse, and it is music – not in any purely aesthetic or intellectual sense, but as something fundamental, essential, visceral. His demand in 'Art poétique', 'De la musique avant toute chose (...) Où l'Indécis au Précis se joint (...) Pas la couleur, rien que la nuance' ('Music before all else [...] Where the Vague is joined to the Precise [...] Not colour, nothing but nuance') (*Jadis et naguère*, 1885, l.1-2, 8, 14), designates something real, which can only be expressed physically, through sound, rhythm and feeling, rather than rhetoric. 'Prends l'éloquence et tords-lui son cou!' ('Take eloquence and wring its neck!') (l.21):

> Que ton vers soit la bonne aventure
> Éparse au vent crispé du matin
> Qui va fleurant la menthe et le thym…
> Et tout le reste est littérature.

> (May your line be your fortune-teller/Scattered to the morning's stiff wind/Which goes fragrant with mint and thyme…/And all the rest is literature.)

The sensuality of mint and thyme contrasts with the dismissiveness of the throwaway final line: as Verlaine declares, '"Art poétique" (...) n'est qu'une chanson, après tout, JE N'AURAIS PAS FAIT DE THÉORIE!' ('"Art poétique" [...] is only a song, after all, I WOULD NOT HAVE MADE ANY THEORY!') ('Critique des *Poèmes saturniens*'). The 'petite sensation', not the theory, governs experience. In Verlaine, intensity speaks through the sensual.

### 3.3.3. Rimbaud

In Rimbaud's verse, the 'things' of the external world, the descriptive and the sensual, are even more prominent. Poems like 'Les

Étrennes des Orphelins', 'Soleil et chair', or 'Le Dormeur du val' combine powerfully descriptive elements with narration. But Rimbaud's description is never innocent: it is the springboard for a message, a reflection, or a vision. So 'Les Étrennes des Orphelins', by focusing on the physical, but fragile, mementoes of the children's dead mother, stresses their absolute desolation, the absence of any spiritual consolation. 'Soleil et chair' makes a similar point via a vigorous, pagan sensuality:

> Le grand ciel est ouvert! les mystères sont morts
> Devant l'Homme, debout, qui croise ses bras forts
> Dans l'immense splendeur de la riche nature!

(The great sky is wide open! The mysteries have died/In the face of Man upstanding, crossing his strong arms/In the immense splendour of rich nature!)

Rimbaud concentrates on the very plastic description of things, but their effect is reverie, reflection – variously suavely erotic ('A la musique', 'Roman'), politically provocative ('Le Mal', 'Le Dormeur du val'), or viscerally shocking, as in 'Vénus anadyomène', where Venus rises from a coffin-like tub, grotesquely deformed, 'belle hideusement d'un ulcère à l'anus' ('hideously beautiful with an ulcer on her anus'), confronting us with the physical reality of decay without any of the countering spiritual consolation of, say, Baudelaire's 'Une Charogne' (*Les Fleurs du mal*, 29).

Rimbaud's greatest poems engage in a more visionary transformation of the real. 'Le Coeur volé' starts – like Lamartine's 'Le Lac' – in mid flow, but on the high seas, with the poet's heart puking over the poop of a ship:

> Mon triste cœur bave à la poupe
> Mon cœur couvert de caporal:
> Ils y lancent des jets de soupe
> Mon triste cœur bave à la poupe: (...)

Ithyphalliques et pioupiouesques
Leurs quolibets l'ont dépravé! (...)
O flots abracadabrantesques,
Prenez mon cœur, qu'il soit lavé! (...)

Quand ils auront tari leurs chiques:
J'aurai des sursauts stomachiques,
Moi, si mon cœur est ravalé:
Quand ils auront tari leurs chiques
Comment agir, ô cœur volé.

('Le Coeur volé', l.1-4, 9-10, 13-14, 17-24)

(My sad heart drools over the poop/My heart covered in shag tobacco:/They throw at it spurtings of soup/My sad heart drools over the poop:[...] // Ithyphallic and squaddyesque/Their jeers have all depraved it![...]/O waves abracadabrantesque,/Take my heart away, to wash it![...] // When their wads have been chewed dry:/I shall have stomachic retchings,/I shall, if my heart is down-broken:/When their wads have been chewed dry/How should I act, O heart stolen?)

There is no easily visible reality here: Rimbaud mixes distress, abandonment and abjection, without apology or explanation. These lines seem to be images, or analogues, of an emotional state, but they are so directly violent and visceral, so devoid of causation (apart, perhaps, from 'leurs quolibets l'ont deprave'), that they cannot be certainly related to any readily identifiable referent, or reconstituted as any conventional narrative. Instead, Rimbaud gives us an emotional state as a physical reality, its victimised, claustrophobic desolation expressed by repetition.

Rimbaud wants reality to be different, but not for him Hugo's consoling God, or Baudelaire's compulsion and despair. His revolt is existential, but conducted with things as they are, yet against their conventional order. *Le Coeur volé* combines the vulgar and the mundane (shag tobacco, soup) with slang and the antiquely obscene ('pioupiou', a colloquial word for soldier, the priapic 'ithyphallique') with a pawky kind of humour but also a visionary transformation in its 'flots abracadabrantesques'. The storm-tossed seas of 'Le Bateau ivre', flowing from the earlier 'Le Coeur volé', but also from previous poetic models (Lamartine's 'Le Lac', Baudelaire's 'Le Voyage'), figure not the poet's melancholy or a moral lesson on humanity, but the shifting deep beneath us, our profound instability of being. What we might see as grounded is for Rimbaud productively mobile, a liberation from the dry land of what is conventionally accepted as reality and a freeing into visionary yet multi-sensory delight:

> La tempête a béni mes éveils maritimes.
> Plus léger qu'un bouchon j'ai dansé sur les flots
> Qu'on appelle rouleurs éternels de victimes
> Dix nuits, sans regretter l'œil niais des falots! (...)
>
> Et dès lors, je me suis baigné dans le Poème
> De la Mer, infusé d'astres, et lactescent,
> Dévorant les azurs verts; où, flottaison blême
> Et ravie, un noyé parfois descend (...)
>
> Je sais les cieux crevant en éclairs, et les trombes
> Et les ressacs et les courants: je sais le soir,
> Et l'Aube exaltée ainsi qu'un peuple de colombes,
> Et j'ai vu quelquefois ce que l'homme a cru voir!
>
> ('Le Bateau ivre', l.13-16, 21-4, 29-33)

(The tempest has blessed my maritime awakenings./Lighter than a cork I have danced on the waves/That we call the eternal twisters of victims/For ten nights, without missing the lanterns' silly lights[...] // And thenceforth, I have bathed in the Poem/Of the Sea, lactescent, infused with stars,/Devouring the green azures; where, like pale/Delighted flotsam, a drowned man sometimes descends[...] // I know skies bursting into lightning, and water-spouts/And backwashes and currents: I know the evening/And the Dawn exalted like a people of doves,/And I have sometimes seen what man thought he saw!)

But this is not some Baudelairian synaesthesia – there is no transcendent unity of sea and sky (as in, say, 'L'Homme et la mer', *Les Fleurs du mal*, 14), but a bringing-down of the sky to the sea (l.22-4) – the reverse of resurrection and ascension into heaven. The visions are intense, but momentary (l.33) ('d'ineffables vents m'ont ailé par instants', 'Ineffable winds have winged me at moments', l.60), their intensity resulting from a sensuality the poet cannot quite relay. For 'Les Aubes sont navrantes./Toute lune est atroce et tout soleil amer' ('The Dawns are appalling./Every moon is atrocious and every sun bitter') (l.89-90), the conventional forms and models of vision and transcendence will not do. What is needed is the breaking of the conventional shell by the greatest force of water on earth:

> Que ma quille éclate! O que j'aille à la mer! (l.93)

> (Let my keel burst open! Let me go to the sea!)

This bursting of boundaries, this altering of experience, marks Rimbaud's later career. 'Voyelles' (1872) answers 'Correspondances', but in a less certain and more material form. Where Baudelaire is in no doubt about the unity of the universe, Rimbaud sounds the more halting note of a child learning its alphabet – with the colours and pictures to match. Where 'Correspondances' is built around the parallel between heaven and earth, and structured around simile (the comparator 'comme' appears seven times), 'Voyelles' is structured around apposition and metaphor: 'A noir, E blanc, I rouge': the words simply *are* the colours and images with which they are identified, an identification reinforced by the juxtaposed images, piled on in appositions where Baudelaire uses simile, and by internal rhyme and alliteration:

> E, cand*eurs* des vap*eurs* et des tentes
> Lances des glac*iers fiers*, rois blancs, frissons d'ombelles (...)
> U, cycles, *vi*brements di*vins* des mers *vi*rides. ['Voyelles', l.5-7; italics added]

(E, candours of vapours and tents,/Proud glaciers' lances, white kings, parasol-frissons[...] // U, cycles, divine vibrations of viridian seas.)

Yet while the essential nature or certainty of the vision might not initially seem in doubt – vowels are the most elemental and visceral sounds in language, the alchemical reference (l.11) suggesting that a great secret is indeed unlocked – 'Voyelles' begins with an explanation no sooner offered than deferred ('Je dirai *quelque jour* vos naissances latentes', '*Someday* I shall tell of your latent births', my italics), and ends with a Last Trump, sounding silently:

> O, supreme Clairon plein de strideurs étranges,
> Silences traversés des Mondes et des Ange;
> – O l'Oméga, rayon violet de Ses Yeux! (l.12-14)

(O, supreme bugle full of strange stridors/Silences traversed by Worlds and by Angels;/– O the Omega, violet ray of His Eyes!)

The Revelation is of contradiction: the trump sounds, but silently, the vision is intense and absolute but also personal and arcane, voiced in Rimbaud's obscurities ('strideurs', 'vibrements'). The scientist's spectrum may be no more than a child's alphabet.

These alternatives of vision and void shape Rimbaud's subsequent output, written not in verse but in prose. Rimbaud described his enterprise as 'un long, immense et raisonné *dérèglement de tous les sens*' ('a long, immense and reasoned disorder of all the senses') (letter to Demeny, 15 May 1871); his prose poetry collections explore this ordered disorder. *Une Saison en enfer* is a kind of diary of Rimbaud's 'season of hell', in May 1872, when he abandoned verse, and of the crisis in his relationship with Verlaine; it is a sort of personal testament, taking on the visionary role to reject it: 'Je devins un opéra fabuleux' ('I became a miraculous opera'), he says in 'Alchimie du verbe', 'J'ai cru acquérir des pouvoirs surnaturels. Eh bien! je dois enterrer mon imagination et mes souvenirs!' ('I believed I was acquiring supernatural powers. Well! I must bury my imagination and my memories!') (*Adieu*).

*Illuminations*, composed of poems probably written between 1872 and 1875, but not collected and published, by Verlaine, until 1886, more than a decade after Rimbaud had rejected literature, reflects the Romantic visionary theme of meditation and contemplation, but abandons personal narrative and continuous discourse in favour of fragmentation and an impersonal perspective. These are illuminations both in the sense of being illustrations of experience, of another text, so to speak (as on an illuminated manuscript: Rimbaud's anglicism for the French *enluminure*), and epiphanic, if momentary, revelations. 'Après le déluge' begins with what, after the images of being washed, 'lavé', in 'Le Coeur volé' and 'Le Bateau ivre', is the most fundamental image of redemption in Rimbaud's work. Yet the vision of animals, minerals, plants coming to life, which gets from prehistory to modernity in half a page, is rapidly dispelled by its end, where the queen or witch lighting her fire in a pot of earth will never want to tell us what she knows and we do not. 'Les Ponts' follows the reverse dynamic, describing the urban landscape in terms of a pattern, apparently factually, without explanation before destroying 'cette comédie' ('this nonsense') with a bolt from the blue, as if to stress the preeminence of light over the charade of modern urban existence, glumly described in 'Ville'. But it is just light, just as the bridges are simply a pattern. Another poem, 'Barbare', magics up phantasmagoria, bizarre but apparently too real to be hallucinations, then tells us they do not exist – twice. There is no transcendence, simply one materiality trumping another; and even less than in Rimbaud's verse is there any overarching system of symbolism, recurrent imagery, or meaning: the *Illuminations* give us fragmentary, seemingly irreconcilable perceptions, and leave us to make of them what we will. Rimbaud's poetry is raw, rough-edged, and intensely visionary, yet deeply rooted in the physical, personal and ultimately opaque. Poetry was, as he wrote when he abandoned it forever aged 19, 'une tentative insensée' ('a senseless attempt'), but the sense lay in its potential. He was a rebel with a hopeless cause.


### 3.3.4. Mallarmé

What for Rimbaud was ultimately an insuperable obstacle to creation – the subjectivity, the inexpressibility of vision, language's opaque plasticity – was for Mallarmé its very conduit. Although both reflect something of Parnassianism's cold, impersonal objectivity, Mallarmé owes far more than Rimbaud to Baudelaire, and to Baudelaire's quest for transcendence. In the early poem 'Les Fenêtres' (1863), under the crucifix of a hospice, a dying man goes to press his face on the windows in quest of the light. But whereas for Baudelaire, in, say, 'La Vie antérieure' (*Les Fleurs du mal*, 12) there is a real memory of transcendence, here there is none. The incense is fetid, Christ distant and dispassionate, reduced to a material emblem, 'le grand crucifix ennuyé du mur vide' ('the big crucifix bored with the empty wall') (l.3); the vision seems to result from the dying man's delirium. The blood bleeding between the tiles (l.15) may be Christ-like, but is, in the end, just blood.

Yet closer inspection reveals the self-reflexiveness of Mallarmé's later work. Although apparently about dualities (inside/outside, temporal/transcendent, death/the unlimited azure or 'heaven'), 'Les Fenêtres' seems also to be about the windows themselves, less transparent panes of glass than, like the crucifix, objects that both proffer and deny transcendence. Both etymology and shape of the 'croisées' (l.25) ('casements' or 'crosspieces') echo the crucifix. The poet hangs himself on them, seeing himself as an angel in their glass, reborn through art or 'mysticity':


> Je me mire et me vois ange! et je meurs, et j'aime
> – Que la vitre soit l'art ou la mysticité –
> A renaître, portant mon rêve en diadème,
>
> Au ciel antérieur où fleurit la Beauté! (l.29-33)

(I look and see myself as an angel! and I die, and I love/– Be the glass art or mysticity –/To be reborn, bearing my dream as a diadem, // To the earlier heaven where once flowered Beauty!)

Either art or mysticism can lead to this transfiguration, but this transcendence is deceptive, for 'Ici-bas est maître' ('Here below is master') (l.33), the deception is a torment, and the attempt to overcome it the opportunity for an Icarus-like quest to 'enfoncer le cristal' ('smash through the crystal') (l.37), threatening a Baudelairian damnation:

> Est-il moyen, ô Moi qui connais l'amertume,
> D'enfoncer le cristal par le monstre insulté
> Et de m'enfuir, avec mes deux ailes sans plume
> – Au risque de tomber pendant l'éternité? (l.37-41)

(Is there a way, O I who know bitterness,/To smash through the crystal insulted by the monster/And to flee, with my two quill-less wings/– At the risk of falling throughout eternity?)

Look more closely, though, and we can begin to read this poem in a different way, which celebrates, as well as laments, the inability to 'enfoncer le cristal', which praises the medium as much as the message. The 'galères d'or, belles comme des cygnes' ('golden galleys, beautiful as swans') (l.17) that the dying man sees lauds not just swans, but also the 'signes' (signs) that sound identical and bring them to mind; 'or' (gold) is present not just as itself (l.12, 17) but also as a sound in other words ('trésor', 'horloge', 'gorgé', 'dore': 'treasure', 'clock', 'gorged', 'gilds', l.10, 14, 16, 28) representing the gold standard of poetry (an 'or-dure', literally 'rubbish', but homophonically 'hard gold' [l.23]), which is not just extracted from the mire of everyday life, as it was for Baudelaire: 'J'ai pétri de la boue et j'en ai fait de l'or' ('I have kneaded mud and turned it to gold') (*Bribes*), but is inherently part of it, and of language. Language is Mallarmé's gold, and the answer to the final question of 'Les Fenêtres' is 'No':

without 'plume' ('feather', but also 'pen'), there is no flight. As Mallarmé declared in 1867: 'Il n'y que la Beauté, et elle n'a qu'une expression: la Poésie' ('There is only one thing, Beauty, and she has only one expression: Poetry').

Mallarmé's contemporary Barrès wrote that one should read him wearing 'des lunettes sur le cerveau' ('spectacles on one's brain') (*Les Taches d'encre*, 1 November 1884). If we read Mallarmé carefully, we can find many moments that both bring into being, and dispel, presence. It is the so-called 'Sonnet en –yx' (1887) that most emblematically encapsulates Mallarmé's quest:

> Ses purs ongles très-haut dédiant leur onyx,
> L'Angoisse, ce minuit, soutient, lampadophore,
> Maint rêve vespéral brûlé par le Phénix
> Que ne recueille pas de cinéraire amphore
>
> Sur les crédences, au salon vide: nul ptyx
> Aboli bibelot d'inanité sonore,
> (Car le Maître est allé puiser des pleurs au Styx
> Avec ce seul objet dont le Néant s'honore.)
>
> Mais proche la croisée au nord vacante, un or
> Agonise selon peut-être le décor
> Des licornes ruant du feu contre une nixe,
>
> Elle, défunte nue en le miroir, encor
> Que, dans l'oubli fermé par le cadre, se fixe
> De scintillations sitôt le septuor.

(Her pure nails most elevated dedicating their onyx,/Anguish, this midnight, upholds, bearing torches,/Many a vesperal dream burnt by the Phoenix/Ungathered by any cinerary urn // On the credenzas in the empty salon: no ptyx/Trashed trinket of auric inanity, (For the Master has gone to draw tears from the Styx/With this one object with which the Void is honoured.) // But next the empty casement to the north, a gold/Is dying according maybe to the décor/Unicorns dashing fire at a nixie, // She, dead, naked in the mirror, even/Though, in the oblivion closed by the frame is fixed/Immediately the septet of scintillations.)

The poem evokes some sacramental act, but it is impossible to say (or translate) exactly what, for surface meaning is at the mercy of significations suggested by repeated patterns and sounds, and interpretations are no sooner established than dispelled. Anguish may indeed be offering the onyx of her nails (l.1), but if we listen, it sounds as if she may be 'dédiant leur ? aux nixes' ('dedicating their ? to the nixies [watersprites]'), hearing 'onyx' as the homophone of 'aux nixes'. But 'dédiant' both means 'dedicating' and suggests its opposite, 'dédisant': unsaying, disavowing, denying meaning. Likewise, the dream is destroyed by the Phoenix (l.3), but homophonically, 'Phénix' sounds like 'fais-nixe' or 'fait nixe': 'make the/made nixie' (l.4). In line 5, the words 'crédences' ('credenzas', etymologically derived from 'croyance', 'belief', designating the tables on which the Holy Sacrament is reserved for Mass), and 'ptyx', evoking the 'pyx' (French 'pyxine'), where the Host is kept, ought to guarantee meaning. Yet here we have 'nul ptyx' or, effectively, no nothing, a sound no sooner uttered than exploded, something negated the very moment it is stated, suggesting that it is in the void that the most precious plenitude is to be found. 'Aboli bibelot' almost palindromically abolishes, then bodies forth, the trinket, whose void ('Néant') is its gold ('s'honore' = 'son or'). 'Or', gold, echoes through the 'no*r*d vacante', in the 'déc*or*', whose lack of embodiment (homophonically and etymologically 'dé-corps', 'debodies') is its very power; in the 'lic*or*nes', unicorns, mythical beasts, but here present; and in 'enc*or*' (l.2), which seems to combine the '*enc*re' (ink) of which the poem is composed with '*or*' (my italics).

The final stanza embodies the dichotomy of presence and absence, for she (presumably the nymph), the dead naked girl in the mirror, is within the oblivion contained by the frame (for which we might read: the meaning contained by the poem). The 'septet' of 'scintillations' suggests a Baudelairian correspondence and synaesthesia, a relation between sight and sound and earth and heaven. But the lack of defined external referent suggests a purely internal, self-referential relationship, while the paradox of fixing a septet of scintillations points to the productive conflict of presence and absence, designation and ambiguity, which is at the heart of Mallarmé's verse:

> Un désir indéniable de mon temps est de séparer comme en vue d'attributions différentes le double état de la parole, brut ou immédiat ici, là essentiel. (...) Je dis: une fleur! et, hors l'oubli où ma voix relègue aucun contour, en tant que quelque chose d'autre que les calices sus, musicalement se lève, idée même et suave, l'absente de tous bouquets. (*Crise de vers*, 1886-96)

> (An undeniable desire of my time is to separate as if for different purposes the double state of the word, raw or immediate here, there essential [...] I say: A flower! and, apart from the oblivion to which my voice relegates any shape, as something other than known calyxes, there musically arises, the very self-same suave idea, the most absent of all bouquets.)

In other words, the very act of utterance conjures up the flower, but the flower that appears must be the very one that is unlike all known flowers ('quelque chose d'autre que les calices sus'). Not for nothing is 'Ses purs ongles ...' known as the 'Sonnet allégorique de lui-même', for it creates what Mallarmé called a 'mirage interne des mots mêmes' ('an internal mirage of the words themselves') (letter to Cazalis, 18 July 1868) with no one fixed or literal meaning, a space for creation more than a creation in itself.

Mallarmé, then, makes a virtue of what, for Rimbaud, was a vice, exploiting the very limitations of language not to cramp his vision in the materiality of the things described, but to show that the potential vision was *in* the material, in language itself, and that this could become, via the symbol, the virtual. For, as he told the journalist Jules Huret's *Enquête sur l'évolution littéraire* (1891)

*Nommer* un objet, c'est supprimer les trois quarts de la jouissance du poème qui est faite de deviner peu à peu: le *suggérer*, voilà le rêve. C'est le parfait usage de ce mystère qui constitue le symbole: évoquer petit à petit un objet pour montrer un état d'âme ou inversement, choisir un objet et en dégager un état d'âme, par une série de déchiffrements.

(*To name* an object does away with virtually all the pleasure of the poem that is made by guessing little by little; to *suggest*, that is the dream. It is the perfect use of this mystery that constitutes the symbol: to evoke an object little by little to show a state of mind, or, conversely, to choose an object and unlock from it a state of mind, by a series of decipherings.)

This was Mallarmé's Symbolism: multifarious suggestiveness mediated by multiplied fragments of meaning. 'Le sens trop précis rature/Ta vague littérature' ('Over-precise meaning out-scratches/Your vague literature') ('Toute l'âme', 1895). Literature's power of suggestion lies in both potential presence and absence: 'litté-rature', the 'rature' (scratching-out) of the letter, or the literal:

Toute âme est une mélodie qu'il s'agit de renouer; et pour cela, sont la flûte ou la viole de chacun. (*Divagations*, I)

(Every soul is a melody to be recomposed; and everyone has his own flute or viol to do it.)

Nous ne sommes que de vaines formes de la matière, mais bien sublimes, pour avoir inventé Dieu et notre âme. Si sublimes (...) que je veux donner ce spectacle de la matière, ayant conscience d'être, et, cependant, s'élançant forcenément dans le Rêve qu'elle sait n'être pas. (Mallarmé to Cazalis, February 1866)

(We are but vain forms of matter, but truly sublime to have invented God and our soul. So sublime [...] that I want to stage this show of matter, having awareness of being and yet throwing itself wildly into the Dream which it knows does not exist.)

Mallarmé's contemporaries found in his poems a kind of Platonic idealism, an intimation of greater realities beyond our senses; ours, a linguistic construct; he himself, a transcendence in the very stuff of poetry, language. It is a moot point as to how real such transcendence can ever be; but the very paradox encapsulates the tension between subjectivity and vision, objectivity and effect, which lies at the heart of nineteenth-century French verse.

## Selected reading

Paul Bénichou, *Les Mages romantiques* (Paris: Gallimard, 1988). Panoramic overview of the visionary poetry of Lamartine, Hugo and Vigny, following *Le Sacre de l'écrivain (1750-1830)* (1973) and *Le Temps des prophètes* (1977).

Richard D.E. Burton, *Baudelaire in 1859* (Cambridge: Cambridge University Press, 1989). Insightful and moving account of the pivotal year in Baudelaire's career.

Albert Cassagne, pref. D. Oster, *La Théorie de l'art pour l'art en France chez les derniers romantiques et les premiers réalistes* (Seyssel: Champ Vallon, 1997 [1906]). Classic study of some of the pivotal paradoxes in nineteenth-century French literature.

James Lawler, *Rimbaud's Theatre of the Self* (Cambridge, MA and London: Harvard University Press, 1992). Close interpretation of selected poems in terms of poetic personae and roles.

—— *Poetry and Moral Dialectic: Baudelaire's 'Secret Architecture'* (Madison, NJ and London: Fairleigh Dickinson University Press, 1997). Observant, sometimes controversial thematic tour of *Les Fleurs du mal.*

Roger Pearson, *Unfolding Mallarmé: The Development of a Poetic Art* (Oxford: Oxford University Press, 1996); *Mallarmé and Circumstance: The Translation of Silence* (Oxford: Oxford University Press, 2004). Two superlative studies.

Lawrence M. Porter, *The Crisis of French Symbolism* (Ithaca, NY and London: Cornell University Press, 1990). Provocative, sometimes idiosyncratic challenge to conventional literary history, interpreting Mallarmé, Verlaine, Baudelaire and Rimbaud in terms of a crisis in communication.

Christopher Prendergast (ed.), *Nineteenth Century French Poetry: Introductions to Close Reading* (Cambridge: Cambridge University Press, 1990). Covers canonical writers while opening wider perspectives.

Jean-Pierre Richard, *Poésie et profondeur* (Paris: Seuil, 1955 and reprints). Penetrating explorations of Nerval, Baudelaire, Verlaine and Rimbaud.

Mary Lewis Shaw, *The Cambridge Introduction to French Poetry* (Cambridge: Cambridge University Press, 2003). Useful overview of genres, versification and forms, as well as of political, philosophical and aesthetic issues, not restricted to the nineteenth century.

# 4

# Drama

Le théâtre est une tribune (...) le théâtre parle fort et parle haut.
(Hugo, *Lucrèce Borgia*, Preface, 1832)

(Theatre is a tribune [...] theatre speaks loud and clear.)

On ne voit pas dans l'âme comme on voit dans cette chambre.
(Maeterlinck, *Intérieur*, 1893)

(You cannot see into the soul as you see into this room.)

## 4.1. Public and private, political and personal

There is a central paradox in nineteenth-century French theatre. On the one hand, theatre was the most public and objective of the literary arts; on the other, writers sought increasingly to represent individual and subjective states of mind. The tension between public and private is mirrored by a second, of popularity and performability, versus an absolute literary ideal: with few exceptions, the most popular plays of the period are not those which are read, still less performed, today. Finally, the inherently public nature of theatre had made it the focus of official attention and control that other literary forms largely escaped, creating a preoccupation with dramatic rules and their subversion that to this day has tended to overshadow the plays themselves.

This process has had no more notable victim than Victor Hugo's first great drama, *Cromwell*. Its preface, in large part not concerned directly with the play, is more of a general Romantic manifesto, outlining the ideal Romantic drama, in counter-distinction to the neoclassical rules that, as in poetry, then still prevailed. After brief liberalisation during the Revolution, which had seen a massive expansion in popular theatre, Napoleon, driven by misguided pedagogy as well as political repression, had closed down all the Parisian theatres except three: the Comédie Française, the Comédie Italienne and the Ambigu-Comique offered a strictly limited diet of great Classical dramas – Corneille and Molière, Racine and Voltaire – which they alone were officially permitted to purvey. Although other rival theatres first timidly, then increasingly boldly, staged pieces from this repertory under the later Empire and Restoration (along with numerous new neoclassical offerings), the mass of the play-going public, largely deprived of the very Classical fare that the Emperor would have fed them, turned to the most popular genre of the moment, the melodrama, whose stereotyped, highly coloured heroes, heroines and villains, racy plots and spectacular staging reflected the insecurities and preoccupations of the time. Pixérécourt's *Victor ou l'enfant de la forêt* (1797), his *Coelina ou l'Enfant du mystère* (1800), both adapted from novels by Ducray-Duminil, and Ducange's *Trente ans ou la vie d'un joueur* (1827), were among the greatest successes of the era.

It was to bridge the gulf between official and popular theatre, and the genre division it represented, between Classical drama, and melodrama, that *Cromwell*, and its preface, set out. Classical rules reflected the needs of the Antique, Classical age; but the modern, Christian age needed a different kind of drama. The Classical division between comedy and tragedy did not conform to nature, where spirit and matter, sublime and grotesque, were combined in a single being or situation; the Classical unities of time, action and place, with a single action involving one group of protagonists over not more than twenty-four fictional hours, did not correspond to real life, where real events were often more protracted and more complex, and compelled dramatists to subterfuges whereby important and dramatic actions were merely reported, rather than represented on the stage. Hugo's new conception of theatre, foreshadowed also by Stendhal's *Racine et Shakespeare* (1823, 25) was of a theatre of freedom, offering a complete vision of reality, where anything, in principle, could be said or represented. Of this bonfire of the unities only verse, 'la forme optique de la pensée' ('the optical form of thought') (*Cromwell*, preface), would remain; for prose, writes Hugo, opens the way to mediocrity.

It was *Hernani* (1830), rather than *Cromwell*, unperformed during Hugo's lifetime, which achieved the public impact necessary for Romantic drama to make its mark as the major avant-garde theatrical form and to supersede Classical drama. *Hernani* was a provocation, showing by its very failings the measure of its ambition. Set in Spain in 1519, at the moment of Don Carlos's (Charles I of Spain's) accession as Holy Roman Emperor, *Hernani* obliquely challenged the contemporary French political status quo, echoing Beaumarchais's ploy of using distant Spain to critique contemporary France in *Le Mariage de Figaro* (1784). Hernani, a bandit, but of noble blood, loves the aristocratic Doña Sol, who is betrothed to her uncle, Don Ruy Gomez; but the man introduced into her chamber with his hat pulled down over his eyes in the very first scene is neither, but the Holy Roman Emperor elect, Don Carlos. Don Carlos hides from Hernani in a wardrobe, later emerging to challenge him to a duel for Doña Sol, only to join him there when Don Ruy Gomez arrives.

Such situations are not infrequent in Hugo's drama. In *Le Roi s'amuse* (1832), King François I loves Blanche, not realising that she is his jester Triboulet's daughter; in *Ruy Blas* (1838), the valet-protagonist loves the queen, becomes prime minister, while a ruined noble, Don César, makes one of his entrances down a chimney. They inevitably invite the charge of melodrama; the most critics have sometimes felt able to do with them is to relate them to Hugo's theory of sublime and grotesque, of their fusion in a single situation or character.

But while Don Carlos, or Don César, behave in ways that no Shakespearian, still less Racinian tragic hero, could have countenanced, that is the point of the *drame*: it fuses actions and events that comedy and tragedy keep separate. And beneath this apparently exclusively aesthetic aim lies one more fundamentally political. The famous 'Bataille d'*Hernani*', which accompanied the première on 26 February 1830, where insults were hurled and missiles thrown, was a struggle not just between Classics and Romantics, but between political reactionaries and progressives, the old and a new regime, only months before the July revolution. The *enjambement* that, scandalously, failed to endstop the first alexandrine ('Serait-ce déjà lui? C'est bien à l'escalier/Dérobé', 'Could it already be he? It's certainly in the hidden/Staircase') (I.1.1), itself interrupted by a knock on the door, mattered because the rules not just of versification, but of Classical seemliness themselves were being overturned; the use of plain language instead of periphrasis, the sometimes comically incongruous speeches – all challenge conventional hierarchies, aesthetic, moral, social, political. 'Quelle heure est-il?' asks Don Carlos, to be answered 'Minuit bientôt' ('What time is it? Soon midnight' – a word like 'minuit' could never have figured in Classical tragedy) (II.1.463). 'Nous sommes trois chez vous! C'est trop de deux madame', says Don Ruy Gomez when he discovers Hernani and Carlos with Doña Sol ('There are three of us with you! Madame, two would be too many') (I.3.220). So when Hugo's heroes hide in a cupboard or come down chimneys, his noblewoman or queen falls in love with a bandit or valet, these actions question our moral certainties, the astonishing behaviour of characters and the extraordinary turn of events pushing back the boundaries of what we can find believable, acceptable or real.

Such excesses spoke specially to audiences tested by turbulent historical realities, and inured to melodrama: it is against these shifting benchmarks that Romantic drama's disconcerting reversals should be set. The frequent use of misrepresented or mistaken identity or disguise, for example, mirrors not just melodrama, but, more fundamentally, a contemporary reality in which it was often difficult to establish exactly who was legitimate, and who proscribed, and in which these boundaries might move at any moment. Hernani is, in the course of the play, bandit, exile and also noble; the queen loves

Ruy Blas, taking him for an aristocrat, but when she discovers his low standing, forgives him nonetheless. The sometimes involved and over-complex plots, or unclear motivation of character or event reflect a reality itself alarmingly unstable. Is it believable that Hernani should mortgage his happiness with Doña Sol to his honour (a debt Don Ruy Gomez calls in when, in Act Five, he says that Hernani must die)? Can we accept that Gomez should defer to his adversary so readily and so cravenly as soon as he discovers he is king? Is it credible that Don Salluste should be exiled for a mere sexual peccadillo, or that he should construct such an elaborate revenge? These questions test both the drama's credibility and our moral standards, querying honour's relevance in a selfish age.

It is in Vigny's *Chatterton* (1834, first performed in 1835) and Musset's *Lorenzaccio* (1834, but, as we shall see, not performed until 1896) that the political role of the aesthetic is most central. *Chatterton* tells the story of the eighteenth-century English poet Thomas Chatterton's social rejection and suicide. Society's dominant values, represented by the avaricious philistine Bell, are so out of tune with the human, and the humane, embodied by his wife Kitty, with whom Chatterton falls in love, that they effectively kill the poet. The poet represents a pure centre of reflection, beyond venality and utilitarianism, which society ought to support. But the only job offered to Chatterton is as the king's first valet: this insult, compounded by the need to write for money, and his inability to voice his love for Kitty, pushes him to his end. But the situation is not entirely one-sided. Although Bell is an ogre, Kitty angelic, and their Quaker mentor saintly, Chatterton himself is a very mixed blessing: if poets are the pilots who steer humanity by the stars, they are also too egotistical to form relationships, or to be integrated into society. His vulnerability makes him totemic. The poet can live neither within society, nor outside it, and the conflict causes Chatterton's death.

In Musset's *Lorenzaccio*, the artist is apparently tangential, explicitly represented only by Tebaldeo. But the link between aesthetics, philosophy and politics in fact forms the play's thematic core. Tebaldeo, a character like Chatterton, outside society, represents the artist's integrity, but in Musset's play's sixteenth-century Florence, no one is uncorrupted by power. Like Chatterton, the hero Lorenzo is undoubtedly different from the dominant nobles, soldiers and merchants. Yet if Chatterton's difference has virtues, Lorenzo's becomes a vice, allowing him to attack society, but making him also ringleader of a plot to murder Alexandre, Duke of Florence. What ought to be an audacious and noble aim, the toppling of a tyrant for a republic, becomes a corrupt undertaking, compromised by deception, using Lorenzo's aunt to lure the duke to his death, destroying the very integrity that prompted it. Lorenzo ultimately commits the murder simply because it is all that remains of his former idealism. The means have become the end. And, as in Shakespeare's *Hamlet*, an apparent choice between words and action soon proves an insoluble dilemma: if Lorenzo has acted too soon, his opposite, the aged Philippe Strozzi, has waited too long. The acts of neither achieve their goal: Philippe simply avenges himself on his daughter, and Lorenzo's act of murder leads merely to his own death. By the end, the populace these deeds were to serve are still as excluded as ever. In Musset's Florence, there is no moral high ground.

*Lorenzaccio*, written, like most of Musset's plays, to be read rather than performed, was too subversive to be put on in 1834, and was not first staged, cut down, until 1896, when the great actress Sarah Bernhardt, cross-dressed, played the title role. But the intellectual seriousness of plays like *Chatterton* and *Lorenzaccio* poses larger challenges of conception and production. Art, poetry and politics, potentially wordy subjects, risk producing wordy dramas, something Musset generally avoids better than Vigny. *Chatterton* was a huge success, but on account of its accessibility, its starkly painted characters and contrasts, and of how much it spoke to current concerns. Where Vigny makes vivid contrasts between only four main characters, Musset's cast list of nearly thirty named parts, plus scores of extras, suggests a wider world of Shakespearian complexity.

The drama in both plays derives from the struggles in the hero's soul. Yet if Vigny expresses these more strikingly, as serial reversals,

the two *coups de théâtre* in *Lorenzaccio*, the murders of Alexandre and
Lorenzo in Acts IV and V, are more truly dramatic, borne of a situation intrinsically concerned with intrigue, emerging from a slow,
meticulously causal crescendo, conforming to the play's fundamental subject. Both writers use prose to create a more modern kind
of drama; but here too, Musset's work creates a tighter convergence
of form and content. Where Vigny's cast list, speeches, even stage
directions, are extensive (with some challenging examples:
'Chatterton, pâle', is more easily imagined than acted), Musset,
although writing for private reading, sketches settings more
economically, placing description, like Shakespeare, in characters'
mouths as a natural function of their thought, expressing the physical presence of the subject, perfectly matching the two terms of
comparison:

> Le vice était pour moi un masque: il est maintenant collé à ma peau.

> (Vice was to me as a mask: now it cleaves to my skin.)

> L'Empereur et le pape avaient fait un duc d'un garçon boucher.

> (The Emperor and the Pope had made a Duke from a butcher's boy.)

'Je ne me suis pas fait écrivain politique' ('I have not made myself
into a political writer') wrote Musset in *La Coupe et les lèvres* (1833).
But in making the political personal, eminently suited to private
reading, he expresses the individualism of the Romantic generation,
creating a drama both historical yet of enduring relevance today. By
exploiting melodrama, in contrast, plays like *Hernani* and *Ruy Blas*
brought serious social and political issues to a wide audience, while
*Chatterton* and *Lorenzaccio* questioned the writer's very purpose in
society. All strive to express a kind of *ne plus ultra* of theatre, and,
like all Romantic writing, an unattainable absolute of both private
passion and public action, most nearly approached in the operatic
adaptations by Verdi (*Ernani*, 1844; *Rigoletto*, 1851, based on Hugo's

*Le Roi s'amuse*). It is a telling irony that the great plays of French Romantic drama should have their brightest afterlife in the multi-media form of opera, for its aspirations were so absolute and transcendent that they could not be satisfied by the mere linguistic resources of the page or spoken drama alone.

## 4.2. Dramas of money and morals

Chaque minute de recueillement est un vol que tu fais; c'est une minute stérile. – Il s'agit bien de l'idée, grand Dieu! Ce qui rapporte, c'est le mot. Il y a tel mot qui peut aller jusqu'à un schelling; la pensée n'a pas cours sur la place. (*Chatterton*, III.1)

(You commit a theft with every minute of reflection; it's a minute of sterility. – The main thing is the idea, for goodness sake! What earns the money are words. Some words are worth as much as a shilling; thought has no value on the market.)

Transaction and reification, the turning of human beings and rela-tions into objects, are two key themes of mid-nineteenth-century French theatre. Whether in the dramas of Scribe, Dumas *fils* or Augier, or the farces of Labiche and Feydeau, feelings that ought to be valid in themselves become the object of negotiations and trans-actions. Less ambitious but more immediate than Romantic drama, this witty, popular theatre can offer vibrant emotional experiences and telling moral lessons.

Dumas *fils*'s *La Dame aux camélias* (1852), adapted and toned down from his novel of 1848, crystallises these themes. The story of the respectable Armand Duval's love for a courtesan, Marguerite, resulting in his father's outraged prohibition and her death, has, via Verdi's operatic version, *La Traviata* (1863), become one of the century's best-known works. But the opera bowdlerises Dumas's drama, which still powerfully challenges our prejudices and assumptions.

At first, the moral boundaries seem clear enough: Marguerite has

an expectedly cynical view of men, her insistence on only one
flower, the camellia, symbolising her exoticism (but also, in
Magnat's 1855 *Traité du langage symbolique des fleurs*, reputation). Her
readiness to deceive both Armand and her current sugar-daddy,
Giray, by seeing Giray to get money to fund her summer in the
country with Armand, apparently seals her corruption: after all, the
courtesan's purpose, the play tells us, is to feed men's vanity. She is
a nineteenth-century celebrity, who lives and dies by visibility: this
is a very modern world, knowing the price of everything and the
value of nothing, where credit (financial and moral) rules all, and
nothing escapes money's domination. Every single act begins with
money, from the opening revelation that Marguerite has been a
laundry-maid, to Prudence's request for a loan, to Armand's
enquiries about the fate of Marguerite's jewellery and horses
(pawned to keep the wolf from the door), to the Act IV opening
gambling scene, to Gaston's gift of money in the last. Even morality
is financial: Marguerite's previous lover, the Comte de Mauriac,
had promised her everything she wanted, as long as she changed
her ways, cutting off half her income when she fails to obey:

> (...) ce à quoi s'engagea Marguerite, qui, naturellement encore, de
> retour à Paris, se garda bien de tenir sa parole; et le duc, comme elle
> ne lui rendait que la moitié de son bonheur, a retranché la moitié du
> revenu; si bien qu'aujourd'hui elle a cinquante mille francs de dettes.
> (I.3)

> ([...] to which Marguerite agreed, and naturally, as soon as she
> returned to Paris, was only too careful not to keep her word; and the
> duke, as she was only giving him half his happiness, cut off half her
> income; with the result that today she is fifty thousand francs in debt.)

This almost Wildean flippancy (particularly shocking, given that the
speaker here, Varville, will become her lover) seems to celebrate
more than criticise established social mores – which, if not moral,
are at least amusing. But this bartering of money and morality fore-

shadows the central dilemma, when Armand's father makes her leave him, starkly illuminating the hypocrisies of conventional moral reasoning on sex. Mauriac has fallen for Marguerite because she resembles his dead daughter; he punishes her when she fails to live up to his fantasy. Armand dumps her when he discovers that she is really bankrolled by Giray; his father makes Marguerite leave him in order to protect the honour of Armand's sister, symbolically named Blanche. Every single one of these responses suggests dangerously simplistic conceptions of morality, indeed misconceptions of the relationship between love and lust, physical feeling and emotion. There is apparently no awareness of the flagrant double standards men apply to women's sexual conduct and their own – set up from the outset in Varville's comment on Marguerite's alleged inconsistency: 'Elle est sage, mais elle a un amant' ('She's a good girl, but she's got a lover') (I. 3). As she does not hesitate to tell him, 'Je suis libre d'aimer qui je veux, cela ne regarde personne' ('I am free to love whoever I want, it's nobody else's business') (I. 4).

Marguerite's position makes her an exception, giving her wealth and power denied to almost all other women. But the freedom of which she boasts is shown to be an illusion when she really does fall in love with Armand, a man whose respectability, or whose family's respectability, makes her unacceptable to them. On one level, this is mere doublethink, hypocrisy on the part of the bourgeois failing to recognise the parallel between her situation and their own. On another, it is an understandable reaction to someone who has sold herself. Yet in the name of respectability she agrees to tell a lie, that she no longer loves Armand, and takes another lover (Varville) both to support her and to leave Armand in no doubt as to her supposed duplicity. It is paradoxical indeed that untruths are told to defend respectability, while Marguerite and Armand's true love is treated like a falsehood. It is Marguerite's death, her status as victim, which gives her moral validation, just as her sickness connoted society's decadence, making her a quasi-saintly Lady of the Camellias, the symbol of an ideal of sainthood and sinfulness combined.

## The farce of objects: Labiche and Feydeau

### 4.3.1. Labiche: Un Chapeau de paille d'Italie

At first glance, Labiche's *Un Chapeau de paille d'Italie* (1851) seems trivial. Fadinard's quest to replace Anaïs's Italian straw hat, eaten by his horse in the Bois de Vincennes, piles complication upon coincidence in a minefield of mishaps and misunderstandings. Fadinard, challenged to replace the hat by Tavernier, supposedly Anaïs's cousin, goes to a milliner who turns out to be Clara, one of Fadinard's old flames, who refuses to oblige unless he promises to return to her. This he does, putting himself in immediate, seemingly irretrievable difficulty – for he is about to marry Hélène, and the wedding party arrives at the milliner's supposing it to be the town hall. Clara, unable to replace the hat, directs Fadinard to the Baronne de Champigny, for whom she has recently made an exactly identical hat; but when he goes to see her, the baronne mistakes him for the tenor Nisnardi, come to give a concert in her salon; meanwhile Fadinard's wedding party, pursuing him like a fury, duly arrives and, thinking itself at the wedding breakfast, consumes the banquet intended for the Baroness's guests. Fadinard, using eccentricity as a pretext, asks for the Italian hat; but the baronne has sent it to her friend, Mme de Beauperthuis, to whom he goes in Act IV. Instead he finds her husband, furious at this stranger's request to see his wife at ten o'clock at night; but Fadinard, undeterred, enters her bedroom just as his father-in-law, Nonancourt, arrives with the wedding party. Both soon catch up with Fadinard, just in time for him to show Beauperthuis the remnant of the chewed-up hat, which Beauperthuis recognises as his wife's; her story of going out to buy suede gloves was a cover for an outing of a different sort. Fadinard and Beauperthuis rush off to find her, to be confronted by Tardiveau, Clara's bookkeeper, doing his duty as a National Guard; Nonancourt, with the wedding party, arrives soon after, and immediately assumes that Fadinard is seeing a mistress on his wedding day. Pursued by a pistol-toting Beauperthuis, as well as by the outraged Nonancourt, Fadinard has to find a way of extricating himself and Anaïs – which he does by disguising Anaïs as a National Guard, enabling her to turn the tables on her husband, and ask him what, precisely, he thinks he is doing out on the streets so late. Thus she covers her own infidelity – for Tavernier was not a cousin, but a lover – and cuts the many knots into which Fadinard had tied himself. As for the hat: the replacement Fadinard had been chasing turns out to be Anaïs's, the very one his horse had eaten. But salvation appears in the shape of one exactly identical, given by his uncle Vézinet on his wedding day. Thus the convenient uncle resolves all difficulties at a stroke, and the wedding breakfast, at midnight, can finally begin.

What is the point of *Un Chapeau de paille d'Italie*? It offers a fast-moving plot, compressed into one day, reminiscent of Beaumarchais's *La Folle journée ou Le Mariage de Figaro*, a surfeit of coincidence and incident, and constant challenges to probability and credulity. On one level, that of action, our attention and emotions are vigorously engaged: we take Fadinard's predicament seriously, and want to see how he will emerge. On another, we can hardly take him seriously at all, if he can declare love to Clara on the day he is to marry Hélène, or neglect his wedding to pursue an unknown woman's hat. Much of the play is purely pleasure, derived from the characters' agony; and much of the pleasure is intellectual, arising from patterning and wit. We delight in the dupes' gullibility and the protagonists' inventiveness, especially Anaïs's spectacular turning of the tables on her husband at the end.

This is the stock-in-trade of comedy: duped husbands, duplicitous lovers, base motives triumphing over the nobler ones we are supposed to seek. But where earlier comedy concentrates on people, Labiche makes people the agents of things, in pursuit of *La Cagnotte* (the jackpot) or, here, the elusive straw hat. His characters are hamstrung by money and the material. They determine Fadinard's decision to marry (I.4), dog Tardiveau via his ailments

(II.2, V.1) and are nowhere more striking than when hobbling Nonancourt's attempts to adopt a tragic stance in the face of another of Fadinard's infidelities:

> Hélène: Papa ... papa ... je vais me trouver mal....
> Nonancourt, *vivement*: Pas par terre, ma fille ... tu flétrirais ta robe de cinquante-trois francs! *(A tous)* Mes enfants, jetons une malédiction sur cet immonde polisson, et retournons-nous tous à Charentonneau.
> Tous: Oui, oui!
> Hélène: Mais, papa, je ne veux pas lui laisser mes bijoux, mes cadeaux de noces.
> Nonancourt: Ma fille, ceci est d'une femme d'ordre.... (*Un Chapeau de paille d'Italie*, V.3)

> (Hélène: Papa ... papa ... I'm going to faint.... // Nonancourt, *force-fully*: Not on the ground, my dear ... you would spoil your fifty-three-franc dress! // (*To everyone:*) My children, let us put a curse on this vile rogue, and let us all return to Charentonneau. // All: Yes, yes! // Hélène: But papa, I don't want to leave him with my jewels and my wedding presents. // Nonancourt: My dear, that is the mark of a well-ordered woman....)

The things we frequently care about are not really important at all, but, like Hélène's dress, or the hat itself, consume our attention. The hat is both all-encompassing (symbolic of infidelity and deception but also, as a wedding present, of their opposite), yet also as insubstantial as the straw from which it is made: the biggest joke in the play is that the much sought-after hat is also a non-hat, the very ex-hat Fadinard had been trying to replace. More disturbingly, the play suggests perhaps that there is not much that we do really take seriously: Fadinard's reasons for marrying are appallingly trifling, like his motives for briefly courting Clara – the plot leads via deceptions and mishaps to a concluding festival of bad faith. We laugh as it treats people as objects, but wonder also whether this might be more truthful than traditional discourses of feeling and fidelity, requiring integrity of a kind that may not be in human nature. The superficiality highlights the illusions of conventional readings of humanity. Labiche makes us laugh at our own void.

### 4.3.2. Feydeau: Le Dindon

Labiche's farces are built around haplessness and fecklessness; Feydeau's compound these elements with cynicism and cruelty. In perhaps his greatest play, *Le Dindon* (1896), the seducer does not hold back when one of his conquests turns out to be his friend Vatier's wife Lucienne. Indeed, he gives her proof of her husband's infidelity: 'C'est un peu canaille ce que j'ai fait là ... mais bah! j'ai une excuse, c'est pour avoir sa femme' ('What I've just done is a bit rough ... but bah! I've got an excuse, I did it to get his wife') (I.17). This 'morality', founded on the dimmest of views of marriage ('Vous savez ce que c'est ... C'est pour la vie', 'You know what it's like ... it's for life', I.2), governs Pontagnac's actions, and runs throughout the play, with a ready libertinage and sexiness in every scene. One feels a liaison could come from almost every encounter. Yet none of the characters is really vicious; they are simply weak and opportunistic, and are often made to lie on beds they have made for themselves in the past.

This is what most differentiates them from Labiche's merely hapless figures. Feydeau's have to endure their fair share of unfortunate coincidence and contrivance, but the most profoundly comic moments come from their compulsion to commit the very acts of love that might supposedly be the pinnacle of self-realisation and free will. Vatelier has to endure his ex-lover Maggy's surprise visit from England, an upshot of their past affair; his wife Lucienne contrives supposed infidelities with Rédillon and Pontagnac simply to avenge herself on her husband. Both spouses treat people as things, means to their own ends, yet end up being used themselves: Maggy forces Vatelier to meet her, threatening suicide otherwise; Lucienne is embroiled in a revenge for which she has no appetite – she is merely going through the motions.

This 'thing'-like status lets us laugh at the characters, and much of the play's comedy depends on the cruelty of treating human beings as things. Maggy's English accent and hopeless French give rise to much humour, like Mme Pinchard's deafness, or certain running jokes (Pontagnac's compulsive purchasing of second-rate art), or Vatelin's absurd explanation to Maggy's husband Soldignac of the presence of her arm (that Soldignac does not recognise), glimpsed through a half-open door:

> Soldignac: A qui ce bras?
> Vatelin: – Je ne sais pas! C'est pas d'ici! C'est un bras qui est là ... alors, il est venu! il est venu sans venir! C'est le bras du voisin!...
> Soldignac: – Blagueur! C'est le bras de votre femme.
> Vatelin: Voilà, vous l'avez dit, c'est le bras de votre femme ... de ma femme ... du voisin qui est ma femme!... (Feydeau, *Le Dindon*, II.12)

> (Soldignac: Whose arm is this? // Vatelin: – I don't know! It's not from round here! It's an arm that happens to be there ... so it came! it came without coming! It's the neighbour's arm!... // Soldignac: – You joker! It's your wife's arm. // Vatelin: There, you've said it, it's your wife's arm ... my wife's arm ... the arm of the neighbour who is my wife!)

This just before the half-dressed Maggy walks straight into the room.

Yet beneath such comic moments lie darker truths, which reach a climax in the last Act when Lucienne makes Pontagnac begin to undress in order to for it to appear that they have committed, or were about to commit, adultery. Pontagnac's feelings begin to carry him away, but Lucienne puts a stop to his ardour by reading the paper, and Rédillon, another of Lucienne's potential accomplices, defuses the whole impending disaster by engineering the over-hearing of Vatelin's confession that his adventure with Maggy was just a fling, and that his true feelings are for his wife. Despite this happy moral ending, the ubiquitous promiscuousness and deception leave us with the queasy feeling that, even if Pontagnac does not suffer, he ends up at the very least being ridiculed for desires which, if short-lived, are genuine. As he says in his parting remark: 'C'était écrit, je suis le dindon!' ('It was predestined, I'm the turkey!') (III.10).

### 4.3.3. Becque: Les Corbeaux

Feydeau's plays, along with those of Courteline and Labiche, represent the major stream of nineteenth-century theatre, a theatre of levity, founded on dramatic incident, often centring on marriage and its mishaps – the popular commercial theatre of Scribe and Halévy that dominated Parisian and provincial stages throughout the century. Becque, in contrast, represents a reaction already begun by Dumas *fils* and Augier towards more serious subjects and realistic presentation. But while they met commercial needs in order to get their work performed, *Les Corbeaux* (1882) was, apart from *La Parisienne* (1885), the uncompromising Becque's only stage success.

This success came at the price of some concessions to popular theatre, evident in dramatic incidents like the industrialist paterfamilias Vigneron's sudden Act I death. Marriage is a major theme, in the shape of his youngest daughter, Blanche's, projected and socially advantageous match with an impoverished aristocrat, Georges de Saint-Genis. But *Les Corbeaux*, the story of how creditors strike and friends desert after Vigneron's death, has a gloomy yet unclouded view of human nature, and of the omnipotence of money, a no-holds-barred quality by which its first audiences were shocked. Scenes like Gaston's mocking of his father moments before he dies (Act I) or Mme de Saint-Genis's cruelty (III.2, III.11) caused such offence that they were cut.

But what really distinguishes *Les Corbeaux* is the presence of an aesthetic, indebted to the novelistic Realism of Balzac and his successors, Champfleury, the Goncourts, and to Zolian Naturalism (see Chapter 5, this volume). Balzacian is the guiding comparison between humans and animals: the predators are crow-like in their sly arrival and unflinching picking of the corpse. This is an inheritance drama like Balzac's *Le Cousin Pons* (1846), but driven by a relentless Darwinian, Zolian, instinct for survival. The descriptive documentation is also Realist: the creditors' letters arriving rapidly in Act II, the partly superfluous Act I exposition of Mme Vigneron's relations with Teissier, or the Act IV dumb-show portraying her grief only through expression and gesture. Such things might work better in a novel, unobtrusively related by a narrator: there is no need, for example, to carry the dead Vigneron on stage at the end of Act I; indeed, the corpse's arrival might diminish believability, and seem motivated by a determination not to be Classical (in French Classical drama deaths always take place off-stage), by the demands of theatrical effect, and above all by a Realist and Naturalist need to be complete, to tell the whole truth, seemingly in every detail. The effect would be of a 'slice of life', were it not that too many momentous events are crammed into the apparently brief, unspecified time frame and too many plot strands left untied. Even the ending is unresolved, with Teissier's final words, 'Allons retrouver votre famille' ('Let us go back to find your family') (IV.10) shedding ironic light on the likely actual outcome. The resolution is thematic more than dramatic. The play appears, like life, to present raw data, leaving us to draw our own conclusions.

*Les Corbeaux* thus does what is nearly impossible on the stage, where form and effect are almost more important than content. It dares to present notation that seems comprehensive, leaving the audience to pick up, or play with, the threads, and to give subtleties and details of behaviour that can usually only feature in the novel. As such, it represents the pinnacle of Realist drama in nineteenth-century France, portraying a credible social context with characters who are particularised types, exploiting an aesthetic mode –

Realism – whose possibilities, in the nineteenth century, would only be more completely exploited in the novel, and whose true potential would only be apparent in the twentieth, via its dominance in film and television.

### 4.4. Dramas of interiority: Maeterlinck, *Pelléas et Mélisande* and *Intérieur*

*La Dame aux camélias* and *Les Corbeaux* represent one model of individualism – the selfishness of capitalism – where humans are driven only by their own desires, and treat others as objects, pawns in marriage contracts and business deals, the drama of Villiers de l'Isle-Adam and Maeterlinck represents another: the suggestive solipsism of the characters' inner worlds. In Villiers's *Axel* (1886), the successively claustral, fortified settings (an old abbey in the first part, a stronghold in the others) represent closedness and reclusion; in *Pelléas et Mélisande* (1893), the servant's difficulty in opening the castle doors at the beginning symbolises the inaccessibility of the world where the drama is set: both the characters' inner worlds, and the physical setting itself. *Pelléas et Mélisande* takes place in a mysterious, quasi-mythic world, whose characters and every detail assume an emblematic and suggestive Symbolic status. The drama's core, Pelléas and Mélisande's adulterous love, is potentially no different from the basic premise of many plays explored thus far. What is very different is the way the characters and details assume portentousness far beyond themselves. From the very opening, when Golaud is trapped in the forest, when he sees Mélisande and instantly falls in love, there is a sense of the urgency of every encounter, event and sensation, of their meaningfulness and transcendence, yet ultimate mystery. From the outset, symbolism of the phenomenal world structures our perceptions, and, it seems, the characters' destinies – the light of the sun rising over the sea (I.1); the forest where Golaud is lost, and finds Mélisande (I.2); the fathomless pool into which she gazes, and where her crown has fallen;

Mélisande's hair, and the light that glints off it, in her central encounter with Pelléas (III.2).

All these and other notations will, through insistent reformulation, gradually gain significance – the forest, where Golaud's dog goes wild as noon strikes, at the very moment that Mélisande, illicitly with Pelléas, drops her ring into the pool (II.1, 2); her hair, as it cascades luxuriantly from the tower, engulfing Pelléas; the light as the sun sets back into the sea when she dies in the final Act. Everything is pregnant with a significance, a purpose, a destiny, which gradually closes in on the characters: the forest seems to symbolise the thicket of desire in which the three protagonists are trapped; the bloodlust of Golaud's hound, or the quiver and arrows he gives his son Yniold, the violence of his own urges; the cellars of the castle, with its pool that Golaud and Pelléas visit, the murky unknowability of feeling; the pool in which Mélisande has lost the ring, and the sea which, Golaud warns, might swamp it, the dangerous depths of desire; the sheep that both he and Yniold see going to town (doubtless to market), the inevitability of death. The servants, the blind men's fountain, the poor dying of hunger towards the end, figure the shadow-side of the lovers' destiny; Mélisande's daughter is born a runt, like a pauper's child (V.1).

Characters, and their destinies, are thus absorbed into a larger picture; yet its meaning remains unclear. Destiny, though scarcely mentioned, encircles them, but why, and to what purpose, we cannot say. That Mélisande cannot be touched by Golaud when he meets her (I.2), that Pelléas cannot look her in the eye, seems to figure the individual's sacred inviolability, yet these same individuals all seem to be playthings of a higher power. The closed room in which Pelléas and Mélisande are cloistered, and into which Yniold looks when Golaud asks him to describe their actions, represents that unknowability; and the grandfather Arkel, who seems to have a hotline to wisdom and destiny, can tell its outline, but not its detail.

This central paradox in *Pelléas* point to a central problem – because we cannot certainly interpret its symbolism, we cannot certainly interpret the play in any sense at all. Golaud is attracted to Mélisande, and Pelléas and Mélisande to each other, by some insuperable force, but whether that force is its own justification is very much open to question. Mélisande's confession of love to Pelléas seems to come 'from the ends of the earth' (IV.4, 32), like the prompting of destiny – or death. In Act V, Scene 1, Pelléas has been found in the blind men's fountain – symbolising his lack of awareness of what he should have done; Mélisande, on the other hand, dies not from her tiny wound but, it seems, from not having been able to satisfy not just her desires, but her destiny: 'on dirait que son âme a froid' ('you would think her soul was cold') (V.2). If the dying Mélisande wants to open the great window, and believes she is attaining wisdom, her selfhood is actually being absorbed into a different order: 'je ne sais plus ce que je sais', she declares, 'je ne dis plus ce que je veux' ('I no longer know what I know, I no longer say what I want'). The light is not that of earthly enlightenment, but of the sun setting into the sea, one infinity being absorbed into another. Golaud, too, misses the truth by being convinced that he knows it already, refusing to believe that Mélisande has not consummated her love for Pelléas. 'Je vais mourir ici comme un aveugle', he says ('I am going to die here like a blind man') (V.2). But his blindness is simply that of all mankind. The only certainty is meaningless torment. With its closing setting sun mirroring its opening dawn, the play suggests an unending destiny of suffering, in which individuals feel intensely but act out an unknown higher design. *Pelléas et Mélisande* suggestively explores the individual's inwardness and solipsism, making it central, yet utterly subservient to a hidden transcendent plan.

'On ne voit pas dans l'âme comme on voit dans cette chambre' ('You cannot see into the soul as you see into this room'). The old man's remark in the one-act play *Intérieur* (1890) expresses an aim that is paradoxically achieved in this and other Symbolist dramas. *Intérieur* begins by allowing us to look literally from outside through the window at a family, parents, daughters and young child, sitting contentedly by the fire. We can see but cannot hear them. Outside two men appear, who, it gradually transpires, have dreadful news to break. A woman has been found drowned; they must inform the family before her body is brought back home, which one of the men, the grandfather, does as the body arrives. We see the dumb-show of the revelation and the family's grief, until they exit the room leaving the child in its chair, and a spectator outside to comment that the child did not wake up.

With this apparently unpromising material, *Intérieur* is a triumph of suspense and suggestion. We do not know who any of the characters are, but instead of compensating for our ignorance with a conventional exposition, Maeterlinck gives merely glimpses of their relations that allow us to build up a complete, but conjectural, picture. The two men, at the start, could be burglars about to commit a crime; only gradually do we learn that one is the finder of the body, the other a friend of the family, and only later still that this friend is their grandfather. We surmise that the drowned girl is perhaps a daughter of the family and, since she was about to speak to the grandfather that very morning, but turned away, that she has perhaps committed suicide. In one way, there is a very modern sense of the anonymity and chance nature of events and individuals: none of us, the play seems to imply, has an inherent identity or necessary existence or relations with others, and any of us could be overtaken by tragedy at any time.

Yet countering this impression of randomness is a powerful sense of destiny that transcends the mere mortals who do its bidding. The grandfather fights the sudden responsibility of having found the body, and having to reveal the news, being compelled to do so only by the inexorable progress and imminent arrival of the crowd carrying the body, driven along, as he comments, by an irresistible force. All the characters are symbolic, designated by their family roles – father, mother, daughter, passer-by; only two, the grand-daughters, have names, Marie and Marthe, which themselves seem symbolic. Are these two sisters, whose namesakes in Luke 10.38, love and worship Jesus, to be taken, in their grief for the family, as feeling for and pitying the sufferings of a humanity whose Christ is absent? We cannot say; but their names are enough to suggest it, as is the final invitation to look at the sleeping infant, with the implication that its innocence will soon be overtaken, like the family's, by the suffering of life. In making us helpless spectators of that suffering, and in emphasising the visual, Maeterlinck achieves the paradoxical feat of using the objectivity of the theatre to suggest the complexity of inner worlds, and the ultimate mystery of life, events and their causation. Maeterlinck thus largely transcends the polarity of objective and subjective that, in the form of conflict between the individual and his context (whether society, history or the cosmos) proved such an obstacle for the Romantic generation. This tension between inner and outer worlds is emblematic of one at the heart of nineteenth-century theatre, between subjective and objective, performance and censorship, artistry and commerce, between the demands of the page and the stage. During the course of the century, the rise in popularity of the novel would know (and indeed, in its rivalling of the drama, prompt) similar conflicts, as we shall now see.

## Selected reading

Gérard Gengembre, *Le Théâtre français du XIX^e siècle (1789-1900)* (Ivry sur Seine: Armand Colin, 2000). An invaluable overview of genres, trends and individual plays.

Henri Gidel, *Le Théâtre de Georges Feydeau* (Paris: Klincksieck, 1979). A systematic study by the principal renovator of Feydeau's reputation.

Albert W. Halsall, *Victor Hugo and the Romantic Drama* (Toronto: University of Toronto Press, 1998). Well contextualised interpretation of the whole of Hugo's dramatic work.

F.W.J. Hemmings, *The Theatre Industry in Nineteenth-century France* (Cambridge: Cambridge University Press, 1993). Groundbreaking exploration of the material conditions of production and performance.

William D. Howarth, *Sublime and Grotesque: A Study of French Romantic Drama* (London: Harrap, 1975). Still the standard work.

Patrick McGuinness, *Maurice Maeterlinck and the Making of Modern Theatre* (Oxford: Oxford University Press, 2000). Authoritative and comprehensive exploration of Maeterlinck and his influence.

Florence Naugrette, *Le Théâtre romantique: Histoire, écriture, mise en scène* (Paris: Seuil, 2001). Clear, well organised and informative.

Leonard C. Pronko, *Eugène Labiche and Georges Feydeau* (London: Grove/Atlantic, 1982). A compact, readable introduction.

# 5

# Novels

Aujourd'hui que le roman s'élargit et grandit, qu'il commence à être la grande forme sérieuse, passionnée, vivante, de l'étude littéraire et de l'enquête sociale, qu'il devient, par l'analyse et par la recherche psychologique, l'Histoire morale contemporaine, aujourd'hui que le roman s'est imposé les études et les devoirs de la science, il peut en revendiquer les libertés et les franchises. (E. and J. de Goncourt, *Germinie Lacerteux*, 1864, Preface)

(Today, now that the scope of the novel is growing and widening, that it is beginning to be the great, serious, living and impassioned form of literary study and social enquiry, that it is becoming, through analysis and psychological research, the contemporary moral History, now that the novel has assumed the studies and duties of science, it may demand science's freedoms and openness.)

The Goncourt brothers' statement represents what was then, and still is, the dominant vision of the novel, represented by Balzac and, apparently, other nineteenth-century Realists, Stendhal and (although he denied it) Flaubert, of the novel as a transcription of social reality, a narrative of characters and events that might credibly have existed and taken place even if, in reality, they did not. 'Un roman, c'est un miroir qui se promène sur une grande route' ('A novel is a mirror carried along a high road') (Stendhal, *Le Rouge et le noir*, II, 19); '*All is true*: il est si véritable, que chacun peut en reconnaître les éléments chez soi, dans son cœur, peut-être' ('*All is true*, it is so authentic, that everyone can recognise its features in his own life, in his heart, perhaps') (Balzac, *Le Père Goriot*, 1834); 'une oeuvre d'art est un coin de la création vu à travers un tempérament' ('a work of art is a corner of nature viewed through a temperament') (Zola, *Les Réalistes du salon*, 1866) – the great nineteenth-century Realist novelists all assert the credibility, even literal veracity of their works. Yet all hedge that view by acknowledging the subjectivity of any description; and few, if any, writers or readers at the beginning of the century would have recognised this ostensibly transcriptive vision of the novel, still less dignified it with the status of history or philosophy. We shall begin by looking at some important pre-1830, pre-Realist novels, before going on to explore Realism, and later reversions to subjectivity, towards the century's end.

### 5.1. From Gothic to modern

From the perspective of posterity, the novelistic landscape of France prior to 1830 looks like a great desert punctuated by a few relatively modest peaks. Yet for contemporaries it was a teeming ecosystem, seething with their sufferings, hopes and regrets. It would be tempting to ascribe the apparent absence of many great French canonical works from this time to the simple fact of Napoleonic censorship, and to the low esteem for the novel in 1800. But such an explanation would be illogical, for censors attended chiefly to kinds of writing that mattered, like theatre and journalism. No: the real explanation of this paradox lies in the definition of what matters. If nineteenth-century and present-day elites define this as writing that gives private, aesthetic, intellectual and emotional and, therefore, not primarily political pleasure, the past and present-day populace define it as writing they can relate to, racy, saucy, readable, reflecting their everyday lives and concerns. So if many of the most influential novelists were foreign, and mostly English, this was not just because of a dearth of home-grown production, but because their works particularly spoke to the French psyche of the times. Works like Radcliffe's *The Mysteries of Udolpho*, Lewis's *The Monk* (1794, 1796, both translated in 1797) or Maturin's *Melmoth the*

*Wanderer* (1820, translated in 1821), with their tales of violence, imprisonment, haunted castles, ruined abbeys, evil forces, improbable reversals and often spectacularly melodramatic plots were devoured by a public living in an age where real life could be, if anything, even more extraordinary. Part of the appeal of Lewis's *The Monk* for French readers was its anticlericalism, its presentation of monasticism as a perversion – a more or less explicit denial of the goodness of God's representatives on earth, and a questioning both of the reasons for the existence of evil and of its very definition; how good and evil can be distinguished. The multiple reversals of ideology and regime, the rapidity and drama of these changes, found fictional expression in such works, soon emulated by a plethora of native writers.

To the ingredients of the Anglophone Gothic novel (or *roman noir*, or, as Nodier called it, the *genre frénétique*), exemplified by Ducray-Duminil, were added, in the first successful novelists of the century, Pigault-Lebrun and Paul de Kock, a French comedy and picaresque, indebted to Scarron and Lesage, with hyperactive plots leavened by levity, and potentially momentous themes ironised by the tongue-in-cheek. Thus was born the *roman populaire* and the *roman gai.* In Pigault's *L'Enfant du carnaval* (1792), a child of the people succeeds, after multiple vicissitudes, in marrying an aristocrat's daughter and making good at last – a little Figaro overcoming prejudice, conquering equality, showing that the ordinary man could now be on top. Ceaseless action mirrors the exuberant, senseless restlessness of post-revolutionary life, its shifting social and political boundaries embodying uncertainties and possibilities undreamt of hitherto. Ducray-Duminil's *Victor ou l'enfant de la forêt* (1796) and *Coelina ou l'Enfant du mystère* (1798) contain altogether more sinister strands: plots equally complex, but involuted, expressing anxiety about the mysterious and seemingly omnipotent victory of evil, coupled with a reassuring if improbably happy end. The villainous Truguelins, by repeated slanders and abductions, try to thwart Coelina's union with her lover. Only at the end are the Trugelins defeated, only then can the abandoned Victor marry the aristocratic Clémence.

Such novels may strain credulity, but then so did current events. The incredible was part of their appeal, bringing the fantastic of real life, the lack of stable meanings, identities and moral boundaries, into the novel. And they introduced a popular readership – still, at this time, via reading rooms, *cabinets de lecture*, and not yet generally via privately purchased volumes or newspapers – to the pleasures of reading fiction.

This was far from Scott's more earnest explorations (in his major works at least), but these lightweight novels touch on weighty issues, and share common ground with contemporary and later 'serious' writers. Many explore motifs – the quest for paternity or social success, reversals of identity, social roles and moral boundaries – that fed melodrama and Romantic drama, as well as the novels of Hugo, Balzac and Sue. Nodier's *Jean Sbogar* (1818), Hugo's *Han d'Islande* (1823), and Balzac's *Annette et le criminel* (1824) explore the nature of good and evil, the relations between the legal and the criminal. In all three novels, the heroine loves an outlaw, and the plot explores problems of defining good and evil, legitimacy and illegality, whether the man society defines as 'criminal' can be redeemed by love. In *Han d'Islande*, the hero Ordener is saved from death by a last-minute reprieve, and executioner and criminal are revealed as brothers – a moral and social reversibility later exploited in Balzac's *Le Père Goriot* and *Splendeurs et misères des courtisanes* (1837-47), and Hugo's *Les Misérables* (1866) (see Section 5.3 below). In *Annette et le criminel*, the criminal, Argow, catches religion from passion, and goes to the scaffold a penitent man. *Han* also confronts, but cannot explain, the mystery of evil. At the novel's centre is the title-protagonist with his grunt-like name, a dehumanised, bestial, cannibalistic dwarf who lives as an outcast, accompanied only by a bear (as will later the human protagonist, Ursus [= bear] of Hugo's *L'Homme qui rit* [1869], who is accompanied by a bear, called Homo). Han is a monster of cruelty, who tugs the novel's centre of gravity away from where we might expect it, with the lovers Ethel and Ordener. Yet excessive as he is, Han is more believable than we might think. His inexplicable, seemingly unmotivated evil, the novel's relentlessly involved, apparently arbitrary reversals, figure the disconcerting instability of real political life; while Argow's expiation of his crime recalls the influential political theorist Joseph de Maistre's doctrine that bloody crimes may only be redeemed by blood (*Soirées de Saint-Pétersbourg*, 1821, afterword).

Built around arduous action and opposition, startling events, cosmic reversals, the sound and fury of these novels voices fears about origins and identities, about the chances of love in a world of hate. Unconvincing as they might seem, we can take them as thousands took them, as expressions of scepticism and uncertainty about moral, legal and social limits, the dubious reality of difference between political regimes, and as stories of individuals striving against the odds to realise their desires, to acquire the promised rights of the *Déclaration des droits de l'homme* and the *Charte*. Jean Sbogar and Antonia, Ethel and Ordener foreshadow Esmeralda and Quasimodo in Hugo's *Notre-Dame de Paris* (1831), struggling to love across social (and, in Quasimodo's case, aesthetic) boundaries. As Nodier remarked, 'Le frénétique ne sera jamais un genre puisqu'il suffit de sortir de tous les genres pour être classé dans celui-là' ('The Gothic will never be a genre, since it is enough to step outside all genres to be classed in that one') (*Bertram*, 1821, preface). And to step outside all genres is to face the real.

All but one of the novels so far mentioned are by men; it is perhaps no accident that the first major contemporary writer to recognise the novel's potential for the treatment of intimate feeling – 'l'âme humaine' ('the human soul'), or what we might now call psychology – is a woman. In her *Essai sur les fictions* (1795), Mme de Staël writes that the future lies in

> ... les fictions naturelles, où tout est à la fois inventé et imité, où rien n'est vrai, mais où tout est vraisemblable (...) Le genre seul des romans modernes est en mesure d'atteindre à cette utilité constante et détaillée qu'on peut retirer de la peinture de nos sentiments habituels.

(Natural fictions, where all is at once invented and imitated, where
nothing is true but all is believable [...] Only the genre of the modern
novel is in a position to attain that constant and detailed utility that
may be gained from the painting of our habitual feelings.)

In her hugely successful novels *Delphine* (1802) and *Corinne, ou
l'Italie* (1807), Staël practises what she preaches – and extends it.
Both are concerned with confinement – not the confinement of the
Gothic novel, but the equally oppressive constraints of society.
Delphine's love for her cousin's fiancé, Léonce, is thwarted, despite
her pluckiness, by both social obstacles and Léonce's prudery and
indecision, ending in her death (by suicide in the novel's first
version, of melancholy in the second). In *Corinne*, published the
year after Staël's lover Constant began *Adolphe*, the conflict between
individuals and social constraints, common to both works, is
presented on a broader canvas. The distinguished Italian poetess
Corinne also dies in despair, abandoned for the virtuous but unre-
markable Lucile by her Scottish lover Oswald, Lord Nelvil. Here,
though, the protagonists are prisms for wider emotional and socio-
political illumination (not least, perhaps, on account of *Corinne*'s
abandonment of *Delphine*'s epistolary form). Corinne literally
enlightens Nelvil, introducing him to Italy and its culture, softening
his Puritanism, and falling in love despite herself: the novel is strikingly perceptive about the vulnerabilities and reticence created by
emotional commitment. But the relationship cannot last. A kinship
and social constraint, namely Oswald's father's death, combined
with guilt about an earlier affair to which his father had been
opposed, prompts Oswald to 'review' his relationship with Corinne.
This leads to a psychologically credible return to the security of the
family after the destabilising experience of death, in the shape of his
marriage with Lucile Edgermond: a choice of the known, familiar
and unexciting over the different, exotic and challenging Corinne.

*Corinne* asks what makes a relationship, an issue indissociable
from the nature of individuals, their potential and development, and
from what society allows them to be. *Corinne* interweaves these

questions in a complex and ambitious way, creating a tapestry stretching between the two key poles of Scotland and Italy, as well as encompassing England and Germany. The affair between the two is a symbolic battle of light and dark, of Italian sun and culture versus repressive northern mists – a battle for enlightenment that for some time Corinne looks set to win. Yet the symbolism is not clear-cut: it is Corinne who is dark, and Lucile blonde, and Corinne is in fact only half-Italian, the daughter of the symbolically named Lord Edgermond's first wife. More than a straightforward opposition of north and south, the novel is about choices, political, cultural, and personal, and how they intermesh: whether Corinne and Oswald can realise their potential by transcending social constraints and their national backgrounds, or whether they will be driven backwards by atavistic forces of nation, nurture and kinship. The novel's very structure answers the question: although it pivots around the protagonists' first-person accounts of their experience (XII-XIV), it ends with testamentary letters setting the seal on their affair, and a poetry reading feebly reflecting Corinne's initial triumphal entry (*Corinne*, II, XX, 4, 5). More memorably than worthwhile but now less-read fictions by other contemporaries like Cottin or Duras, Staël makes real points about women's difficulties in achieving self-fulfilment in society, using the novel as a social as well as personal fresco, nearly a decade before the arrival of Scott's work in France.

The conflicts of north and south, passion and reason, individual and society, are central to key later works. In Latouche's *Fragoletta; ou Paris et Naples en 1799* (1829), the contrast between the two cities points to geopolitical tensions, caught in the cusp year, 1799, of the Corsican (Italian or French?) future Emperor Napoleon's coup as First Consul, as well as to conflicts between desire and consummation, passion and reason, art and life, the ideal and the real (see also Section 7.3 in Chapter 7, this volume). Stendhal's *La Chartreuse de Parme* (1839) turns on comparable questions but assimilates history far more deftly, beginning with France's invasion of Milan in 1796 and its hero Fabrice's hapless attempts to find a role on the field of Waterloo, which is soon abandoned for even more picaresque adventures – there could be no sharper example of the difficulties of social insertion. Social conflicts, the dichtotomies between the novel's Italian setting and its French reader, between French vanity and Italian passion as contrasting modes of political and public behaviour, challenge the reader as urgently, but more subtly, than in *Corinne* or Stendhal's earlier novel *Armance, ou quelques scènes d'un salon en 1827* (1827). Here, the metropolitan French subject and social constraints marking most of the narrative – Octave de Malivert's passion for his cousin Armance – contrasts at its end to his departure for the Greek War of Independence (although tellingly, his death is a suicide occasioned by psychosexual crisis, not military bravura). The omnipresent social oppression is offset, or rather symptomatised, by some surprising moments, like Octave's scarcely provoked throwing out of a window of a valet who seemed to cross him. The violence writ large in the *roman noir* has become miniaturised, domesticised (if not domesticated), in the stifling oppressions of respectable social and emotional life in the Restoration, to emerge in the private sphere, in alarming moments like this, or, earlier in the July Monarchy, in the festering marital conflict of George Sand's *Indiana* (1832). In *Armance*, the treatment of inhibition is still symbolic and displaced; the novel's real subject was impotence, inspired by Latouche's 1826 novel *Olivier*. But what sticks in the mind is Stendhal's treatment of social awkwardness, of the infinitesimal nuances of emotional transaction between individuals who are unsure. As a medium for treating human psychology, Staël's 'âme humaine', and human relations, the novel had come of age.

## 5.2. Fiction: a women's genre?

Superficially, the nineteenth-century novel might look like a masculine genre: the story of ambitious *arrivistes* like Julien Sorel or Rastignac, or gutless failures like Frédéric Moreau. Yet in the first third of the nineteenth century, and certainly up to the vast expansion in novel production and circulation created by serialisation in the 1840s, the novel, especially of private life, the *roman sentimental*, to use the term apparently invented by Mme de Flahaut, was thought of as a genre largely written, and read, by women. Since the 1804 *Code civil*, women were effectively minors, denied citizenship, the vote, divorce (prohibited in 1816, and not restored until 1884), control of family property, finance or children, and imprisonable for adultery. Untrammelled by the conventional shackles of the noble genres, poetry and drama, driven by women's extreme subordination, the novel was a private space where women writers and readers could freely explore their concerns. Not that these are 'women's issues' in any modern exclusive sense. Some of the most penetrating fictions about women were written by men – Balzac's first stories, the *Scènes de la vie privée* (1830: written, says the afterword, in hatred of the 'silly books hitherto given to women' – the moral tales of Genlis or Montolieu), or later novels like *Eugénie Grandet* (1833), whose heroine, her mother and servant, are kept in penurious oppression by her Bluebeard-miser father; a huge fan-mail shows how much women readers valued his insights. And Flaubert's *Madame Bovary* (1857) is more concerned with the thoughts and feelings of its protagonist Emma, than with her husband Charles, whose subjective viewpoint is strikingly absent for most of its duration. Flaubert was prosecuted for Emma's blasphemously enthusiastic adultery – for attacking the very institution of marriage. Yet his famous (if apochryphal) declaration, 'Madame Bovary, c'est moi', says how much Emma's yearning for fulfilment in love and life belongs to the universal human condition. The feminisation of sentiment, the ghettoising of novels dealing with feeling within supposedly predominantly female author and readership, can be seen more as a masculinist rearguard action against evolving emotional and moral parameters than as an accurate reflection of the gender make-up of real writer and readerships of the time.

Nonetheless, the really radical voice is a woman's. George Sand's enduring success, *Indiana* (1832), born of her own disastrous arranged teenage marriage, lays it on the line, blaming 'les lois barbares qui régissent encore l'existence de la femme' ('the barbaric laws that still rule woman's existence') (1842, preface), declaring that 'le malheur de la femme entraîne celui de l'homme, comme celui de l'esclave entraîne celui du maître' ('women's unhappiness brings about men's, just as the slave's brings about the master's'). The novel certainly proves the first. Indiana's husband, Colonel Delmare, transplants Napoleon's militaristic brutality to his home, treating her with a mixture of indifference and contempt, embodying in miniature the repression of women that the *Code civil* wrote large. His misogyny reaches a logically horrific conclusion when, discovering her diary about her lover Raymon, he beats her. But whether men suffer because women suffer is left very much open to doubt. Delmare dies in his sleep, unaware that Indiana has left him for Raymon. And Raymon, a different kind of misogynist (like the later Rodolphe in *Madame Bovary*), sees women as dispensable conquests, seducing first Indiana's servant Noun, then Indiana, before making a respectable, lucrative marriage. Noun, meanwhile, has killed herself, and Indiana's life is wrecked. Only her cousin, Ralph, is really distressed by her wretchedness, because he has secretly loved her since she was a child. They decide to commit suicide when she is finally freed from both Raymon and Delmare, but take a wrong turn to the river, and live to find happiness at last. *Indiana*'s ending has long been found unconvincing: the blatant contrast between the causally justified misery of the core narrative, and the miraculous chance denouement challenges our credulity, to say the least. But what might be found really unreal is what passes for normal in this world: Delmare's insane hardness, Raymon's reckless neglect. Yet we go so native in this madness that mutual respect between the sexes and emotional contentment come to appear absurd, resulting from only the most improbable event. Perhaps *Indiana* is suggesting that happiness depends on chance; that unhappiness, in her world, is the law.

Both Balzac and Sand, then, combine two distinct and contrasting veins: real women's experience (gained, by Balzac, from his mother and sisters), and the *roman noir*, shocking, but also moving and shaking, by showing what was Gothic about private life

– how the *Code civil* wrought public oppression on the domestic. Brutality stamps Balzac's *La Duchesse de Langeais* (1834), where Montriveau abducts and threatens to maim Antoinette de Langeais when she resists him. After she has retreated to a monastery and died, he contents himself with abducting her corpse. For this 'pupil of Bonaparte', 'punir, n'est-ce pas aimer?' ('Is not to punish to love?'): a matter of man's power over woman. Sand's *Mauprat* (1837) recounts the tempestuous passion of Bernard, scion of the notoriously brutal Mauprat family, for his cousin Edmée. But where Balzac's work is marked by a materialistic pessimism, Sand's strives increasingly towards the ideal. Balzac's 'heroes' kill the thing they love, stymied by the real in their pursuit of the ideal. *Mauprat* tells a different story, of the individual's victory over his instincts. Bernard has to prove himself worthy of Edmée, educating and civilising himself before she will accept him; only thereafter can she confirm her love for him in all its conflicted complexity. This overcoming of bad blood takes a Gothic theme, the curse, and overturns it, rendering the reversal all the more effective by putting the story in Bernard's words: reform from the horse's mouth, in contrast to the unreformed views of *Indiana*'s male narrator.

*Mauprat* embodies 'les progrès dans la science de l'homme' ('progress in the science of man'), and its rationalistic conviction both of the individual's progress over himself, and of a more general advance in human relations, informs Sand's key later works. Her women stand up to their men, and, with goodwill, triumph over endemic brutality. In *La Mare au diable* (1847), it is only after Marie resists a lecherous exploiter, and Germain assists her, that she sees Germain's qualities and takes him as her spouse. In *François le Champi* (also 1847), the miller's wife Madeleine confronts her boorish husband, after his death marrying the foundling *champi* ('field-boy') François, who she has raised against his will. For the Naturalist novelist Zola, heredity would be fate; but Sand's protagonists, through love, transcend their backgrounds, Marie marrying the farmer Germain even though she is a servant, Madeleine marrying François even though he is an outcast. Indeed, the families that supposedly guarantee cohesion turn out to be sources of evil, blood curses (as in *Mauprat*), nests of schemers plotting to stop individuals connecting with the ones they love. In contrast to Balzac's reactionary conservatism, social progress, in Sand, is seen as a good, explored in works whose simplicity conceals much art, aimed at the social issues and audiences shared by the serialised novel.

### 5.3. Serialisation and seriousness: the *roman-feuilleton*

In 1836, the year before Sand's *Mauprat*, Balzac brought out *La Vieille fille*, the first *roman-feuilleton* (serialised novel) ever to appear in the French press. *La Vieille fille* caused a scandal. This story of an old maid's attempts to get married, with its scarcely veiled accounts of her sexual frustrations, showed, critics said, the novel's immorality – the way it would do almost anything to get read. There was something in this. Émile de Girardin, the press-magnate who pioneered serialisation, a kind of nineteenth-century left-wing Rupert Murdoch, did so to sell as many copies of his paper, *La Presse*, as possible, using fiction to reach readers across the political boundaries that had divided and restricted newspaper sales hitherto. So Girardin chose Balzac's sensational novel to launch his paper. And although Balzac had done nothing especially unusual (at least for Balzac), simply taken one of his stock themes, frustrated celibates, and written the novel before it was split into episodes, it did set the tone for the serialised novel, which with theatre was the dominant form of popular fictional entertainment from the 1840s until cinema took over from the century's end.

The genre took a few years to become established, the great examples appearing from the 1840s – Sue's *Les Mystères de Paris* (1842-3) and *Le Juif errant* (1844-5), Féval's *Les Mystères de Londres* (1844), Balzac's *Splendeurs et misères des courtisanes* (1837-47) and *La Cousine Bette* (1846) – with those of Dumas, today still France's bestselling novelist, from 1844: *La Reine Margot, Le Comte de Monte-Cristo, Les Trois Mousquetaires* (1844-5), and *Vingt ans après* (1846).

But *La Vieille fille* has in embryo some of the key features that would be developed later on: a sensational subject, stark oppositions, a concern with social tensions. If nineteenth-century popular theatre was like television today, the prevalent mode of public mass entertainment, then serial novels would be like soap operas, a private space where ordinary readers could find real life reflected, but in a displaced and heightened way. The appeal was the daily 'fix' of adventure, and following a highly coloured, starkly contrasted cast of characters over an extended length of time. 'La suite au prochain numéro' ('to be continued in the next number') was a lure for getting readers to read on. But they did not need much persuading: the next number was often the next day, and they had been hooked when renewing their subscriptions, when new serials were announced. Although serial novels often bore no more relation to their lives than (hopefully) *Dynasty*, *EastEnders* or *Desperate Housewives* to our own, they magnified, and made visible, issues latent in society. Of these, foremost was the nature of society itself – the question of individual identity and social role, and the definition of good and evil. In a sense, these were continuations of the earlier Gothic and popular novel, and they were as much a response to an unstable social and political situation. The increasingly insecure circumstances of the 1840s are reflected in a series of key novels expressing anxiety about social polarisation, criminality and secret networks within society, with sometimes extreme, fairy-tale resolutions – saviours who emerge to save the day (as Louis-Napoléon apparently would after 1848). Prince Rodolphe descends into the capital's lower reaches in *Les Mystères de Paris* to save the prostitute Fleur de Marie from the grasp of le Chourineur. Dastardly Jesuits attempt to wrest the wealth from the heirs of Sue's *Juif errant* before it is destroyed. Balzac's arch-criminal Vautrin goes through multiple disguises before finally appearing as Chief of Police, in a stunning reversal at the end of *Splendeurs et misères*. The Bonapartist conspirator Edmond Dantès, like Vautrin a master-manipulator, escapes from prison, discovers the treasure and becomes Count of Monte-

Cristo, the self-styled agent of relentless providential revenge on
the successful but corrupt Restoration figures who first imprisoned
him. And – although it is not a serialised novel, despite being, like
*Les Mystères* or *Le Juif*, a *roman social* – in Hugo's *Les Misérables*
(1866), Archbishop Myriel saves the criminal Jean Valjean, who, if
he becomes a successful businessman, is pursued by inspector
Javert and thrown back into prison (in some sense, a reversal of
Balzac's *Splendeurs et misères*), but escapes, saves Cosette, and dies
with her and Marius.

These fairytale outcomes fed a public avid for satisfaction in an
age when the real was often less than ideal. In this sense, they
played the role of the happy, or at least moral, ending in melodrama. But what we make of these endings, and how seriously we
take them, depends very much on our interpretation of stock
devices common to many *feuilletons*. First of these is opposition, and
reversal, because of its inherent association with moral contrasts of
good and evil; but it has different implications for different writers.
For the liberal Sue, Rodolphe's transcendence of social limits shows
their iniquity, a sign, as in Sand, that they ought to go. *Les Mystères*,
like *Les Misérables*, makes clear that crime results from poverty and
misfortune rather than vice; in *Le Juif errant*, goodies and baddies
are clearly labelled – the novel ends allegorically, with the principal
inheritor Baudoin retreating to a peaceful rural life, and the
Wandering Jew symbolically pardoned and allowed to die at last. In
contrast, Vautrin's spectacular apotheosis as Chief of Police serves
to query moral boundaries, to suggest that what official discourse
calls 'right' and 'wrong' may well be equal, that there is something
amoral at society's heart. If identities can be swapped as easily as
this, then perhaps, for the reactionary Balzac, social mobility has
gone too far, or authority is a scam. As for Dantès/Monte-Cristo, his
very name attests the ambiguity of his quest: dubiously providential,
climbing the mountain where Christ (and, Dantès says, he himself)
was tempted, usurping the Lord's vengeance in the Dantesque hell
of the protagonist's compulsive urge for retribution. However
morally weighted (or weightless) these oppositions, the thrill is ulti-

mately in the chase. Linearity of plot enacts the desire to get figuratively and in fact to the bottom of society, to discover its ultimate truths. This is why the detective, either actual or figurative (Corentin in *Splendeurs*, Rodolphe in *Les Mystères*, Javert in *Les Misérables*) is such a perennial figure, persisting in the work of later *feuilletonistes* like Ponson du Terail or Gaboriau. He allows, as in televised crime series, bourgeois readers safe encounters with otherwise unknown and threatening social forces, and the satisfaction of seeing problems always solved.

### 5.4. Reality and Realism

These novels all deal, directly or by displacement, with the real, but they could scarcely be called Realist. Even those of Balzac, conventionally classed as a Realist, contain significant heightenings of reality: the use of chance and contrivance; strikingly monomaniacal characters, starkly opposed; highly imagic language and strikingly organised metaphorical description. 'J'ai mainte fois été étonné', remarked Baudelaire, 'que la grande gloire de Balzac fût de passer pour un observateur. Il m'a toujours semblé que son principal mérite était d'être visionnaire, et visionnaire passionné' ('Many a time have I been astonished that Balzac's great glory should have been to pass as an observer. It has always seemed to me that his principal merit was to be a visionary, and a passionate visionary') (*L'Art romantique*, 'Théophile Gautier', II). We cannot for a moment believe that Balzac's (or any other writer's) novels are mirrors, reflections of reality in any straightforward sense, or Balzac the impartial secretary of French society he claims to be in the 'Avant-propos' to *La Comédie humaine*: 'La Société française allait être l'historien, je ne devais être que le secrétaire' ('French Society would be the historian, I was only to be the secretary'). Although his novels abound in description of people and places, and his characters are representative types, they are also highly individualised, hyperreal, often surreal, concentrations of traits. Many are monomaniacs: Père Goriot or the miser Grandet in

*Eugénie Grandet*, to name but two. Add to this often strikingly coor-
dinated symbolism and imagery, and Balzac's belief in
transcendent systems of scientific, philosophical and social
meaning (physiognomy, phrenology, thought ranging from
Enlightenment materialism to Swedenborgianism, and what he
called *vestiognomie* – the science of deducing character from the
wearer's clothes), and it is not difficult to share Baudelaire's view,
neither to see why the next generation of writers, headed by
Champfleury and Duranty, driven by progressive social concerns,
should have been dissatisfied with the Romantic, over-visibly
stylised aspects and limited social coverage of this vision. 'Le
Réalisme conclut à la reproduction *exacte, complète, sincère*, du milieu
social, de l'époque où l'on vit (...) Cette reproduction doit être aussi
simple que possible pour être compréhensible à tout le monde (...)
il faut qu'il ne déforme rien' ('Realism chooses the *exact, complete,
and sincere* reproduction of social milieu, of the age in which we
live.[...] This reproduction must be as simple as possible in order to
be understandable by everyone [...] it must distort nothing') wrote
Duranty in the first number of his manifesto-review *Réalisme* (15
November 1856). The aim was to provide low-key, accessible
coverage of types of people and situations hitherto romanticised or
ignored. Champfleury's story *Chien-caillou* (1847) explicitly
contrasts Romantic treatments of the artist figure with harsh reality;
his novel *Les Bourgeois de Molinchart* (1855), like Duranty's *Le
Malheur d'Henriette Gérard* (1860), or many of Sand's (like *La Mare
au diable*) has a pre-eminently Realist subject: provincial marriage,
and love against convention or class boundaries.

    Yet the handling is far from strictly documentary. The practice
could not live down to the theory. These novels challenge stereotypes, but draw on them. Sand's farmer Germain and peasant Marie
fall in love, against the social odds; Champfleury's opens with the
mad romp of a hunted deer through the shops of Molinchchart,
taking refuge with a lawyer's wife, Louise, which is how she meets
the Count, her future lover. (The rest, although comic, gets
grimmer.) And – although Champfleury was much more explicitly

a Realist than Sand – neither refuses the mythic or symbolic. It is by a haunted pond, *La Mare au diable*, that Sand's characters fall in love; Champfleury's chase is both actual, and satirical. And both show something fundamental about Realism, most apparent of all in Balzac: that this is a vision of reality, rather than reality itself; that Realism needs to be more than a document, to have an imaginative focus, to be effective; to make connections, via symbolism, imagery and coincidence, in order to reveal a truth; that the novel is an enterprise of vision and synthesis.

## 5.5. Objectivity and vision

Realism was a dominant doctrine until the mid-1860s, in visual art, in the paintings of Courbet and Manet, and in fiction, where the Goncourts' early novels (*Charles Demailly*, 1860; *Soeur Philomène*, 1861) most successfully embody the twin aims of putting contemporary people centre-stage and using quasi-journalistic objectivity. The exercise is both ideological and aesthetic: exploring alien social classes, Edmond later notes, has the exotic charm of travel to distant lands (*Journal*, 3 December 1871). Their *Germinie Lacerteux* best reconciles the twin quests for objectivity and vision, adopting flat documentary Realism, without Balzac's symbolism and humour, but with a coordinating style and aesthetic. Like their other novels, it is a case study, based on their own servant Rose, underpinned by science (Brachet's *Traité de l'hystérie* of 1847), yet its heroine's slide into depravity has the coherent relentlessness of Classical tragedy. The Goncourts demonstrate that truth, and even the sordid and ugly, need not exclude beauty; indeed that they could be a kind of beauty, redeemed through art, as Baudelaire had already shown. Edmond's cultivation in the later novels *La Fille Élisa* (1877, on provincial prostitution) and *Les Frères Zemganno* (1879, on the circus) of a mannered *écriture artiste* inverting usual syntax, relying heavily on metaphor, represents an ultimate development of the dichotomy between objective and subjective, social reality and the style that presents it.

Édouard Manet, *Le Déjeuner sur l'herbe* (1863),
Paris, Musée d'Orsay.

In a different way, this painting, Manet's scandalous 1863 sensation, *Le Déjeuner sur l'herbe*, encapsulates this central tension of
Realism. The men wear contemporary dress, enjoying a plausibly
modern picnic, but the subject and poses are thoroughly Classical,
going right back to Giorgione and Raphaël – sending up, as well as
saluting, history. And in the midst of this conflict between what, and
how, we see, the female figures loom like visions in a dream. The
scene is flatly unreal, yet strangely present, more juxtaposition than
composition. It is a telling paradox that the greatest Realists,
Flaubert, who consistently refused the label, and the Goncourts –
thought reality (and strict doctrinal Realism) an abomination,
retreating into art, for it is only through art that the real can be most
completely apprehended.

Yet only the real provides the richest source for art. Flaubert's
major novels of the contemporary, *Madame Bovary* and *L'Éducation*

*sentimentale,* focus on credible, mundane, typical characters (a bored, provincial wife, an ambitious but feckless young man) in closely described and believable settings, have few, if any, extraordinary events, and a wealth of precise, evocative, seemingly objective descriptions. However, this apparently flawless Balzacian method – a kind of 'Balzac plus', Balzac but visited on mundane protagonists – is in fact a systematic subversion of Balzac's method, relying on our measuring of the ironic distance between Flaubert's texts and their precursors. *Madame Bovary,* initially written in Balzac's dual-focus way, alternating the perspectives of the two leads Emma and her husband Charles, was in fact rewritten so that Charles was effectively lobotomised for most of the novel, depriving him of one of a fictional character's most basic rights – a mind of his own. *L'Éducation sentimentale* begins with its protagonist, Frédéric Moreau, heading not up to Paris, like those of *Le Rouge et le noir* or *Le Père Goriot,* but back to his provincial parents.

At the opening of *Madame Bovary,* the mind-boggling description of Charles's cap, combining features of five different sorts of headgear, produces not a Balzacian certainty revealing its owner's character, but 'une de ces pauvres choses dont la laideur muette a des profondeurs d'expression comme le visage d'un imbecile' ('one of those poor things, in short, whose mute ugliness has expressive depths like an imbecile's face') – in other words, which means precisely nothing. The plot of *L'Éducation sentimentale* – rather like the figures in Manet's painting – seems to have been devised in order to ensure that none of the conventional connections work at all. When Frédéric sees his future lover, Mme Arnoux, he exotically imagines first that she is Creole, then Andalusian; in fact she comes from Chartres. When Julien calls on Mme de Rênal, or Rastignac on Mme de Beauséant, Stendhal or Balzac make sure they are in; but when Frédéric seeks Mme Arnoux, she is out, and Flaubert allows him only to break what he supposes to be her parasol, which turns out to belong to her husband's lover – as we are reminded when Frédéric presents the baffled Mme Arnoux with a replacement later on. Objects, events and language, instead of expressing meaning and certainty, as they are supposed to in Realist novels, reveal only void and doubt. Flaubert's list of the love-tokens Emma has given to her lover, Rodolphe, is mirrored by the later scene when Rodolphe rifles through the biscuit bin containing them before scattering water on his letter ending the affair to make her think that he has wept. For, like these objects, 'la parole humaine', language, 'est comme un chaudron fêlé où nous battons des mélodies à faire danser les ours, quand on voudrait attendrir les étoiles' ('Human words are like a cracked kettle where we beat out tunes for bears to dance to, when we would wish to touch the stars') (*Madame Bovary*, II.12).

Flaubert, then, reveals objectivity not to be unimportant, but attainable only in the impersonal description of a narrator who, while notionally authorial, scarcely ever speaks in his own voice. What we might suppose to be authorial perceptions are exported to the characters via *style indirect libre* (reported speech or thought), Emma's dreams falling one by one into the mud like wounded swallows, the narrator tells us, her life as cold as an attic whose window faces north, Charles's conversation as flat as a pavement. The absence of explicit authorial comment was a major plank of the prosecution case in Flaubert's 1857 trial for *Madame Bovary*, his failure to condemn Emma's adultery suggesting apparent approval. This was overstating the case (which Flaubert won): the novel simply relates what might plausibly have happened with quasi-scientific detachment. But there is no doubt that the absence of authorial narrator parallels the absence of God. Emma takes her life into her own hands, claiming the sexual and emotional freedom inside and outside marriage normally restricted to men, and that is what Napoleon III's representatives, the judges, could not bear. Flaubert described *L'Éducation sentimentale* as 'l'histoire morale des hommes de ma génération' ('the moral [i.e. psychological] history of men of my generation'). For Flaubert, reality is ultimately in the mind of the beholder.

## 5.6. Naturalism and the novel

Flaubert's novel far transcends those of any contemporary self-acknowledged Realist, and it is no accident that it is focused through a woman, Emma, whose perceptions (often implicitly, and not always consistently) question official, 'male', hierarchical views of reality. Many of the major novels of the next twenty years, although written by men, would take as their protagonists women in depraved or abject situations: the Goncourts' *Germinie Lacerteux*, *La Fille Élisa*, Zola's *Thérèse Raquin* (1867), *L'Assommoir* (1877) or *Nana* (1880). It is as though the desire for objectivity were asserting itself through a righting of the wrongs that had made men heroes too often in the past, even if most of these novels, especially the Goncourts', contain elements of misogyny. Their major works, and Zola's, together with Huysmans's early novels (*Marthe*, 1876 and *Les Soeurs Vatard*, 1879), and those of lesser writers like Céard and Alexis, are generally labelled 'Naturalist'. Naturalism is Zola's term for, and development of, Realism, with a greater stress on scientific method and objectivity and, in Zola's case, on deterministic physiology and heredity, inspired by the positivist critic and historian, Taine.

The principal theorising of Naturalism, Zola's *Le Roman expérimental*, was not published until 1880, and the only Naturalist collection, *Les Soirées de Médan*, a group of stories by Zola's acolytes, known as the Groupe de Médan (where he lived) – Zola, Huysmans, Maupassant, Alexis and Céard – appeared the same year. But what were effectively Naturalist principles had been embodied in novels for many years, notably in *Germinie Lacerteux* and *Thérèse Raquin*, treating low-class, usually scabrous characters and subjects, with vivid description and scientific objectivity.

It is the stress on science, and in particular, the kind of science, which is new. Balzac's *Comédie humaine* was inspired, its author's *Avant-propos* declares, by 'une comparaison entre l'Humanité et l'Animalité' ('a comparison between mankind and the animal world'); and it was in Balzac that Zola found the analytical, scientific method that was to inspire his work. Zola's 'science', never much more than a flag of convenience for plying the subjectivity of art, was embellished by two scientific writers in particular: Lucas, whose *Traité philosophique et physiologique de l'hérédité naturelle* (1847-50) helped make heredity the bedrock of Zola's enterprise, and Bernard's *Introduction à la médecine expérimentale* (1865), which advocates systematic experiment rather than random observation in physiology. These Zola strives to combine. His twenty-novel series *Les Rougon-Macquart* (1871-93) is subtitled *Histoire naturelle et sociale d'une famille sous le Second Empire* – an organised account of a whole family, based around heredity. The empirical method was earnestly applied, Zola visiting a colliery for *Germinal* (1885), riding a railway engine for *La Bête humaine* (1890).

Nonetheless, Zola's method, if empirical, was not nearly as systematic or experimental as publicly claimed. The image that links him to Bernard, of the novelist at work on his subject like a surgeon dissecting a corpse, was a captivating aspiration more than it could ever be reality: the doctor, unlike the novelist, cannot invent his subject or his results. If he was long taxed for this illogic, painted as disingenuous, or aesthetically naïve, the very title of his series acknowledges the relation between heredity and the extraneous variables – the social and historical context – that would invalidate scientific experiment. This relation is precisely his subject. His characters wrestle with their inherited destinies: Lantier, Coupeau and his wife Gervaise fall prey to the alcoholism that dogged her father and helped put her daughter Nana on the streets; Gervaise's son Étienne's temper has lost him his job by the beginning of *Germinal* (1885); the same bad blood makes her other son, Jacques, a psychopath in *La Bête humaine* (1890). Yet Nana's 'fate' comes as much from parental neglect caused by alcoholism as from alcoholism itself, and Etienne's fire will make him a worker's leader as well as a loser; only Jacques seems to fall totally prey to his genes (although other factors weigh here too: see Section 6.1 in Chapter 6, this volume). And Zola's definition of the art-work as 'un coin de la création vu à travers un tempérament' acknowledges the subjectivity inherent in any would-be objective depiction of reality, stressing its unavoidably partial and selective treatment of the external, pointing back to the tensions between subjective and objective outlined at the opening of this chapter.

Zola's novels exploit these tensions to electrifying effect. Their peculiar force comes from the conjunction of 'scientific' method and mythical impact. So *Germinal* encompasses both factually accurate and intense impressions of miners and their work, and archetypal scenes of conflict or renewal – the destructive, rampaging mass revolt, the spring shoots appearing as Étienne trudges off at the end, above all the dominating image of the all-devouring mine with its 'voracité de bête goulue' ('voraciousness of a gluttonous beast'), an image of the all-consuming nature of capitalism itself. *La Bête humaine* convincingly evokes nineteenth-century railway working, but its opening quasi-physiological image of the tentacular railway system is also a symbolic counterpart to the central subject, murderous desire. *Au Bonheur des dames* (1883), set in a Parisian department store, turns it into a giant physiological system (like the lodging house in *Pot-Bouille*, 1882), but ends essentially as a love story between the owner, Octave Mouret, and a shop assistant, Denise, with a spectacular (and ironic) burgeoning of wedding whites on the day of the sales.

In every case, Zola brilliantly exploits that feature inherent to the novel: that to understand it, we must empathise, identify with it and internalise, creating a virtual reality halfway between the external world and our own. His novels enlighteningly exploit a symbolism seemingly natural to the environment, even if in fact artfully chosen to illuminate or make a point. So his glamorous courtesan Nana first appears on stage as Venus, a device that uses plausible factual presentation – she is described as a Venus simply because she is playing the role on stage – to make a symbolic point. And his first big success, *Thérèse Raquin*, plays at once on proto-Naturalist, physiological notation – Thérèse's *sang africain*, the 'effluves' and the 'flammes qui s'échappaient de sa peau' to appeal both to the medical, the scientifically objective, and, via 'flammes',

to the traditional language of love, as it describes her first adulterous kiss:

> Laurent, étonné, trouva sa maîtresse belle. Il n'avait jamais vu cette
> femme. Thérèse, souple et forte, le serrait, reversant la tête en arrière,
> et, sur son visage, couraient des lumières ardentes, des sourires
> passionnés (...) On eût dit que sa figure venait de s'éclairer en dedans,
> que des flammes s'échappaient de sa chair. Et, autour d'elle, son sang
> qui brûlait, ses nerfs qui se tendaient, jetaient ainsi des effluves
> chauds un air pénétrant et âcre.
>
> Tous ses instincts de femme nerveuse éclatèrent avec une violence
> inouïe; le sang de sa mère, ce sang africain qui brûlait dans ses veines,
> se mit à couler, à battre furieusement dans son corps maigre, presque
> vierge encore. Elle s'étalait, elle s'offrait avec une impudeur
> souveraine. Et, de la tête aux pieds, de longs frissons l'agitaient.
> (*Thérèse Raquin*, ch. 7)

> (Laurent, astonished, found his mistress beautiful. He had never
> before seen this woman. Thérèse, strong and supple, clasped him,
> throwing her head backwards, and, on her face, ran ardent lights,
> passionate smiles.[...] One might have said that her face had just been
> lit up from within, that flames were escaping from her flesh. And,
> around her, her burning blood, her tautening nerves, threw out like
> hot vapours an acrid, penetrating air.[...] // All her nervous woman's
> instincts burst forth with unheard-of violence; her mother's blood,
> this African blood that burnt within her veins, began to flow, to pulse
> furiously in her thin, still almost virgin body. She spread herself out,
> offered herself with a regal impropriety. And, from her head to her
> toes, long tremors ran right through her.)

In *Germinal*, the phrases applied repeatedly to the mineshaft, its
'air mauvais de bête goulue', its 'tassement de bête méchante'
('unpleasant air of a greedy beast; squatting of an evil beast') not only,
by repetition, imprint themselves on the memory, but, in their geni-
tive formulations ('de bête …'), deftly project onto the thing described

what is essentially an authorial perception about it. In other words, the perception becomes part of the object, and the object becomes the perception. The technique is akin to that of Impressionist painting (with which Zola was deeply engaged) in its emphasis on painters painting what they see, rather than what they know, and, in its stress on sensation as the interface between subject and object, as the place where perception actually occurs. Along with Flaubert, it was Zola who most successfully moved the novel from the Realist rut of spurious, unattainable objectivity, fusing earnest social and political purpose with conventional literary devices in riveting fictions of tremendous popular appeal. But the dichotomy of subject and object, of real and symbol, and the transcendent virtuality of perception, were also to be determinant tensions in the work of many other writers in the century's last two decades.

## Selected reading

Colette Becker, *Zola: Le Saut dans les étoiles* (Paris: Presses universitaires de la Sorbonne, 2002). Magisterial overview; contains extensive extracts from Zola's work.

Peter Brooks, *Reading for the Plot: Design and Intention in Narrative* (Cambridge, MA and London: Harvard University Press, 1984 and reprints). Humane, rigorous, wide-ranging treatment of canonical novels, serialisation and desire.

―― *Realist Vision* (New Haven, CT and London: Yale University Press, 2005). Authoritative and insightful on what Realism is and why it matters.

Margaret Cohen, *The Sentimental Education of the Novel* (Princeton, NJ: Princeton University Press, 1999). Pioneering exploration of the role of women writers and feeling in the emergence of the Realist novel.

Jonathan Culler, *Flaubert: The Uses of Uncertainty* (London: Elek, 1974, revised edition, Ithaca, NY and London: Cornell University Press, 1985). A groundbreaking study.

Madelyn Gutwirth, *Madame de Staël, Novelist: The Emergence of the Artist as Woman* (Urbana, Chicago, IL and London: University of Illinois Press, 1978). Feisty feminist bio-literary investigation.

Pierre Laforgue, *1830: Romantisme et histoire* (2001). Perceptive discussions of Stendhal, Hugo, Sand and Balzac in context.

Christopher Prendergast, *The Order of Mimesis: Stendhal, Balzac, Flaubert, Nerval* (Cambridge: Cambridge University Press, 1986). Sophisticated theorising of nineteenth-century Realism.

—— *By the People for the People? Eugène Sue's 'Les Mystères de Paris': A Hypothesis in the Sociology of Literature* (Oxford: Legenda, 2002). Intriguing exploration of the extent to which readers may have influenced the nature of Sue's novel.

Naomi Schor, *George Sand and Idealism* (New York: Columbia University ress, 1993). Persuasive, personal restoration of Sand to the canon.

# 6

# Modernities

Centuries have a way of starting late; but they also have a way of starting early, of foreshadowing things far in advance of their time. Developments we can recognize as modern – technology and science, burgeoning capitalism, urbanisation, increasingly rapid transport, communications and change – begin to mark France from the Restoration. And reactions to the modern – utopian fantasies of nature, religion or society, or their opposite, rejection of religion, fervid embrace of science, social alienation or refuge in dream, art or the self – can be found from Romanticism onwards. Romanticism *is* modernity: 'Qui dit romantisme dit art moderne – c'est à dire intimité, spiritualité, couleur, aspiration vers l'infini, exprimées par tous les moyens que contiennent les arts' ('He who says romanticism says modern art – that is to say intimacy, spirituality, colour, aspiration towards the infinite, expressed by all the means the arts contain') (Baudelaire, *Salon de 1846*). We shall be exploring modernity in earlier writers, Nerval, Baudelaire and Hugo, later in this chapter. But it is in the century's last three decades, the 1870s, 1880s and 1890s, that we find modernity in its most patent form, in the tensions between science and spirituality, subjectivity and fiction in the work of Zola, Huysmans, Villiers de l'Isle-Adam and Verne.

## 6.1. Science, subjectivity and fiction

The dominance of the scientific, particularly evolutionary, model, and its threat to traditional conceptions of the individual as a moral being in command of his own destiny, is plainest in Zola's Naturalism. Zola's characters, as we have seen, are subject to their heredity, to their selfish genes, and to the forces of 'natural' (but really, economic) selection that mimic them in modern capitalism. In *L'Assommoir*, Gervaise's hope of improving her lot by running a shop are dashed by atavistic alcoholism, which virtually pre-scripts Nana's depravity. The very physical attractiveness that ensures her success as a courtesan also guarantees her dissolution as an individual. Zola's characters are primarily physical organisms, driven by instinctual urges. 'Vous mettez l'homme dans le cerveau', he wrote to Jules Lemaître on 14 March 1885, 'je le mets dans tous les organes. Vous isolez l'homme de la nature, je ne le vois pas sans la terre, d'où il sort et où il rentre' ('You place man in the brain, I place him in all his organs. You isolate him from nature, I cannot conceive of him without the earth from which he comes and to which he returns'). Nana, like most of his characters, has only as much of a mind as she needs: we see much more of her body. And that body causes her to become part of the capitalist system of rich and powerful men, like Baron Muffat, who become her lovers, and of the decadence and decay it represents. Nana, 'la Mouche d'or', 'une mouche couleur de soleil, envolée de l'ordure' ('The Golden Fly', 'a sun-coloured fly, flown up from the filth' (*Nana*, ch. 7), as a journalist dubs her, who excites bestial behaviour in all men, ends by being consumed by the decay on which she has lived, her face dissolved by syphilis on her death-bed:

> Vénus se décomposait. Il semblait que le virus pris par elle dans les ruisseaux, sur les charognes tolérées, ce ferment dont elle avait empoisonné un peuple, venait de lui remonter au visage et l'avait pourri.

> (Venus was decomposing. It seemed that the virus she had caught in the gutters, from the carcasses she had borne, this fermentation with which she had infected a whole people, had just risen back up to her face and rotted it.)

The fate of Zola's characters is to be absorbed by the milieu from which they come. The cry of 'To Berlin!' which ends the novel, sending French troops to disastrous defeat in the Franco-Prussian war, symbolises how *thanatos*, death, is indissociable from *eros*, and how Nana herself is a product, as well as producer, of a wider decadence. *Germinal* opens with Étienne's approach to the mine and closes with his departure, *La Terre* (1887), with Jean sowing grain, ending with him rushing off to fight a fire, casting a last look at the earth he has grown to love. Zola's vision is entropic, moving from the physiological (and evolutionary) system to the social, charting disorder, dispersal of energy, transformations from one material state to another. Zola shows the human as constantly threatened by the bestial, the civilised by the natural, generation by degeneration and decadence (as in Gervaise's, or Nana's, rise and fall), regeneration being only timidly present, as in the small shoots of hope emerging at the end of *Germinal* or *La Terre*. Man-made systems may mimic natural systems – as is the case with the quasi-sexual commercial desires that drive the protagonists of *La Curée* (1871) or *Au Bonheur des dames* – but the result is alienation. (The latter's happy ending, where the shop girl Denise marries her oversexed boss, seems too convenient to convince.) The tentacular railway lines opening *La Bête humaine* figure the surrogate physiology of capitalism – a system that links individuals, yet keeps them apart, as Jacques's glimpsed witness of Grandmorin's murder in the compartment of a railway carriage shows; a system which creates the emotional distortion that leads Jacques to treat his engine La Lison like a mistress, which offers a false promise of progress, to which the novel's resurgent, murdering human beasts give the lie. The railway is central to *La Bête humaine*, because, in bringing distant people together, yet without any sense of community or emotional link, it symbolises the disconnection inherent in modern society, of which the psychopathic Jacques is the pre-eminent case.

Des Esseintes, the hero of Huysmans's 1884 novel *A rebours*, represents one possible modern response to alienation: a retreat into aesthetic solipsism. Des Esseintes, the degenerate last of a line of

French aristocrats, over-stimulated and exasperated by the omnipresent vulgarity of the modern world, sells his château and withdraws to a refined retreat in the country outside Paris. There he surrounds himself with ever more arcane delights: a library of rare books; exotic flowers, a symphony of perfumes to enchant the senses; a tortoise whose shell he has first gilded to match the décor, then encrusted with precious stones. He is a disciple of Schopenhauer, whose *Die Welt als Wille und Vorstellung* (*The World as Will and Idea*), published in German in 1818 but particularly influential in the *fin de siècle*, held that the world was only our imagining of it, an illusion, subject to an irrational, selfish will, producing an eternal, purposeless cycle of desire, pain, love and loss that can only be relieved by the will's destruction through self-abnegation, withdrawal into nothingness or aesthetic contemplation. Des Esseintes revels in the subjectivity of impression, wallowing in sensory experiences that are virtual substitutes for the real. Cunning devices replicate the feelings of a sea-journey – the sounds, the sights, the smells. A proposed actual journey to London gets no further than the waiting room in the Gare du Nord, where, finding himself actually confronted by the awful English, Des Esseintes concludes that he has had the experience already and – on the basis of a past actual journey to Holland, which fell far short of his imaginings because it failed to live up to the promise of Dutch painting – decides to go home.

In its substitution of the virtual for the real, of subjective imagining for actual experience, *A rebours* is the quintessential text of French Decadence, a term that describes many major writers of *fin de siècle* France, exemplified in differing ways by Rimbaud, Mallarmé, Corbière, Verlaine and Villiers de L'Isle-Adam. Yet if, on the face of it, *A Rebours* appears to be at the opposite pole to Naturalism, it can be seen as its utmost development – the development, in fact, of a lineage beginning with the Romantics. Its *Notice*'s account of Des Esseintes's lineage parodies both the archetypal Romantic autobiographical text, Chateaubriand's *Mémoires d'outre-tombe*, and also the heredity that damns any Naturalist hero. Description, cataloguing – defining features of Realist and Naturalist

writing – are so exaggerated that they produce a fantastical, halluci-
natory experience of reality that loosens our hold on any firm
external truth. Des Esseintes's tortoise, potentially the absolute
Naturalist creature (an object-lesson in evolution) is turned into the
opposite, the artificial, when Des Esseintes has it gilded and bejew-
elled. Yet nature gets its revenge. Des Esseintes's attempt to live life
'à rebours' ('back to front, against nature') is taken so far that it
pushes nature beyond its limits. The gilded tortoise is so over-
embellished that it expires; the exotic garden withers, because Des
Esseintes forgets to tend it; he himself almost dies, developing ever
more extraordinary allergies and intolerances as he removes
himself from ordinary life. His love for the androgynous Miss
Urania and, briefly, for a female ventriloquist, founders on the fact
that his subjective delusions, however vivid, cannot change an unco-
operative reality. *A rebours* seems to subvert the Schopenhauerian
idea that the egotism of enclosure within the self could be transcended through art: Des Esseintes ends up enclosed within art,
which makes him more solipsistic and egotistical than ever.
Ordinary life has the last laugh, nature compelling Des Esseintes to
abandon unsustainable artifice and return to the real world. *A
rebours* gives an ironic twist on the very artifice it purports to
promote; in its extremity, it reveals the flaws and inconsistencies
inherent both to Naturalism and to Decadence.

   If reality, the material, undermines the ideal in *A rebours*, it is the
material that creates the ideal in Villiers de l'Isle-Adam's *L'Eve future*
(1886). Written in the wake of the *Contes cruels* (1880), which
lampoon bourgeois pretensions to literalism in matters of the
imponderable, *L'Eve future* questions the relations between the physical and the material, between the scientific and subjectivity,
producing some unorthodox answers. Lord Ewald, smitten by the
physical perfection of an opera singer, Alicia Clary, but distressed
by her stupidity and mundane sensibility, recounts his plight to the
great American inventor Thomas Edison. Edison proposes an
innovative solution. He will construct an 'Andréïde', an exact like-
ness of the disappointing Alicia, an automaton which, using

Edison's electric light and phonograph technologies, will replicate Alicia's physical beauties and movements, but who, thanks to many hours of Alicia's recorded voice, and the infinite number of possible combinations of her utterances, will be superior to this real human model, capable of infinite imagination and sensitivity of response. In response to Ewald's incredulous misgivings about this artificial Eve, Edison demonstrates that women's attractions are in any case artificial, recounting the story of his friend Anderson's fatal infatuation with Evelyne Habal, a dancer, whose charms were entirely synthetic, producing her hairpieces, padded corsets, false teeth, high heels and make-up as evidence. In response to his objections to the limited scriptedness of this new Eve's utterances, Edison shows that all human exchanges are scripted, and, as if to counter the objection that the automaton will, of necessity, not be human, we are shown the extreme subtlety with which Edison replicates, with wires, batteries, cylinders and solenoids, false hair, eyelashes and Alicia's recorded voice, the flesh and blood of the real human being. His 'Andréide' is a material system – but so are we.

The whole narrative combines science fiction, fantastic tale and Faustian pact. Hadaly, the automaton, represents, as her Persian-derived name indicates, 'la limite supérieure', the ceiling of both physical beauty and scientific and spiritual perfection. Ewald's prizing of physical perfection, Alicia's own thirst for stardom and Edison's earnestness in pursuing them, all suggest parallels with our contemporary cult of celebrity, with the quest for a uniform and universal physical perfection which, today, feeds the celebrity culture and beauty and fashion industries. He even proposes mass-producing his 'Andréides', as a way of meeting the modern thirst for the ideal in the real. Yet, while fully aware of the artificiality of his enterprise (as his cynical presentation of Evelyne's 'beauties' shows), Edison uses the very same materials (false hair, eyelashes, padding), as he has condemned in Evelyne to produce Hadaly (a superior version of Alicia) for Ewald. Ironically, base materials, through Edison's skill, let Ewald reach his ideal. At their final meeting, Alicia reveals untold depths of feeling, declares her love, makes Ewald think himself crazed to abandon this gorgeous flesh-and-blood mistress for a machine. Only then does Edison reveal that this 'Alicia' *is* the machine, Halady, his 'Andréide', in every way superior to the woman on whom she was based: eternally beautiful, never banal, tailored – because so programmed – to Ewald's fancies, and always ready to respond.

The objections to the misogynist, male-centred nature of this fantasy are obvious. But it also sounds a serious warning about the materialism, egocentrism, inhumanity and dangerously subjective virtuality of this already modern conception of desire. Ewald, having teetered on the brink of madness at the discovery of Hadaly's mere material nature – she is not a person, but a doll, a thing – then accepts his great good fortune and revels in the rapturous feelings she provokes, in this creation of a material ideal. What matters is not the reality, but the illusion. Subjectivity, not objective truth, is supreme. He is another Schopenhauerian gone to the bad. In our own terms, for Ewald, virtual reality trumps reality itself. Hadaly replaces the physically perfect, but spiritually imperfect Alicia. Yet after Hadaly has been placed in her symbolically woman-shaped coffin, symbolic of the death of real woman and her replacement by a machine, and embarked with Ewald on the sea voyage back to England, the ship is wrecked and the precious automaton lost, and the crazed Ewald has to be physically restrained from going to the bottom with his 'ideal'. Is the shipwreck an act of God, a punishment for a Promethean stealing of fire? Whatever sense we make of it, the novel's references to Prometheus, alchemy, magic and Satan point to the dangers of solipsism, of an obsession with physical perfection and of the snare of a material ideal.

We find an apparently much more optimistic science in the novels of Jules Verne. Still the world's most translated author, many of his scores of *Voyages extraordinaires* – *De la terre à la lune* (1865), *Vingt mille lieues sous les mers* (1870), *Le Tour du monde en quatre-vingts jours* (1873) – are enduringly popular. Verne put science fiction on the map. The phrase was coined in 1851, the year of the London

Great Exhibition which, with its Paris counterparts of 1855 and 1867, showcased the achievements of modern science, industry, technology, art and craft. Verne's novels celebrate their potential. His heroes (invariably men) take on improbable tasks against impossible odds: Captain Nemo's journey to the bottom of the sea in the submarine *Nautilus* (a real *Nautilus* had been built by Fulton in 1797), a journey to the moon in *De la terre à la lune*. Their exploits are driven by impulses that are nothing less than macho: the project of flying to the moon emerges from a meeting of a North American gun club: it is a product of Imperialism, of geopolitical conquest, as the means of achieving it, a giant canon, amply attests. The artificial 'island' (in fact, a giant ship) inhabited by the protagonists of *L'Île à hélice* (1895) both foreshadows comparable enterprises of our own (underwater hotels in the Gulf, the 10,000 person nomadic island envisaged by Jean-Pierre Zoppini for 2010) and the ecological questions they raise. Speed, science, knowledge, drive his heroes: their adversaries, their difficulties, are mainly not human but natural, the physical laws that must be accommodated, or conquered, in order to make the journey to the bottom of the sea or to the moon. Their journeys are accompanied by detailed accounts of the preparations and technical difficulties that must be overcome; the moon journey itself is interspersed with descriptions of the physical constraints, cosmic forces or geography that govern the trip. Unlike Villiers, this is science for the masses, doses of technological information (or, given its frequent literal impossibility, misinformation) in sweetly sugared fictional pills. Verne, a left-wing sympathiser and firm believer in the improving value of education, saw fiction as a means of achieving it. Whether it did so is another matter; there is something of the worthiness of the pop-science of David Attenborough or Jacques Cousteau in his work, the natural as fodder for the voyeur.

In 1856, after reading Poe, and without using the term 'science fiction', the Goncourt brothers had presciently described the kind of fiction Verne was to write as *maladive* ('sickly', *Journal*, 16 July 1856). The word is telling. It suggests both the alienation from the human that is a mainspring of science fiction, and the malaise that lies at its heart. The underemployed members of the gun club take on the conquest of the moon as an exploit; they fall happily but haplessly to earth, breaking the bowsprit of the ship sent to track them, and are fêted as heroes – but for what? Verne's millionaire protagonists may have their *Ile à hélice*, but it is ultimately (like much of our own modern virtual technology) simply a surrogate for, or imitation of, nature: the dramatic plot provides a solution, but their ingenuity opens, via its destruction, onto a void.

For all its apparent optimism, a deep pessimism underpins Verne's work. The hero of *Robur le conquérant* (1886) is a kind of super-Nemo, operating in air and on land as well as in the sea. But he is also a megalomaniac, who in the sequel, *Maître du monde* (1904), becomes a tyrant, challenging the powers that be. Robur is both the Gothic novel evil genius (like Han d'Islande, a mysterious wandering outsider, endowed with malevolent powers, like the devil to whom he is compared), and a James Bond baddie, with mysterious hideouts and wonderful machines – a speedy airship, a car that is also a submarine, boat and plane. But above all, Robur is the spirit of technology. For the major part of the novels in which he appears he is invisible, manifest only in his seemingly supernatural and incredible effects: the ghost at the heart of the machine, especially in *Maître du monde*, which makes him (and it) truly sinister. *Paris au XXᵉ siècle*, written in 1863, but so controversial it was not published until 1994, describes with seemingly visionary foresight a world of skyscrapers, world communication and rapid transport, which brings its anti-modern artist hero only marginalisation and despair. It shows an astonishingly familiar set-up where education has been privatised, where nobody reads, where money and technology are the prime values, and the guardians of canonical culture are impoverished, vilified and excluded. Any nineteenth-century reader, and any later student of the nineteenth century, would know that these alienating human consequences, not to mention the technological 'developments', belong at least as much to Verne's age as to our own – products of nineteenth-century keenness to peek into the future, and useful if only to show not Verne's prescience, but how much our own technological and social 'modernity', with its attendant alienations, distresses and dysfunctions, began at least a century and a half ago. Yet although Verne's inventions were inspired almost entirely by his own time, only scholarship can reveal this for posterity; for the vast majority of readers who choose to ignore it, his magical appeal remains undimmed. Verne may seem strikingly prophetic, foretelling, like, in a different way, the visionary Hugo, an endlessly burgeoning void. Yet his value lies not in his prescience – dubious, and in any case for us old news – but in the presence of very modern forms of doubt.

A striking contrast to Verne, significant for his influence on the contemporary intellectual and aesthetic elite rather than the masses, is Bourget. A major conduit for the work of the German thinker Hartmann on the Unconscious, for Buddhism (seen by Schopenhauer, on account of Nirvana, as the highest religion), and for the dilettantism that would thrive in the nineties, he was also one of the first French readers of Freud. But this Unconscious is, unlike Freud's, not peculiar to the individual, but a blind, unknowing, purposeless force akin to Schopenhauer's will. Bourget, as struck by science as Zola, Villiers or Verne, by focusing on psychology looks forward to our own time. Moving from criticism to fiction, from the *Essais de psychologie contemporaine* (1883) examining contemporary mentalities through major writers, to novels whose zenith is *Le Disciple* (1889), Bourget's fiction melds psychological dissection with moral puzzles and primal impulses. *Le Disciple* tests and breaks the arrogance of the professor who sets himself above the world when this disciple puts his inhuman theories into practice; ironically, it is the misguidedness of the disciple that sets the master back on the road to faith. If the psychology seems mechanistic, this is precisely the point: in this novel, life is an experiment conducted on real human beings.

Bourget was important for contemporaries' view of themselves, and for posterity's view of writers like Flaubert and Stendhal, seen not as Realists but as psychological analysts embodying modern pessimism. There is a faint echo of Bourget in Gide, who, in the *Cahiers d'André Walter* (1891), sees a novel as a theorem, and whose *Les Nourritures terrestres* (1897), like, later, *L'Immoraliste* (1902), is in some ways a kind of anti-*Disciple*, a 'manuel d'évasion' ('escape manual') (1926, preface), an exhortation to self-realisation rather than the self-oblation that ends *Le Disciple*. Barrès, Bourget's junior by 10 years, Gide's senior by only seven and Proust's by only nine, had even more impact as the voice of a generation. His novel-trilogy *Le Culte du moi* (1888-91) heralds nothing less than a new, egocentric, view of experience. 'La réalité varie avec chacun de nous puisqu'elle est l'ensemble de nos habitudes de voir, de sentir et de raisonner', declares the first novel's preface ('Reality varies with each of us, as it is the sum of our habits of seeing, feeling, and reasoning'). This 'bréviaire d'égoïsme', a 'roman de la vie intérieure' ('breviary of egoism, novel of interior life') explores the egotistical development of the self. Drawing on Constant, Stendhal and also Nietzsche, *Le Culte du moi* was admired by the young (and excoriated by the older) Gide, whose work draws on an economy of impulse and restraint, sensation and spirit, authenticity and hypocrisy, sincerity and lies. From *Les Nourritures* to later fictions, *Les Caves du Vatican* (1914) and *Les Faux-monnayeurs* (1926), its technical devices and moral boldness owe much to a Barrès they have overshadowed.

Barrès finds reflections, but above all reactions, in Proust, whose plumbing of the self in *A la recherche du temps perdu* (1913-27) embodies a quest to convey the very sensation where Barrès, in his view, has failed, but who, like his friend and model, makes the perceiving self the centre of attention and organisation, rather than the objective external world. Bourget, rejecting Naturalism, creates a 'psychologism' paradoxically redolent of Zola's mentor Taine, who saw literature as a living system; Barrès explores an instinctual world wherein the individual in different ways both needs and must resist absorption, fighting misguided (usually sexual) instincts yet requiring roots in his own home soil, a divided egotistical parallel to the Naturalist physiological vision. *Les Déracinés* (1897), written a decade after *La Terre,* deals not with an outsider taking on the land, but with the psychological and moral trauma wrought on seven men, uprooted from their native Lorraine by modernisation, urbanisation, and socio-economic change. It is, politically, a call for the individual's absorption into a unified, homogenised nation and, morally, a threnody on its consequences. Gide and Proust (despite his memories) were forward-looking, Proust becoming a convinced *dreyfusard* (see Section 7.3.3 in Chapter 7, this volume), appalled by the bigotry of the anti-semitic elite, Gide individualism's pre-eminent evangelist. But both Bourget and Barrès have got on history's wrong side, being associated with the reactionary Catholicism of the Nationalist *Action française* movement, founded in 1899, prominent during both twentieth-century world wars, and which still has an afterlife in French right-wing extremism today. And both writers are telling examples of a central modern phenomenon, begun with Napoleon's Empire: the tension between progress and reaction, innovations and atavism, the modern and its opposite.

### 6.2. Dreams, prose poetry, subjectivity and the Unconscious

#### 6.2.1. Dreams: Nerval

*Les Chimères,* the title of the sonnet cycle that closes Nerval's 1854 story-sequence *Les Filles du feu,* could aptly describe much of his work. For a consistent theme is the vision of an absent loved one – the other as virtual, rather than embodied, as intangible ideal. In his novella *Sylvie* (1853), the beloved is 'une apparition', a 'fantôme' ('an apparition', 'a phantom'): 'C'est une image que je poursuis, rien de plus' ('I am pursuing an image, nothing more'). The emphasis on the image seems to announce a modern and egotistical stress on the subjective – on the individual's own mental response to the beloved, rather than her supposedly objective being. Others, in other words, are what we make of them, rather than who they 'really' are. *Sylvie*'s narrator pursues Aurélia because she resembles the pure girl Adrienne he had loved in the past; in chapter 1 he gasps: 'Je touchais du doigt mon idéal' ('My finger was on my ideal'). Yet at the same time, Aurélia is an actress (whereas the unsatisfied Adrienne will go to a convent), and the narrator has been taught that actresses were not women. For him, indeed, every woman is an actress, the mere means to attaining his dreams. Refusing to buy Aurélia's favours, he retreats into dreams of his childhood love Sylvie, temporarily abandoned for Adrienne, but ultimately accepted.

It is tempting to see Sylvie's narrator, like *L'Eve future*'s Ewald, as the willing victim of self-delusion, all three women feeding a notional, fantasy, composite ideal in which each only plays a part. The interchangeability of roles, its totemic, fetishistic nature, seems particularly emphasised when Sylvie dons her aged aunt's eighteenth-century dress (*Sylvie*, 6). The reference to the past shows how atavistic the narrator's quest is. But the fitting of these women into the role of lover is not just a selfish indulgence: it is an act of reverence and remembrance, each one corresponding to different personal archetypes (queen, mother and actress/whore) but also, as Freud's concept of the Oedipus Complex has since shown, to more universal archetypes.

The near excess of meaning in Nerval's archetypes seems almost absurd in a story where the pursuit of the ideal leads only to a void – to the narrator's ultimate disappointment in love. But this yoking of sense to absurdity is precisely the point. In *Aurélia* (1855), a greater insistence on transcendent meaning joins a greater stress on dream. *Aurélia*'s opening sentence, 'Le rêve est une seconde vie' ('Dream is a second life'), foregrounds dream's importance as a preeminent mode of perception – not just Freud's means of access to a psychological or psychoanalytical truth, but as the way to an absolute truth. Via dream, and vision, the narrator has far-seeing and apocalyptic insights: of beholding before him all his loves and relations, past and present, foretelling the end of time or the end of the world, or stopping the flood that will drown it.

Yet these insights are shadowed by their opposite. Although he believes himself to be a visionary, his visions (as he suspects) are actually schizoid delusions, the products of his madness. The narrator may think that he has stopped the flood that will drown the world, but his action and the rain's ceasing were merely coincidental. Dream may apparently offer redemption, a way of restoring lost unity and meaning to a fallen creation, but it is paralleled by its contrary, fragmentation, and by the negation of meaning, absurdity and void.

This pairing of meaning with its opposite makes *Aurélia* a supremely modern text. The dream of spiritual transcendence is underpinned by the nightmare of existential angst, by the corresponding temptation of suicide that the narrator feels in *Aurélia*, and to which Nerval succumbed in 1855. The centrality of these dichotomies is enshrined in the story's structure, where Part I is a descent to despair, and Part II a recovery to redemption – a pattern mirrored in *Les Chimères*. Yet the Christian belief he finds in Part II is not a pat answer to an insoluble existential problem, but a reasoned faith, reached by rational struggles, tormented by doubt, an edifice he has constructed himself from various revolutionary and scientific beliefs, and a Christianity encountered only belatedly. In *Les Chimères*, the business of construction is made central, as writer and reader retrace, via an intriguing series of arcane, mythical and legendary references, an experience of woman, and of life and memory, which is both personal, and universal. Nerval's concept of the redemptive power of dream as the way to absolute truth can be taken on its own, mystical, nineteenth-century terms, but can also be read more agnostically, as a way of retreating from anguish. His questioning Christianity is combined with a mix-and-match attitude to belief, involving Classical, oriental and pagan references in what seems a very modern, eclectic (but also syncretic) kind of faith. It is perhaps Nerval's proto-Deconstructionist awareness that meaning is shadowed by its opposite, plenitude by void, that makes him truly modern.

### 6.2.2. Prose poetry: Baudelaire, Lautréamont

The uncertain status of the objective, the emphasis on the image, the mingling of past and present, the creation of meaning through patterns, all move Nerval's prose beyond the narrative towards the poetic – towards the *poème en prose*. But it was Aloysius Bertrand, author of *Gaspard de la nuit* (1842), the first collection of canonical prose poetry in France, rather than Nerval, who inspired Baudelaire's landmark collection of prose poems, *Le Spleen de Paris* (1861), also known as the *Petits poèmes en prose*. Rather than using prose in short strophes bordering on free verse (like most of the pieces in *Gaspard de la nuit*), or mixing verse and poetic prose (like Nerval's *Petits châteaux de Bohème*, 1853), Baudelaire's collection grows out of verse poetry. Its earliest pieces ('Un Hémisphère dans une chevelure', 'L'Invitation au voyage') transpose earlier versified poems: 'Les Veuves' reconfigures 'Les Petites vieilles' from the *Tableaux parisiens* section of *Les Fleurs du mal,* using repetition to parallel emphases of rhyme, rhythm and metre in verse. But later ones introduce effectively a completely new aesthetic, based on things we might now recognise as quintessentially modern: rapidity, change, chance, the contingent, the fantastic, the fragmentation and alienation of the self – themes that, in *Le Spleen de Paris,* are indissociable from the locus of modernity, the urban. The theme of change, which Baudelaire had already explored in the *Tableaux parisiens* part of *Les Fleurs du mal,* in, for example, 'Le Cygne':

Paris change! mais rien dans ma mélancolie
N'a bougé! (*Fleurs,* 89, l. 29-31)

(Paris is changing! But nothing in my melancholy/Has moved!)

here becomes a much more radical aesthetic, almost a philosophy of contingency and alienation, of the paradoxical mixture of solitude and yet submersion in the city and the crowd that characterises modern urban life. The first piece of the *Petits poèmes* is tellingly enti-

tled 'L'Étranger' ('The Outsider'), its subject an enigmatic man
without friends who answers the question 'Who do you love most?'
'J'aime les nuages ... les nuages qui passent ... là-bas ... là-bas ... les
merveilleux nuages!' ('I love the clouds ... the passing clouds ... over
there ... and there ... the marvellous clouds!). Among its most telling
pieces are 'Les Foules', 'Les Veuves' and 'Les Fenêtres'. 'Les Fenêtres'
begins with the emblematic assertion that 'Celui qui regarde du
dehors à travers une fenêtre ouverte ne voit jamais autant de choses
que celui qui regarde une fenêtre fermée' ('He who looks from
outside into an open window never sees as many things as he who
looks through one which is closed'), and gives us a penetrating picture
of the poet looking from the outside into, not just a room, but into its
inhabitant's private space. 'Les Foules' talks about the pleasure of
immersing oneself in the crowd, for the poet a source of inspiration
and of moral empathy born, paradoxically, of detachment:

Le poète jouit de cet incomparable privilège qu'il peut à sa guise être
lui-même et autrui. Comme ces âmes errantes qui cherchent un
corps, il entre, quant il veut, dans le personnage de chacun. (...) Le
promeneur solitaire et pensif tire une singulière ivresse de cette
universelle communion. (...) Il adopte comme siennes toutes les
professions, toutes les joies et toutes les misères que la circonstance
lui présente.

  Ce que les hommes nomment amour est bien petit, bien restreint
et bien faible, comparé à cette ineffable orgie, à cette sainte prostitution de l'âme qui se donne tout entière, poésie et charité, à l'imprévu
qui se montre, à l'inconnu qui passe.

(The poet enjoys that incomparable privilege of being able to be, as
he pleases, himself and another. Like those wandering souls in search
of a body, he enters, when he wishes, into the character of each
person.[...] The pensive solitary walker draws a singular intoxication
from this universal communion.[...] He adopts as his own all the
professions, all the joys and all the miseries that circumstances
present. // What men call love is very little, very restricted, very

weak, compared to that ineffable orgy, to that holy prostitution of the soul that gives itself entirely, poetry and charity, to the sudden appearance of the unpredictable, to the stranger passing by.)

Whatever the practical value of this empathy, it is the next poem, 'Les Veuves', which expresses it most completely. Beginning with the eighteenth-century aphorist Vauvenargues's observation that public gardens are haunted by aborted glories and broken hearts, the poem focuses on one widow, and ends with the reflection that, despite the presence of her child, she will have returned home, as always, alone, for children are selfish and, unlike animals, cannot be the confidants of solitary pain. Baudelaire's 'double postulation', tending towards both the sublime and the base, the *spleen* and the *idéal* in mankind, is evident both in the dignity of the widow and the baseness of the child, and also, perhaps, in the poet's paradoxical mix of identification and detachment.

Both identification and detachment are, of course, functions of a seeing poetic eye, or 'I', and might suppose the transcendence of that subjectivity, of that perception, over reality. Yet a poem like 'La Chambre double' juxtaposes 'une chambre idéale' with 'une chambre réelle', very much to the latter's detriment, and many others contrast ideal and real, beauty and ugliness, art and life. In 'La Soupe et les nuages', as in 'L'Étranger', the poet much prefers the clouds to his more corporeally-sustaining soup; in 'Le Chien et le flacon', the dog, like the public, prefers to the suggestiveness of perfume 'des ordures soigneusement choisies' ('carefully chosen filth'). Brutal reality intrudes on, and threatens, the ideal: the most striking pieces of *Le Spleen de Paris* are those that form some shocking anecdote expressive of the contingent, inharmonious and brutal quality of modern life, the way base events constantly threaten the serenity, plenitude and potential sublimity of the self: 'La Corde', where a mother will sell the rope with which her child has hanged himself; 'Assommons les pauvres', where the poet beats a beggar, getting him to thrash him back and conquer his liberty and equality; 'Le Vieux saltimbanque' or 'Une mort héroïque', exploring the artist's alienation. The only responses to this predicament are escape, expressed in 'La Soupe et les nuages' or 'Anywhere out of this world'; but as the very title of the last poem suggests, the hope of eluding *spleen* is ultimately just a dream.

The themes of cruelty present in Baudelaire's prose poems are taken to an extreme by Lautréamont, whose *Chants de Maldoror* (printed in 1868-9, contemporary with *Le Spleen de Paris*, but not published until 1874) set out deliberately to shock. The *Chants* are the poetic narratives of an ill-characterised Gothic prowler, part melodramatic villain, part nightmare vision of Baudelaire's *flâneur*, wandering Paris seeking victims or voyeuristically enjoying cruelties, driven by uncontrollable hate. Its world is the Gothic novel's (gallows, mad women, tortured babies), its narrative sustained without apology or explanation, only repeated initial warnings, marrying the factual with the apocalpytic – as shown by the following extract, on how to assault a child:

> On doit laisser pousser ses ongles pendant quinze jours. Oh! comme il est doux d'arracher brutalement de son lit un enfant (...) Puis, tout à coup (... ) d'enfoncer les ongles longs dans sa poitrine molle (...) Rien n'est si bon que son sang (...) nourris-toi, nourris-toi avec confiance des larmes et du sang de l'adolescent (...) alors, t'ayant écarté comme une avalanche, tu te précipiteras de la chambre voisine, et tu feras semblant d'arriver à son secours. (...) Comme alors le repentir est vrai! L'étincelle divine qui est en nous, et paraît si rarement, se montre; trop tard!

> (The nails must be allowed to grow for two weeks. Oh! how sweet it is to rip a child brutally from his bed.[...] Then, suddenly [...] to plunge the long nails into his soft breast.[...] Nothing tastes as good as his blood [...] feed, feed confidently on the adolescent's tears and blood [...] then, having rushed aside like an avalanche, you will fly in from the neighbouring room, and you will pretend to come to his aid.[... ]. How genuine repentance then is! The divine spark within us, which appears so rarely, shows itself; too late!)

This perverse and schizophrenic passage is like some mad, blasphemous parody of Christian redemption. Maldoror is tormented
by his evil, but succumbs to it. He is aware, in a beautiful eulogy of
the purity and truth of mathematics (*Chant* II), of his insignificance
before the Almighty, but mathematical reason gives him the power
to unseat Him, to entrench himself in revolt. Most striking of all,
however (and this is what makes Lautréamont truly modern), is the
means by which this is explored. In another passage, recalling the
strange visions of the book of Revelation, Maldoror sacrilegiously
breaks the lamp in the temple. But, Magritte-like, it sprouts wings
and turns into an angel, flying up to pursue him before plunging
down and floating away along the Seine. A little later comes an
extended account of watching struggling survivors from a shipwreck, and his delight when a shoal of sharks descends on, and
consumes, this 'crème rouge' ('red cream'), this boiling human soup.
His pleasures climax when the last, a pregnant female, voraciously
consumes the scraps and, seeing in Maldoror a kindred cruel soul,
joins with him in ecstatic aquatic congress, her flippers embracing
his arms in 'un accouplement long, chaste et hideux' ('a long, chaste
and hideous coupling'). The bestiality is shocking enough. But, what
it really reveals, at a more fundamental level, is a spiritual or psychic
yet physical kinship between man and animal, revealing a truth
about our shared nature, our joy in suffering, and moving on from
Baudelaire in the psychic Realism, or rather Surrealism, of his
vision. (Lautréamont, with Nerval and Rimbaud, was among twentieth-century Surrealism's inspirations.) Where Baudelaire, like, as
we have seen, Hugo, fixes experience to a symmetrical scaffolding
of absolutes, to a metaphorical, metaphysical system outside
himself, Lautréamont gives us a pathological truth. The sinking ship
is replayed three times, the phrase 'le navire tire des coups de canon
d'alarme' ('the vessel fires cannon-shots in alarm'), foreshadowing
disaster-movie replay or slow-motion cliché, but also replicating
something of psychological obsession, of the *idée fixe* that just will
not go away – the voyeurism that had billions watching planes
flying into towers after 9/11, over and over again. And the weirdness

of his images foreshadows both Surrealism's proto-Freudian obsession with the sexual and the unconscious, and what the
twentieth-century theorist Barthes called, in an entirely different
context, the mind's capacity to 'tirer tout de rien' ('draw everything
from nothing'). Lautréamont conducts a revelation of strangeness
that does not need the alibi of madness or of dream. The *Chants*
represent the furthest nineteenth-century development of the literature of evil, running from Sade via Barbey's 1874 *Diaboliques* to the
Surrealists and Georges Bataille, the cry of the unspeakable and the
unsuspected beneath society's polite veneer.

### 6.2.3. Subjectivity and the Unconscious: Laforgue

Many poems of *Le Spleen de Paris* are concerned with the fragmentation of modern life, the loss of any sense of integrity or
wholeness. Lautréamont's *Chants* certainly suggest disconnection,
and this sense of subjectivity as threatened or dispersed appears
perhaps most completely in the poetry of Jules Laforgue. Born in
1860, and, like Lautréamont, in Montevideo, the early death of
both his parents, which left Jules, the second eldest, responsible for
his nine siblings, no doubt made Laforgue peculiarly aware of his
isolation and vulnerability, of his status as an outsider. But his three
main collections of verse give scant hint of this biography: there is
little sense of an individual, poetic 'I', in the way that it is encountered in Romantic poets, or of a Baudelairian personal yet
representative destiny. Instead, subjective, no doubt initially individual experience is externalised and projected as a series of
universally-applicable themes. The personal becomes a persona
(principally Pierrot or Hamlet), a mask behind which the poet can
hide. In 'Complainte de Milord Pierrot', 'Pierrots' ('L'Imitation de
Notre-Dame la Lune'), in the *Moralité légendaire* 'Hamlet', the sad
clown or the Shakespearian protagonist are expressive of the poet's
own predicament. 'J'ai le coeur triste comme un lampion forain'
('My heart is as sad as a fairground lantern'), says the Pierrot of
'Complainte de Milord Pierrot'.

These Pierrots, or Hamlets, are elusive, fleeting, defined by nega-
tivity and nihilism, 'de la secte du Blême' ('of the sect of the Pale')
('Pierrots', I), 'dandys de la lune' ('moon dandies'), 'gens blasés'
('blasé folk') ('Pierrots', II), 'maquillés d'abandon' ('carefree-
painted') ('Pierrots', IV). Not linkable to any biographical actor or
clown, the Hamlet is less a version of Shakespeare's character than
Laforgue's mythification of him (which is no doubt why Hamlet
recognises the author immediately when he visits him in Elsinor in
the *Moralités légendaires*). The Pierrots, like Laforgue's Hamlets and
the *Complaintes* themselves, are, in fact, fragments, multiple splin-
terings and refractions of experience, rather like the splinters,
shards, facetings and reprises of reality that we find in Cubist
painting.

So the Pierrots and the Hamlets are less masks than personae
within which the poet is subsumed, and these personae are themselves less personae, than externalisations, objectifications, of a
universal human predicament. Just as, for Shakespeare, 'All the
world's a stage/And the men and women merely players' who 'have
their exits and their entrances' (*As You Like It*, II.7), so man, for
Laforgue, is but the toy of far larger, blind, impersonal, universal
forces: evolution, biological determinism, natural selection, the
reproductive urge, Chance, the Will, and also the Unconscious.
Laforgue takes his lead from Darwin, Schopenhauer and Hartmann,
but mentions none of these writers or universal forces by name: to
have done so would have been to ascribe to them an authority (and
in the case of these abstract forces, a personification) profoundly
alien to his and our modern, impersonal world view.

The one exception is the Unconscious. By the Unconscious,
Laforgue, like, as we have seen, Bourget, means not the psychoanalytical substratum of an individual's personality, but an impersonal,
ruthless, universal life-force embracing all the other life-forces just
mentioned. 'Inconscient, descendez en nous par reflexes'
('Unconscious, descend within us by reflexes') says Lord Pierrot in
the first of his *Complaintes*, 'Brouillez les cartes, les dictionnaires, les
sexes' ('Muddle the cards, the dictionaries, the sexes'). The poet,

'vermine des nébuleuses d'occasion' ('vermin of chance nebulae') ('Climat, Faune et Flore de la Lune') is beholden to that chance; history and nature are prodigal, 'Ces foires/Aux ratures' ('Those blow-outs/Of crossings-out') ('Locutions des Pierrots', 14), signs of an omnipotent, but unknowable, Unconscious.

There is no place for the individual within this schema, other than as its victim: no God, no love, and, for the individual as a transcendent centre of consciousness, no hope. Man is the victim of his own material, physical, being, and in particular, the victim of woman as the agent of the reproductive urge:

> L'Homme et sa compagne sont serfs
> De corps, tourbillonnants cloaques
> Aux mailles de harpes de nerfs
> Serves de tout et que tout détraque
> Un fier répertoire d'attaques.
>
> > Voyez l'Homme, voyez!
> > Si ça ne fait pas pitié! (... )
>
> Mais ce microbe subversif
> Ne compte pas pour la Substance,
> Dont les déluges corrosifs
> Renoient vite pour l'Innocence
> Ces fols germes de conscience.
>
> > Nature est sans pitié
> > Pour son petit dernier.
> > ('Complainte du pauvre corps humain', l. 1-7, 36-42)

(Man and his companion are body-bondsmen/Whirling sewer channels/With meshes of harps, of nerves/Serfs of all, whom all derails/A fine old game of soldiers. // Look on Man, just look! Doesn't it make your heart bleed![... ] // But this subversive microbe/Just doesn't count for Substance/Whose corrosive deluges/Quickly drown again for Innocence/These mad germs of consciousness. // Nature is without respite / For her latest little mite.)

Despite the obvious misogyny – Laforgue is one of the authors Simone de Beauvoir quotes, without approval, in *Le Deuxième Sexe* (1949) – it is clear that both sexes are subject to their own physical being: 'allons,/Ma bell, nous nous valons' ('come,/My love, we're only as good as each other') (ibid.). In a disconcertingly provisional, modern way we can recognise, Laforgue talks of relations, not relationships, temporary alignments subject to flux and change: 'L'homme, avec ses relatifs "Je t'aime"' ('Man, with his relative "I love yous"') ('États'). Elements of stability are removed. Religious faith is questioned by a string of images presenting faith as illusory. In 'La Lune est stérile', the only redemptive ideal is Art: 'L'Art est tout [...] Après lui, le déluge!' ('Art is all.[...] After it, the flood'), an impersonal echo of Rimbaud's 'Après moi, le déluge', and the only consolation, man's smallness before the Unconscious. Laforgue is emblematic of an ironic vein in contemporary French writing, represented also by other outsiders like Cros, Corbière and Lautréamont. And a similar emphasis on irony and experiment characterises the avant-garde theatre of the later nineteenth century.

### 6.3. Modernity and experiment in theatre

In a sense, every performance of a play is both modern and an experiment: a new, and unpredictable, creation happening in the here-and-now. As we have seen, Romantic drama experiments with the modern in breaking free of Classical constraints, and in tackling contemporary concerns, while mid-century theatre, like that of Dumas *fils*, is modern in facing them head on in plays like *La Dame aux camélias*.

We can find this kind of modernity in other contemporary plays, such as Balzac's *Le Faiseur* (1847; also known as *Mercadet*), where the protagonist is pursued by creditors (as was Balzac himself); Dumas *fils*'s own *La Question d'argent* (1857), which turns on the question of whether a respectable girl can decently marry a speculator; or Hugo's *L'Intervention* (striking in its depiction of poverty, and its topical references), or his *Mille francs de récompense* (both 1866), at the beginning of which the characters' property is about to be seized by bailiffs. But real modernity and experiment in form is only found in plays which, like this one, were written without constraints of censorship, audience expectation or performance; which allowed, in other words, free rein to the author's imagination.

*Mille francs de récompense* forms part of *Le Théâtre en liberté* (1886, republished, ed. A. Laster, 2002), a collection of plays written by Hugo in the 1850s and 1860s, while he was in exile from the repressive regime of Napoleon III. Originally entitled *Théâtre dans l'esprit*, the collection is just that: a 'mind' or 'imaginary' theatre, mixing genres (some of its pieces were eventually published as dramatic poems), taking drama beyond the limits of stageability. The idea of 'imaginary' theatre, written to be read rather than performed, was pioneered by Musset in *Un Spectacle dans un fauteuil* (1832) – a response to the poor reception of his first drama, *La Nuit vénitienne* (1830). *Un Spectacle*'s first play, *La Coupe et les lèvres*, like *Le Théâtre en liberté*, straddles genres. In 'Sur le théâtre', Musset describes how theatre should transport us into a new sphere, so that it seems that there is only a single thought, and a single man speaking to another. For Musset, theatre, the most public of the arts, can also be the most intimate; while Hugo wrote, 'je prolonge mon théâtre dans tous les sens vers l'idéal' ('I extend my theatre in every direction towards the ideal') (Letter to F.-V. Hugo, 17 April 1866). For Hugo, this involves not only the transcendence and fusing of existing genres, already proposed in *Cromwell*'s preface, but also giving fantasy carte blanche. *La Forêt mouillée* (1854) not only refuses a conventional conclusion, leaving the protagonist, Denarius, with his love unconsummated; it also includes, among its cast of characters, talking flowers, trees, birds and insects, and – perhaps most difficult of all to stage – a speaking pond, stream and pebble. On one level, this fantasy echoes the Shakespeare of *A Midsummer Night's Dream*: here, too, there is an element of moral correction as Denarius, a misanthropist who loves all nature but not woman, is made to see the error of his ways. On another, there is a conscious effort to dissolve all verisimilitude or everyday Realism, and place the reader on a completely transcendent level: repeated puns, anthropomorphic jokes comparing mankind and animals undermine any sense of normal reality and bring home the very strangeness of Hugo's (and other Romantic poets') pantheistic vision. Animals, vegetables and minerals routinely speak in Hugo's poetry (in *Les Contemplations*, for example), but it is quite a different matter for them to do it on stage. *La Forêt mouillée*, first performed in 1930 (accompanied with music by Fauré, Debussy and Ravel, which no doubt echoed its strangeness), can claim to be France's first absurdist drama. Hugo fills his stage with articulate plants, just as Ionesco was to do with chairs (*Les Chaises*, 1952) or rhinoceroses (*Rhinocéros*, 1960); Hugo's Baron Giprevac babbles incoherently, and surreally (*L'Intervention*, 1866), just as would the Smiths and the Martins, or the fireman, in Ionesco's 1950 *La Cantatrice chauve*. And although Hugo's plays have an overarching logic where Ionesco's do not, it is all but vestigial: the lovers of *L'Intervention* threaten to part, but reunite; Denarius falls in love, but does not consummate it; the Marquise of *La Grande-mère* threatens to disown her children, but does not. Their events are audacious non-events.

These proto-modern features are more pronounced in *Le Théâtre en liberté*'s other strikingly innovative play, *Mangeront-ils?* (1867). Superficially, it echoes themes familiar in both Shakespeare and Hugo: the king, presiding over an island (here, the Isle of Man) with quasi-supernatural beings (Aïrolo and the sorceress Zineb) recalls Prospero, Ariel and Caliban in *The Tempest*, while the antithesis of the ruler (the king) and the outcast (Aïrolo), between 'legitimate' authority and the underdog, parallels those in many of Hugo's other works, notably the opposition of Javert and Valjean in *Les Misérables*, and of Gwynplaine and the establishment in the novel *L'Homme qui rit*. Beyond this familiar Hugolian social criticism, there is a blacker, more metaphysical absolute, taking the play closer to twentieth-century Existentialism or absurdism, here voiced by Zineb. Just as Winnie, in Beckett's *Oh les beaux jours* (1963), is buried in sand, so Zineb is wearing a sack:

> J'entends dans ce branchage une aile qui palpite.
> C'est le tressaillement d'angoisse d'un oiseau.
> Car l'homme et l'animal sont le même roseau;
> L'éternel vent de mort nous courbe tous ensemble.
>
> (*Mangeront-ils?*, I.1)

(I can hear in these branches a beating wing./It's a bird's fluttering in distress./For man and animal are the same weak reed;/the eternal wind of death bends all of us together.)

This speech is the antithesis of Hugo's usually sunny view of nature. The grim image of the wind of death has far more in common with the paradoxically Pascalian view of man's condition of Beckett's *En attendant Godot* (1952), Hugo here recalling Pascal's description of him as a 'roseau pensant' ('thinking reed') (*Pensées*, ed. L. Brunschvicg, fragment 347). As Beckett contrasts his protagonists' desire to leave (to quit the human condition) with their inability to do so ('Allons-y'/*Ils ne bougent pas*, 'Let's go./*They do not move*', *En attendant Godot*), so the king and his prisoner Aïrolo are similarly entrapped:

> A quoi bon avoir vécu? (...)
> Roi, même en la forêt, je me sens en prison.
> Parfois je cherche à voir plus loin que l'horizon.
> Je gravis une cime.
>
> (*Mangeront-ils?*, II.3).

(What is the good of having lived?[...]/King, even in the forest, I feel myself in prison./Sometimes I seek to see further than the horizon./I climb to a treetop.)

The circularity of Beckett's play, where the natural cycle is represented by the paralleling of its two acts, and the tree, leafed in Act I, leafless in Act II, is present in germ in one of Aïrolo's speeches:

> Dieu, l'avare qui fait semblant d'être prodigue
> Fait toujours resservir le même mois d'avril.
> Je connais son décor.
>
> (*Mangeront-ils?*, II.3)

(God, the miser who pretends to be prodigal/Always uses again the same month of April./I know his scenery.)

The premise of Hugo's title, that lovers need also to eat (Aïrolo tells the fugitive Lord Slada and Lady Janet that they are two angels, but also two stomachs) recalls both Hugo's own juxtaposition of sublime and grotesque, and also Beckett's collisions of the spiritual and the material in the cerebral Vladimir and the earthy Estragon. The chance meeting of two opposites, Aïrolo and the king, the powerless and the powerful, parallels the meetings with Pozzo and Lucky in *Godot*. The reduction of both men to the status of prisoners of death makes both outsiders, strangers to life, like the Meursault of Camus's *L'Étranger*, and confronts them with the absurd he was to address in *Le Mythe de Sisyphe* (both 1942) or *La Peste* (1947). The 'man' in his 'Isle de Man' symbolises the human condition as much as does the absent or perhaps merely invisible God in Beckett's play.

The 'symbolism' of *Mangeront-ils?* is taken much further in Maeterlinck's *L'Intruse* (1890). This play, described by the poet Paul Fort as the *Hernani* of the Symbolist movement, was, in fact, far less well trailed than *Hernani*: it was initially cast without a venue, and then performed only once. But *L'Intruse* was so radical that, via the press and word of mouth, news rapidly spread, and Maeterlinck was the most sought-after playwright in Paris.

*L'Intruse*'s radicality lies in its symbolism. A sense of uncertainty pervades the whole play, centred on the blind grandfather, whose blindness forces him to hypothesise about what is really going on. On one level, his blindness is a disability, placing him at a disadvantage in relation to the sighted characters; on the other, the absence of one of his senses not only makes his others more acute (his daughter remarks that he has sharp hearing), it also endows him with a sixth sense, an inner vision, which gives him a kind of foresight, a gift of prophecy about the action's ultimate outcome.

It is in these terms that *L'Intruse* can be described as Symbolist – in its expression of emotional, psychological or visionary states through non-specific symbols and suggestion. The grandfather is filled with a sense of foreboding about the outcome – that his daughter will die in the wake of giving birth to her child. But this outcome is, during the course of the play, suggested yet not explicitly articulated as the characters flounder in the midst of the action. The dialogue, devoid of conventional exposition, brings out this absurdity to the full. It has a proto-Pinterian quality, its clichéd non-sequiturs echoing the banalities of everyday speech, yet carrying a vague but omnipresent menace:

La Fille aînée: Grand-père s'est endormi. Il n'a pas dormi depuis trois nuits.
Le Père: Il a eu bien des inquiétudes. (... )
L'Oncle: On ne sait pas ce qui peut arriver. Il est drôle à certains moments.
Le Père: Il est comme tous les aveugles.
L'Oncle: Ils réfléchissent un peu trop.
Le Père: Ils ont trop de temps à perdre.
L'Oncle: Ils n'ont pas autre chose à faire.
Le Père: Et puis, ils n'ont aucune distraction.
L'Oncle: Cela doit être terrible.
Le Père: Il paraît qu'on s'y habitue.
L'Oncle: Je ne puis pas me l'imaginer.

(Eldest daughter: Grandfather has fallen asleep. He hasn't slept for three nights./Father: He's had a lot of worries.[...]/Uncle: You don't know what could happen. There are times when he seems funny./Father: He's like all blind people./Uncle: They think a bit too much./Father: They've got too much time to kill./Uncle: They've nothing else to do./Father: And also, they've got nothing to distract them./Uncle: That must be awful./Father: It seems you can get used to it./Uncle: I can't imagine how.)

Here, however, the threat lies not in Pinter's power struggles between characters, but in an ambient yet omnipotent fate: the dislocated dialogue mimics the non-sequiturs of real speech, but suggests the characters' abstracted terror in the face of an unpredictable yet certain dénouement – death. Seemingly trivial circumstances assume potent import – the gardener sharpening his scythe at night (the long grass around the house signalling a life about to be cut down), the preternaturally loud ticking of the clock, announcing transience. Such factors betoken the strangeness of the real, the potential transcendence of the trivial. These representative characters' lives (although they have proper names, they are cast primarily as family roles, grandfather, father, uncle, etc.) could also be our lives, too. The smallness of the cast, the exiguity of means, the stasis yet absolute momentousness of the action (in one sense nothing happens, hardly anyone moves; in another, the most absolute happens as the mother dies and the sister of charity appears at the end) – all foreshadow the audaciously inactive drama that would emerge only after the Second World War.

Nineteenth-century theatrical experiment reaches its zenith with Jarry, but the result is not some symbolic transcendence, but fragmentation, disorientation and doubt. Jarry's Ubu plays – *Ubu roi*, *Ubu cocu* (both 1896), and *Ubu enchaîné* (1899), along with their spin-off, the *Almanach du Père Ubu* (1899, 1900) – are built around his creation Père Ubu, a kind of monstrous everyman figure who is (as his name, with its echo of the Latin 'ubique' suggests) everywhere. In some ways – in his compendious, phantasmagoric, Protean qualities, in his gluttony (12 meals a day in *Ubu enchaîné*), in his clowning, in his no-holds-barred send-ups of everything, *Ubu* reworks

Rabelais's *Gargantua* (1534) for the modern world; in others, he echoes Flaubert's *Bouvard et Pécuchet* (1881), whose impermeable stupidity embodies the very spirit of nineteenth-century positivism.

Yet Ubu, as his name tells us, is not reducible to any single character or preceding literary model: he is omnis, all, and also everywhere, like God the father (Père Ubu). The spiral that, in Jarry's sketch of him, begins at his navel, symbolises an ego in endless expansion, from which it is no more possible to escape than it is not to be stupid, or not to sin (as *Bouvard and Pécuchet*, and Christ's invitation to cast the first stone [John 8.7] tell us). Ubu is, indeed, as Jarry says (*Questions de théâtre*) less a character than a type (the miser), and less a type than an archetype – an archetype of human sociality and psychology. His name suggests both the primitive and the infantile, its palindromic reversibility the state from which we cannot emerge. And his acts, in their selfishness and cruelty, suggest an ego on the loose. But, like a child, Ubu takes fright at a bear, then displays completely reverse behaviour once the danger is past. This is why there is no consistency of characterisation in *Ubu roi* – because there can be no consistency of character. Individuals are simply neurotic types or responses.

We are in a world where there is no overarching meaning, only contradiction, fragmentation, incoherence. The *Gesamtkunstwerk*, or total artwork, embracing music, language and the visual in a single unified whole – a conception of the German opera composer Wagner, influential in France at this time – promises to be a cacophony. Any notion of consistent characters is undone by their inconsistencies and self-contradictions: Ubu is a king in the first play, and a slave in the third. Referentiality is undermined by the constant use of puns and word play. Jarry described writing as a 'syzygie des mots' ('a syzygy [conjunction or opposition] of words'), suggesting an almost chance convergence of individual terms, their fortuitously Mallarméan interaction. But Jarry goes beyond this, neologising, bastardising and extending the word-field beyond anything previously encountered in theatre. 'Merde' ('shit') becomes, as the famous first word of *Ubu roi*, 'merdre', suggesting 'mordre' ('to bite'), individuating but also adding a decidedly sinister note: it is almost as if the word itself is smudged. 'Cornedigouille' suggests both the horns of the cuckold and of the bull, but also 'couilles' ('balls'). Language, referentiality, everything is up for grabs. There is no absolute; there are only relative truths: 'Le dramaturge, comme tout artiste, cherche la vérité, dont il y a plusieurs' ('The dramatist, like any artist, seeks the truth, of which there are many') (*Questions de théâtre*). Relativity, fragmentation, incoherence: welcome to the modern world.

This new content requires a new expression. On the purely political level, this new expression sets out to shock: 'C'est parce que la foule est une masse inerte et incompréhensive et passive qu'il la faut frapper de temps en temps' ('It is because the crowd is an inert uncomprehending passive mass that it must be struck from time to time') (*Questions de théâtre*). But the Ubu plays are far from purely political. The new form also vitally embodies content. Performance of the plays by puppets, or by actors wearing masks, creates an air of unreality, and makes possible effects difficult if not impossible to realise with human actors: the cutting-up of a bear in *Ubu roi*; the impaling of Achras in *Ubu cocu*; the splitting of Pissembock into two (*Ubu enchaîné*). It also expresses the alienation that underpins the plays – people become things. Expressive of alienation, too, is the strange voice of Ubu himself, described by Jarry as a monotonous delivery, like that of a mechanical man. These features, combined with minimal non- (or anti-)realistic staging (as when, for example, the salon in *Ubu enchaîné* is turned into a prison) correspond to what Jarry saw as the true condition of theatre, dependent not on a theatre or on externals, but on what he called, in *Douze arguments sur le théâtre*, an active pleasure of the mind.

In its cruelty, anarchy and surrealism, Jarry's theatre is often said to anticipate the twentieth-century Theatre of the Absurd. Certainly, its clowning and slapstick, its anti-realistic characters and minimal staging look forward to Beckett, as do its running jokes (for example, Ubu's preferred form of torture, reminiscent of a teacher's formula, involving, *inter alia*, twisting of the ears), while its word play might evoke the Ionesco of *La Cantatrice chauve* (Ionesco was a member of the *Collège de 'Pataphysique* ('*Pataphysique* is the science of imaginary solutions, which Jarry invented).

But there is a far more fundamental way in which Jarry's work is modern, and that is in its exploration of the fundamental indeterminacy of meaning. As if anticipating the binary oppositions of structuralism, or the insights of Derridean deconstruction, the Ubu cycle is built around antithesis and reversal, around the oppositions that are creative of meaning being undone. This is true on a macro-level, where Ubu-king in the first play becomes Ubu-slave in the last; but it is also true on a micro-level. The 'jokes' in the Ubu plays depend on a pattern of contradiction and reversal, on what is said being immediately undermined by what follows. It is as if they had been written by Hugo on speed. This pattern is, it seems, for Jarry as for Hugo, inherent to experience. But instead of creating a firm basis for meaning, in the widest, most transcendent sense, it creates only aporia, an insoluble contradiction, a pattern that is ever more developed in *Ubu enchaîné*, the last of the Ubu plays. It is this exploitation of aporia, the indissociability yet incompatibility of opposites, which makes Jarry the most modern writer of nineteenth-century France; and it is the tension between the legitimate, the established, and its opposite that we shall be exploring in the final chapter.

## Selected reading

*General*

Jean Borie, *Archéologie de la modernité* (Paris: Editions Grasset & Fasquelle, 1999). Fascinating long view of the paradoxes of emergent modernity, from 1815 to Baudelaire, Flaubert and Butor.

*On specific subjects*

David Baguley, *Le Naturalisme et ses genres* (Paris: Nathan, 1995). Accessible treatment of ideas developed in *Naturalist Fiction: The Entropic Vision* (Cambridge: Cambridge University Press, 1990).

Patrick Besnier, *Alfred Jarry* (Paris: Editions Fayard, 2005). Comprehensive critical biography.

Antoine Compagnon, *Les Antimodernes* (Paris: Galllimard, 2005). Sophisticated account from the Revolution to the present, covering Bourget, Barrès, Maurras and Péguy.

Philippe Destruel, *Les Filles du feu de Gérard de Nerval* (Paris: Editions Gallimard, 2001). Compact, comprehensive guide.

Anne Holmes, *Jules Laforgue and Poetic Innovation* (Oxford: Oxford University Press, 1993). Lucid, detailed, well contextualised overview.

Marie Lathers, *The Aesthetics of Artifice: Villiers's 'L'Eve future'* (Chapel Hill, NC: The University of North Carolina Press, 1996). Challenging analysis in terms of science and sexual politics.

Patrick McGuinness (ed.), *Symbolism, Decadence and the fin de siècle: French and European Perspectives* (Exeter: Exeter University Press, 2000). Probing essays covering *inter alia* Mallarmé, Villiers and Verne. Valuable both for definition of key terms and anticipations of modernism.

Michel Nathan and Roger Bellet, *Lautréamont, feuilletoniste autophage* (Seyssel: Champ Vallon, 1992). Clearly organised close analysis, based on the intriguing premise of Lautréamont as a subversion of the serial-novel.

Michel Raimond, *La Crise du roman: Des lendemains du Naturalisme aux années vingt* (Paris: Editions José Corti, 1966, republished in 1993). Classic study of the emergence of the modern novel within the contemporary intellectual context.

Sonya Stephens, *Baudelaire's Prose Poems* (Oxford: Oxford University Press, 1999). The most interesting recent overview.

Timothy A. Unwin, *Jules Verne: Journeys in Writing* (Liverpool: Liverpool University Press, 2005). A radical reassessment.

# 7

# Margins, Peripheries and Centres

Il n'y a pas de Vrai! Il n'y a que des manières de voir. (Flaubert to L. Hennique, 2-3 February 1880)

(There is no truth! There are only ways of seeing.)

## 7.1. Space, place and perspective

This remark by Flaubert is understood nowadays primarily as an observation about narrative technique. 'Eccentricity' or 'extrinsicality' of perspective is certainly important in nineteenth-century France. Nodier's 1830 novel *Histoire du roi de Bohême*, for example, takes an episode in Sterne's novel *Tristram Shandy* (1760-7, VIII) and makes it the pretext for the whole novel. But in Nodier's work, the King of Bohemia's story is never fully told: instead, we get endless digressions, enumerations and diversions. They amount to telling us that reality is never a matter of a single story, but of a multitude of potential stories, told from an infinity of possible perspectives. Balzac's *Comédie humaine* does something similar, using short stories to illuminate the action of its main novels from various viewpoints. And Flaubert's own *Un Coeur simple* (in *Trois Contes*, 1876) takes the unusual step of relating the whole life-story of a servant, Félicité, via what, given the sympathy with which she is seen, we might take to be her own outlook. But the story is in fact told in the third person, from an external perspective. The conflict between apparent and actual viewpoint creates a tension between critical distance and identification. Perspective is then not just a technical matter: it is a major thematic issue, determining one's whole mindset. In this final chapter we shall explore margins, peripheries and centres, looking at issues of social, historical, gender and race perspective (however problematic this last concept: see Section 7.4. below), as a way of assessing the alternative viewpoints, values and hierarchies they might offer; of finding the relativities, but also relevance, of the writing of nineteenth-century France.

### 7.1.1. Paris and the provinces

Si tout arrive à Paris, tout passe en province. (Balzac, *Eugénie Grandet*)

(If everything happens in Paris, in the provinces, everything passes.)

En province, la fenêtre remplace le théâtre. (Flaubert, *Madame Bovary*)

(In the provinces, the window replaces the theatre.)

The polarity of Paris and the provinces is a major structuring tension of nineteenth-century France. In Chapter 1 we saw how a generation of young men, *arrivistes* like Sorel and Rastignac, came from the provinces to Paris to make their fortune. This bourgeois mobility contrasts starkly with the stasis of the country nobility, landowning bourgeois notables and peasants. Even mid-century, three-quarters of France's population was still rural, although this had shrunk to nearer two-thirds by the late 1860s. Bourgeois mobility was the way things were going, the sign of developing capitalism and a larger social movement from the country to the cities (in the July Monarchy in flight from an overburdened land, during the Second Empire as a result of economic and industrial growth) that would only seriously slump under the Third Republic.

Balzac's *Eugénie Grandet* (1833) reflects these patterns, foreshadowing the parallel development that would come to prominence under the Second Empire: the rise of finance. Eugénie's miser father makes a fortune from his vineyards and land acquisition in the Loire, putting the money into real estate and gold. Exploiting his

Parisian wine merchant brother's bankruptcy and suicide, he sells his gold, doubling his money, and makes a fortune in treasury bonds. He is thus an object-lesson in the virtualisation of finance, its move from land and property to intangibles – money, stocks and shares. Balzac's story *La Maison Nucingen* (1838) pursues a further development in finance, relating how the banker Nucingen made his fortune by speculation, in part at the expense of Grandet's brother. The contrast between intangibles and real estate mirrors Paris and the provinces, the virtual versus the actual; at the other end of the spectrum is the harsh rural milieu depicted in the unfinished novel *Les Paysans* (1844). Even here, though, the peasants, anxious to acquire land, are at the mercy of the usurer Rigoult – an outcome Marx saw in fact as a victory for the bourgeoisie.

Zola's Rougon-Macquart series is organised perhaps even more fundamentally than Balzac's work around the Paris/province contrast. From its first novel, *La Fortune des Rougon* (1871), set in Plassans (Aix-en-Provence), the Rougon-Macquart clan radiates to cover some of the key points, historical, geographical, social and political, of Second Empire France. Novel 2, *La Curée* (1872), recounts the financier Aristide Rougon's, now called Saccard's, profit-making assault on Paris after Napoleon III's *coup d'état*. After a second metropolitan novel, *Le Ventre de Paris* (1873), set in the capital's perishables market, Les Halles, Novel 4, *La Conquête de Plassans* (1874), returns to the originating province to narrate Marthe Mouret's conquest by the zealot priest Faujas, while Novel 18, *L'Argent* (1891) shows the unholy alliance of finance and faith in Saccard's recruitment of a prosetylising Catholic, Hamelin, in a corrupt banking operation, the *Banque universelle*, and his undoing by the Jewish banker Gundermann. Based like the later novel *Paris* (1897) on a real scandal (in *Paris*, the Panama Canal; in *L'Argent*, the Catholic financier Eugène Bontoux's *Union générale*, a church money-raising scheme that fleeced believers who had invested in, literally, good faith), *L'Argent* pits Catholic against Jew, the forces of reaction and racism against reason, as would, from 1894, the Dreyfus affair (see Section 7.3 below). Saccard's credulous victims, like Bontoux's, own a very virtual commodity – shares Saccard's bank purchases itself to keep prices artificially high – but other novels, *Le Ventre de Paris, Germinal* or *La Terre*, deal in far more solid wares: *La Terre* shows a backward, rural world in slump (as it was in the 1880s), and a family, the Fouans, doomed to schism through a property struggle. The two worlds, Paris and the provinces, or very schematically, progress and reaction, are confronted in the Franco-Prussian war novel *La Débâcle* (1892; Zola's best-seller in his lifetime), where Jean Macquart, peasant protagonist of *La Terre*, and the effete Maurice, comrades in battle, find themselves on opposite sides when Versailles, and the country, march on the capital to end the Commune. Maurice, emblem of the decadence that has caused the fall of France, is unwittingly murdered by Jean, her more authentic and vigorous half.

Paris, then, is opposed to the provinces as movement to stasis, dynamism to inertia, spectacle to retreat, the virtual to the real. On one side is the constantly active city of Balzac's *La Fille aux yeux d'or* (1835), or Baudelaire's 'fourmillante cite, cité pleine de rêves' ('teeming city, city full of dreams') ('Le Cygne', *Les Fleurs du mal*, 89), its people actors in a human comedy, a realm of make-believe, financial and personal, in the bedroom as on the stock exchange floor or the tribune of the Assembly – for Balzac's Esther (*Splendeurs et misères des courtisanes*, 1838-46), her banker lover Nucingen; for Zola's Nana, for his Interior Minister *Son Excellence Eugène Rougon* as for Rougon's exploitative love-object Clorinde. On the other is the world for which Paris is a mirage of realised dreams, a world where women wait, Emma Bovary's world, the contrast to her limited life and its uncomprehending entourage, to whom Rouen comes to seem an exciting, pseudo-metropolitan substitute for the capital, the zone of provincial stagnation deathlessly sent up in Huysmans's 1887 novel *En rade*. Yet, as the Versaillais' march on Paris would show, out of the apparently backward provinces came paradoxically modern forces, bodying forth Royalist, Catholic, anti-democratic reaction with a powerful impact on the nineteenth century and its successor – forces explored in *Les Chouans* (1829), Balzac's novel of the 1799 Royalist revolt in the Vendée, or Barbey d'Aurevilly's novels on his native Cotentin – *Une Vieille maîtresse* (1851), *L'Ensorcelée* (1854) and *Le Chevalier des Touches* (1864; also on the Chouan revolt), which were to have been grouped together under the collective title *Ouest*. Barbey's Normandy is a nostalgic evocation of the landscapes and feelings of his youth, the desolate setting for his isolated, passion-wracked heroes. In the twentieth century such forces would take shape in right-wing politics, embodied variously by Barrès and the writers of *Action française* and reactionary Catholicism, Maurras, Bloy and Péguy.

But nothing is ever clear-cut. Barrès was a mystic and an agnostic; Péguy, a socialist and a Catholic; and from a much humbler provincial background than the aristocratic Barbey came the republican Jules Vallès. *L'Insurgé* (1882), the last of his autobiographical *Jacques Vingtras* trilogy, describes a provincial revolutionary's assault on the forces of order during the Commune. Vallès was an outsider, not just geographically, but politically and aesthetically, refusing to ally himself to any established group. Alphonse Daudet would celebrate Provence in *Lettres de mon Moulin* (1866) and *Tartartin de Tarascon* (1872), while his compatriot the Occitan language poet Frédéric Mistral (1830-1914) would, via his movement, *Le Félibrige*, and his most successful creation, the 12-canto epic poem *Mireille* (*Mirèio*, 1859, adapted as Gounod's opera, 1864), and his dictionary, the *Trésor du Félibrige* (1876-86), promote provincial linguistic and cultural separatism – a reminder of the fine line between romantic regionalism and nationalism. Daudet's son, Léon, and Barrès would later be tribunes of the right, Barrès exploiting the nationalist political capital of his native Lorraine, lost, with Alsace, to Prussia in 1870. If the Paris/provinces opposition has its roots in history, its political and cultural repercussions are still very much alive today.

### 7.2. Artists and bourgeois, bohemians and dandies

The Paris/province opposition is mirrored by others just as fundamental to nineteenth-century France, between artists and bourgeois,

Bohemians and dandies. With the confirmation of bourgeois power after the 1830 Revolution, the artist (a term that now meant writers, as well as visual artists and musicians, of all kinds) was stifled by the dominant bourgeois (which, for artists, meant philistine) demand for utility, profit and progress. We have already seen in Chapters 3 and 4 how Gautier's preface to *Mademoiselle de Maupin* and Vigny's *Chatterton* protest against prevalent bourgeois ideals. But these works are but summits of a literature of difference. The cultivation of an Ideal, memorably praised in Chapter 10 of Gautier's novel, is the goal of the dandy. Inspired by aristocratic English exquisites like Beau Brummel (1778-1840), the dandy, a species present in France from the Restoration, sought to embody the exquisite in manners and dress as a means of marking difference from the bourgeois. Dandies populate Balzac's novels, where Rastignac and Marsay (in, say, *Le Père Goriot* and *La Fille aux yeux d'or*) reflect this real social phenomenon, mirrored also in Musset's 'Mardoche' (*Contes d'Espagne et d'Italie*, 1830) and Gautier's *Fortunio* (1838). But Barbey d'Aurevilly's 1844 essay *Du dandysme et de George Brummel* elevates dandyism into an art form, making the conscious cultivation of artifice an end in itself, the creation, and index, of individuality, the dandy as self-contained setter of fashion marking his opposition to a world of mundane uniformity where, as Musset and Baudelaire noted, all men are dressed in black.

It was Baudelaire who definitively stamped contemporary conceptions of the dandy. In *Le Peintre de la vie moderne* (1863), via a study of the illustrator Constantin Guys, he associates dandyism with decadence, making it a protest against a rising democratic tide. The cult of perfection in impeccable, yet unobtrusive, dress, and absolute self-control, is not a superficial preoccupation with material externals, but a form of spirituality bordering on religion, a marker of originality and removal from conformism. Dandyism is, indeed, central to Baudelaire's conception of the artist, who must be 'un saint pour soi-même' ('a saint for himself'), and, by counterdemonstration, a phenomenon of modernity, representing what he calls, in the same essay, the eternal in the transitory. Yet the hapless, ultimately hopeless decadence of Des Esseintes in Huysmans's *A rebours* shows that the transcendent cannot escape nature. Dandyism is art for art's sake made flesh – the dandy is an artwork in, and for, himself – but, in Huysmans, unlike in Wilde's *The Picture of Dorian Gray*, it is nature, not the artwork, which decays.

A kind of dandyist difference is also at the heart of Bohemianism. *Bohème*, a term originally applied to gypsies from central Europe, was first used to describe impoverished artists of extravagant habits and manners by Sand in 1837, but did not become current until a decade later. The young Romantics who had fought the 'Bataille d'*Hernani*', first among them Gautier, centred on the Impasse du Doyenné, an artist-colony in festering hovels later demolished by Napoleon III's extension of the Louvre, and were distinguished by waist-length hair and extravagant Renaissance dress. Bohemians, like dandies, sought to shock; there is something of both in Flaubert's later wish to 'épater le bourgeois' ('shock the bourgeois'). But where the dandy, especially for Barbey, was distinguished by detachment and self-containment, the Bohemian was excessively expressive. Nearly all, bar Nerval, were both writers and painters (Gautier, Borel, Murger), throwing wild parties, sharing lovers, playing pranks on the bourgeois unlucky enough to be their neighbours. But they were also highly impecunious, living from hand to mouth from journalism, poetry, painting, sharing tiny lodgings, often too poor to eat or pay the rent. Murger, immortaliser of Bohemia in *Scènes de la vie de Bohème* (1851), often could not go out because he had pawned nearly all his clothes. If the dandy was an aggressive, arrogant aesthete, the Bohemian, for all his bravura, was a bourgeois victim, the living indictment of society's philistinism and indifference to art.

Some bohemian narratives indict the bourgeois by exposing hypocrisy or stupidity, or simply trying to shock. In *Champavert, contes immoraux* (1833) by the lycanthrope (wolf-man) Petrus Borel (so-called because of his outrageous political and moral provocations), one of the stories is about a girl condemned to death for infanticide by a prosecutor who turns out to be her seducer, another about an old man who dissects his young wife's lovers. In *Les Jeunes France* (also 1833), co-authored with Nerval, Gautier mocks the bourgeois but also the artist, nonetheless scattering preface and stories with what are virtually style-tips on how to be bohemian. Yet the preface of Murger's *Scènes*, the most famous bohemian stories of all, starkly criticises those who, after *Chatterton*, use society as an alibi for their own artistic void. *Chatterton*, indeed, the preface implies, is responsible for an excess of 'artists' who would be better employed doing other more mainstream things. And that is indeed what happens to Murger's heroes. Although the poet Rodolphe and his painter flatmate Marcel experience the vicissitudes Murger really knew, although their mistresses are unfaithful (Mimi dies in poverty and Musette makes a different marriage), their adventures and their poverty are recounted poignantly, and whimsically, as a matter for slightly patronising amusement, rather than any serious ideological challenge. By the end, Rodolphe and Marcel 'see sense', establishing themselves in society, leaving Bohemia behind. Murger claims to be giving us real Bohemia, not some stage make-believe – but, although his novel is harsher than Puccini's opera *La Bohème* (1896), he had already made a successful theatrical version of his Bohemia in 1849.

The most authentic forms of Bohemia celebrate failure, assert the right not to be bourgeois (useful, productive, conformist), the right to be as you please: to live on, and tell tales from, the margins. Nerval's *Petits châteaux de Bohème* (1852) celebrate the freewheeling joys of bohemian life in a matching freewheeling form. The 'bohemian castles' are 'châteaux de cartes, châteaux en Espagne' ('houses of cards, castles in the air'), reminding us of the fragility of happiness and its subservience to chance. Nerval's *Petits châteaux*, his *Nuits d'octobre*, his *Promenades et souvenirs* are all loosely linked short articles containing memories of bohemian life or his wanderings around Paris, their fragmented, flexible form recalling Diderot's bohemian outsider *Le Neveu de Rameau* (c. 1760) or Sterne. They celebrate serendipity and the offbeat, an openness to experience and a refusal to fit it into convenient or would-be convincing forms. Nerval's marginals and oddballs – the experts whose exchange consists chiefly of 'heuh! heum!', the fairground attraction of the woman with merino hair – are fascinating enough in themselves, without being squeezed into the corsets of the 'possible' or the 'probable'.

It is this combination of thematic and formal eccentricity that constitutes Nerval's ideological protest. 'Normal' (or 'normalised') lives and narratives do not convey the true nature or potential of experience, and Nerval refuses to force his experience into set moulds. In art, 'Le vrai, c'est le faux' ('the true is the false'). Realism is a distortion of reality, a tyranny to be escaped, which is why Nerval lets his experiences do the speaking. The merino woman's supposedly exotic assistants should have dared admit they were really French provincials, for their truth is stranger and more chal-lenging than their fiction. 'Monsieur ... est au cabaret' ('Sir ... is in the bar') is as much self-justification as is required: no one should apologise for simply being. But few get paid for it either: Murger died in a hospice; Nerval, taking experience further, went mad and killed himself. Bohemia's stark opposition of artistic enterprise and grinding material need reminds us that life on the margins is also life at the centre, a cutting-edge, truer-than-conformist encounter with the realities of being.

### 7.3. Gender and sexuality

Sex may be defined as the biological division of the sexes; gender and sexuality as the psychological, social and relational expressions of sex. In view of the very few women who have become major writers for posterity (essentially Staël, Sand, Desbordes-Valmore and Rachilde), one could almost be forgiven for thinking that there were hardly any women writers in nineteenth-century France. In fact, of course, considerable numbers of significant (if now largely unread) female writers, novelists like Cottin, Genlis and Duras, the novelist play-wright Delphine de Girardin, or the radical political activist Flora Tristan, were important in giving contemporary women a voice (not always radical), and raising awareness of their situation.

It is symptomatic of women's subservience that the voices of sympathetic men (like hostile ones) were louder, if not stronger, and are among those still heard today: Balzac's and Flaubert's (see Section 5.2 in Chapter 5, this volume), Dumas *fils*'s in his didactic plays (*Le Demi-monde*, 1855; *Les Idées de Madame Aubray*, 1867) and in his essays (*Les Madeleines repenties*, 1869; *La Question du divorce*, 1880), paradoxical in loving the 'sinner', woman, if hating the 'sin' of prostitution. Education, privilege and prejudice combined to give men a stronger voice than women; it was only in the twentieth century that writing authoritatively on women became belatedly accepted as women's prerogative alone. Yet, even at his most progressive, Dumas *fils*, if well intentioned, aims to normalise, gloss over difference ('fallen' women, illegitimate sons), rather than accommodate or respect it: something 'commun et bas' ('common and base') according to Flaubert, who much preferred Zola's *Nana* (18 April 1880, letter to Edma Roger des Genettes).

The view from the margins is often clearer than from the centre: alternative sexualities can offer a truer view of the mainstream. The emblematic nineteenth-century French exploration of gender and alternative sexuality was Gautier's *Mademoiselle de Maupin*. This novel of a cross-dressed female protagonist (based on an eponymous real seventeenth-century actress), pursued by both men and women, shocked the bourgeois and wowed the bohemes, seeking a truth higher than conformism, a love that transcended the gender divide and strove for the ideal, that went beyond utilitarianism and the 'moral'. Its archaic pretext removed it from the contemporary, connoting a freedom unavailable in the reign of Louis-Phillipe, the *roi bourgeois*. For Gautier, and for Balzac and Stendhal in the *Contes drolatiques* (1832-7) and the *Chroniques italiennes* (1837) respectively, the past, Renaissance or baroque, was an age of authenticity unlike their own.

Other fictions use distance in time and place to explore alternative sexualities. Latouche's novel *Fragoletta; ou Paris et Naples en 1799* (1829) combines history with a bisexual love story emblematising gender as well as geopolitical dilemmas. Balzac's *Sarrasine*

(1830), set in eighteenth-century Rome, recounts its hero's unwitting pursuit of Zambinella, a cross-dressed castrato opera singer; his *La Fille aux yeux d'or* (1835), although occurring in near-contemporary Paris, has bisexual protagonists whose Spanish and English connections evoke dark passions, the baroque, and the powerful perversity of the dandy.

In all these narratives, sexual ambivalence expresses the quest for a higher ideal. Their androgynes seek, or at least seem, to unite the features of both sexes in supernatural perfection. It is this that links *Mademoiselle de Maupin*'s attack on the limitedness of bourgeois utilitarianism with its discovery of alternative sexuality, or the social polarities of *La Fille aux yeux d'or*'s Paris with its quest to transcend sexual opposites, something echoed in Balzac's *Séraphita* (1835), whose protagonist's androgyny represents a transcendence of earthly limits and profane love, and the reaching of a spiritual ideal. *Séraphita* contains visions of heaven, but even it ends with only striving. The androgyne, ideal in principle, is a catastrophe in reality – for the hermaphrodite who embodies, but does not combine or transcend, the sexual features of male and female. No consummate sexual love is possible for Zambinella, for *La Fille aux yeux d'or*'s Paquita or (up to a point), for the male-dressed Maupin, who cannot return her female suitor's advances. The androgyne's theoretical perfections elude the hermaphrodite in practice, doomed – as in Ovid's *Metamorphoses* – to suffer the curse of being both and (n)either male (n)or female. For the Romantic writer, gender and sexuality, rather than being ways of individual self-realisation, are simply means to a transcendent end.

Something different, hinting at a more modern, subjective, individualist conception of sexuality, can be found in Flaubert. In *La Tentation de Saint-Antoine* (begun 1848, but not published until 1874), the saint's sexual, violent, sadomasochistic temptations can be read as displacements of physical desire under the cover of metaphysical yearning. In *La Légende de Saint Julien l'Hospitalier* (*Trois contes*, 1877), it is homosexual desire that seems to be displaced: if the saint's closing embrace of a leper can be read as the pinnacle of loving

Christian self-abnegation, the ultimate victory of the spiritual over the physical, the extreme sensuality of the description with its whole-body embrace and ecstatic delirium also suggests a more viscerally same-sex desire. The story's protracted gestation (over twenty years), its closing sentence (the only one in his mature work where this relentlessly impersonal writer speaks apparently in his own voice) are enough to suggest its closeness to his heart. Later in the century, in a *fin de siècle* bohemian milieu, Rachilde's *Monsieur Vénus* (1884) pushes to its furthest limit a bisexuality only belatedly unveiled at the end of Balzac's *La Fille aux yeux d'or*. Rachilde's story of a trans-vesting aristocrat, Raoule de Vénérande, who picks up Jacques, a working-class boy and makes of him her feminised love-creature, tellingly shifts the emphases in Balzac's story. Where, at the end of *La Fille aux yeux d'or*, Paquita's jealous protector Mariquita murders her in revenge for her infidelity with Marsay (even though Marsay is transvested in remembrance of Mariquita), Raoule contrives Jacques's death in a duel when, like Paquita, he shows signs of inde-pendence, or rather dependence on the gay role she has cast him in, by trying to seduce her male friend Raittolbe. But she worships his effigy, made of wax, rubber and the hair, teeth and eyelashes she has torn from his corpse. Balzac's story ends with what is, at root, conventional jealousy, showing in addition the material limits to would-be spiritual and gender transcendence: the lover's ideal meets with the ultimate finite, death. But Rachilde's makes death an end in itself. The hideous phantasmagoric Jacques-statue that Raoule visits and makes love to, both as a woman and cross-dressed as a man, parodies the statue as emblematic of the androgynous ideal, found in Balzac (whose Sarrasine falls in love with his castrato, more perfect than any woman, as Pygmalion, the sculptor of antiquity, fell in love with this sculpture) and Gautier (whose 'Contralto', in *Émaux et camées*, unites male and female). And Raoule's apparent oblivious-ness to its phantasmagoria underlines her egotism and the way in which, in the modern psyche, the virtual transcends the real. The other is just an object, a tool for private pleasure, as is Hadaly for Count Ewald in Villiers's *L'Eve future*. Marginal, perverse and alternative sexualities question gender difference, but above all, query the otherness of behaviours at the centre.

## 7.4. Travel, the exotic and race

To treat travel, the exotic, and race under the same heading may seem provocative. For while travel and the exotic both imply a euro-centric 'white on black' outlook, with the metropolitan French writing about the cultures they exploit, race could suggest the opposite, with host communities responding to those from outside. 'Race', although now a discredited concept, is employed in what follows as being consistent with the nineteenth-century mindsets and usages. Yet none of these cateogories is straightforward, or a simple matter of black and white. French writers are changed by the cultures they explore, but also present outsiders' views from within.

### 7.4.1. Travel and the exotic

The nineteenth century is a great age of French travel-writing – and not just about the foreign or the exotic. Taylor and Nodier's monumental 20-volume architectural and historical survey, the *Voyages pittoresques et romantiques dans l'ancienne France* (1820-80) journeys into the homeland as into a strange land, travelling in space but also into the past. Stendhal's *Mémoires d'un touriste* (1838) and Flaubert and Du Camp's *Par les champs et par les grèves* (1847) make the provincial exotic, different, curious, an implicit contrast to the ever more dominant Parisian norm. As at *Le Rouge et le noir*'s opening, Stendhal's seemingly impartial traveller's gaze veils ironic social comment; Flaubert's *Par les champs* is as much anthropology as topography, strung between Balzacian observation and Flaubertian irony, mocking its subjects, itself and its contemporaries as much as it informs: the legitimist laments in the visitor's book at Chambord, the current taste for ornament and kitsch (the tailor, Flaubert says, is the century's king), our imbecilic astonishment at those living in other places with other habits than our own. I would give much, the author writes, to know who invented for the statues on Nantes museum white-metal vine leaves 'qui ont l'air d'appareils contre l'onanisme' ('which look like anti-onanism devices'). Yet marvellous evocative passages (the church at Plomelin, for example) are warm-ups for the *tours de force* of the great novels.

Contemporary writing on foreign travel, in contrast, reflects both personal daring (especially of earlier travellers like Chateaubriand, whose *Itinéraire de Paris à Jérusalem* [1811] was arduous) and France's colonialist expansions. Chateaubriand's *Itinéraire*, like the Taylor-Nodier *Voyages*, typifies earlier travel-writing in stressing geography, topography and history, here routes to ideology, attacking the Ottoman Empire and Islam, foreshadowing the philhellenism that would peak in 1826 after the capitulation of Missolonghi. But it also contains in embryo a trait that becomes more prominent in later examples: a reflectiveness that would turn to egotism (self-exploration) in quintessentially Romantic travelogues like Stendhal's *Rome, Naples et Florence* (1817, revised in 1826) and *Promenades dans Rome* (1838). Neither is a straightforward travel guide, as the end of *Rome, Naples et Florence* demonstrates. After a patchwork of anecdotes, reflections and digressions, many unrelated to the title cities, socio-cultural and aesthetic observations and implicit political critique, Stendhal, back in Frankfurt, encapsulates what he has taken from Italy, and what Romantic travel-writing is all about: the quest for an away that is truly home:

> J'ai senti la possibilité d'un nouveau bonheur. Tous les ressorts de mon âme ont été nourris et fortifiés; je me sens rajeuni. Les gens secs ne peuvent plus rien sur moi: je connais la terre où l'on respire cet *air* céleste dont ils nient l'existence; je suis de fer pour eux.

> (I felt the possibility of a new happiness. All the wellsprings of my soul have been fed and strengthened; I feel rejuvenated. Cold-hearted people can no longer do anything against me: I know the land where is breathed that celestial *air* whose existence they deny; I am as of iron towards them.)

Italy has become an analogue for happiness. Romantic travel is wandering less of the body than of the soul.

Stendhal's retreat into ecstatic, fully-realised introspection is characteristic of a more generalised flight from reality, where the quest for the specificities of difference, the particularities of otherness that Hugo had dubbed *couleur locale* in *Cromwell*'s preface, becomes both a celebration of diversity to pit against bourgeois, *classiques*, and conformity, and a search for an increasingly elusive authenticity. Gautier's *Voyage en Espagne* (1843), Nerval's *Voyage en Orient* (1843, published in 1851), and Flaubert's of the same title (1849-51), exemplify this in different ways. For Nerval and Flaubert, the Orient offers the way to an ideal, to be accessed through woman for Nerval, and, for Flaubert, in her. It is a quest for authenticity through subjectivity (the reader's, and writer's own reflections) that travels both in space and time – in Flaubert's novel *Salammbô* (1862), for example, set in ancient Carthage, and whose object, its author declared, was to 'faire rêver', and in Anatole France's more directly erotic and exotic *Thaïs* (1890).

Yet, for both Nerval and Flaubert, the ideal is constrained by the real – by Muslim mores for Nerval, revealing the gulf between the writer and his desires, and by crass reality for Flaubert, whose very lust for a prostitute, Kuchouk-Hânem, is challenged when he finds her more infirm (and less beautiful) on the return leg of his trip – not to mention his fantasy of being loved by her, which is constantly confronted by the sordidness of the real – syphilis, bed-bugs, and the like. The oriental dream is always countered by reality, the white man's imagined supremacy by empires that bite back. The polarities of self and other, metropolis and Europe, are in reality dichotomies, figuring the traveller's constant struggle with the real. Ironically, the desire to escape from modernity is also an index of modernity, the very condition that makes escape impossible: the ubiquity of westernisation, the increasing ease of travel, making escape from the West unlikely. 'Avez-vous vu, dans Barcelone/Une Andalouse au sein bruni?' wrote Musset ('Have you seen, in Barcelona/An Andalusian girl with burnished breast?')

('L'Andalouse', *Contes d'Espagne et d'Italie*). But in *L'Éducation senti-mentale*, Frédéric Moreau's Andalusian turns out to be Mme Arnoux from Chartres, as we have seen (see Section 5.5). The traveller and writer Pierre Loti encounters genuine mysteriousness and difference in his Turkish lover in *Azyiadé* (1879), or in his Japanese mistress *Madame Chrysanthème* (1886), yet at the same time is distressed to find Osaka as occidentally industrialised as the France he thought he had left. As Baudelaire puts it in *Les Fleurs du mal*'s final poem, 'les vrais voyageurs sont ceux-là seuls qui partent pour partir' ('real travellers are those who leave just for the pleasure of leaving'). To arrive is to face certain disillusion, to find somewhere little different from the place you tried to escape. The splendour and wretchedness of nineteenth-century travel writing is its inevitable reflection of the self, the familiar and the known.

### 7.4.2. Race

The few canonical nineteenth-century fictions that deal centrally, and explicitly, with race explore conflict more overtly. Mme de Duras's *Ourika* (1824) tells the story of a black slave's hopeless love for her white aristocratic master, exploring race and class bound-aries at once. This first-person narrative gives its female, black, slave protagonist her own voice, daring to ask why she should renounce her feelings for Charles, a white man of higher class, simply because he is married, and shows her optimistically able to empathise across racial and class boundaries – she understands the plight of the aris-tocrat Thénaïde, whose whole family are guillotined during the Terror. But it does not provide an upbeat answer: Ourika is treated so cruelly that she retreats into a convent, providing only an extreme example of Romantic agony with local colour, owing more to Bernardin de Saint-Pierre's classic love-story *Paul et Virginie* (1788) than to black liberation. Hugo's *Bug-Jargal* (1820, revised in 1832) builds on a similar theme, a black slave's love for Marie, the daughter of a white master – in fact, of the uncle of the narrator, Léonard d'Auverney. The story is more precisely contextualised than *Ourika*, in the 1791 black uprising on St Domingo (then a French colony, now Haiti), pitting Léonard against the black leader, Bug-Jargal – a fictional analogue of the real leader of the uprising, Toussaint-Louverture. But Bug's affection for and protection of Marie brings the men together, in what is ultimately a celebration of the Revolution's trinity, *Liberté, Égalité, Fraternité*. It minces no words about colonial racism, giving a voice to the excluded as would, later, *L'Homme qui rit* (1869). And, like its near contemporary, Hugo's *Le Dernier jour d'un condamné* (1829, written against the death penalty), its chief value is as an act of provocation, revisiting the Revolutionary period when slaves were, briefly, liberated, foreshadowing the ultimate abolition of slavery in 1833.

But it is Dumas's *Georges* that provides perhaps the most satisfying exploration of race. *Georges* (1843), like *Ourika* and *Bug-Jargal*, employs conventional generic frameworks (the love story, the adventure novel, exploited in *Monte-Cristo* the following year) for exploring issues of race. In a way, race issues are genre issues, for both deal with the rights and wrongs of classification and affiliation. In *Georges*, Dumas (himself mixed-race) uses the story of a mixed-race family in Ile de France (now Mauritius) – the father, Pierre Munier, a slave owner; his sons Georges and Jacques, who is a privateer – to question the validity of rigid racial boundaries. The novel is built around a series of dramatically contrasted, but telling, oppositions: between the subservient Munier and his courageous sons; between the devil-may-care Jacques and the upright Georges; between Munier and Lord Murrey, and between their pairs of sons; between the heroic Georges and Malmédie's vain and arrogant son, Henri, Georges's rival for Malmédie's beautiful niece, Sara.

In some ways, the novel's treatment of race may seem caricatural. But its admittedly stark contrasts do no more than express the brutality of its subject, slavery, and of the hard-bitten racial prejudice that accompanies it (slaves, we read, were machines who had to be whipped). Dumas uses contrast to drive the action on, to confront his audience with a vision of subjects – race and slavery – still very much taboo. The central conflict in *Georges*, between mixed-race and white, between the Muniers and Malmédie, is crystallised in Georges's love for Sara. Malmédie's sudden acceptance of Georges's marriage proposal, after an initial and predictable refusal, is inexplicable until it emerges that the whites have learnt of the black revolt that Georges is to lead, and are using Sara as a peace offering. Georges's equally surprise refusal arises from his commitment to his people, from an absolute inability (unlike her family) to use his lover as a pawn. He is imprisoned, sentenced to death, but makes a dramatic eleventh-hour escape with Sara.

*Georges*'s contrasts are sharp enough, its thrilling clichés perhaps too familiar. Yet the meaning of these contrasts is often far from clear, and the more we look at its clichés, the less stereotyped they appear. *Georges* begins with what looks like a conventionally exotic description of Mauritius, and a sexist one into the bargain: the island is like a native girl, waiting to be ravished. Yet when we discover how readily Sara's relatives would trade her in marriage, our acceptance of these clichés is challenged. The text is scattered with received opinions on black *mores*, on their laziness and sensuality, giving signal examples of such behaviour in support: Jacques's is one example, but the most telling is the defeat of the revolt by leaving casks of rum and spirits that make the insurgents hopelessly drunk – the kind of cliché of supposed black inadequacy we also find in Mérimée's story *Tamango* (1829) where slaves mutiny, take control of, but cannot sail, their owner's ship. Georges himself initially appears as a counter-example to this cliché of black indulgence – a man who trains himself, through sheer willpower, never to give in to his feelings or show weakness (he makes himself gamble a fixed amount, in order not to be tempted to gamble more, and resists the temptation to seduce Sara, even when she is panting in his arms). But his discipline and integrity can also be read as pride, as can his refusal of Sara's hand when he desperately desires it. Munier senior may be kinder to his slaves than Malmédie (not difficult), but the only consequence of this kindness is that they fetch better prices on the market. *Georges* uses conventional boundaries to transcend them, to suggest, through Georges's interracial marriage, that prejudice can be overcome. It is a possibility of which Dumas was perhaps peculiarly aware. Yet the in some ways fairy-tale ending also challenges the achievability of that possibility, placing it more within the realm of the Romantic than of the real.

### 7.4.3. Anti-Semitism and the Dreyfus affair

Although these works challenge received ideas, they can nonetheless be placed in the category of what L.-F. Hoffmann has called 'le nègre romantique' – Romantic, idealised presentations of blackness as otherness, to be placed in the same category as more readily recognizable 'exotic' presentations of the other. Yet they can also be seen as implicitly betraying racial tensions that were explosively to surface in relation not to blacks, but to Jews, in the Dreyfus affair of 1895. In one respect, *L'Affaire*, as it has become known, was quite different in character, at least in racial character, from the other works dealing with race discussed here: Jews, with the notable exception of Balzac's Esther (*Splendeurs et misères des courtisanes*) were not, strictly speaking, exotic, at least not in the same way as blacks or orientals. They could not be: they were already part of the fabric of French society, by definition not foreign. But this was paradoxically precisely what exposed them to racism, made them foreigners on the doorstep, whose otherness could be identified and stereotyped as financiers or prostitutes in texts as diverse as Zola's *L'Argent*, Balzac's *Splendeurs et misères* or Baudelaire's 'Une nuit que j'étais auprès d'une affreuse juive' (*Les Fleurs du mal*, 32).

A 'respectable' racism had been theorised by Gobineau's *Essai sur l'inégalité des races humaines* (1853-5), which posited that the decline of civilisation was due to interbreeding. And France's latent, Catholic-driven anti-Semitism was ignited by Drumont's enormously successful *La France Juive* (1886), which attributed Christian civilisation's moral decline to a Jewish plot for world domination. Anti-Semitism came to a head in the condemnation for treason of Captain Alfred Dreyfus, a Jew, for passing military secrets to the Germans, and to life imprisonment on Devil's Island, a penal colony off French Guiana, in 1894. In 1897 it emerged that a different officer, an aristocrat, Commandant Esterhazy, might be to blame. In 1899 Dreyfus was tried, again found guilty, this time with extenuating circumstances, and only completely cleared in 1906. Rather like Iraq, the apparently strictly legal issue snowballed. The *Affaire*, as it became, revealed the fault-lines in *fin de siècle* France. It split the country, broadly into the camps that had marked French politics since the century's start: republicans and anti-clericals versus militarists, Catholics and monarchists, *dreyfusards* versus *anti-dreyfusards*. Zola was among the captain's chief defenders, in his tract *J'accuse* (1898). Dreyfus was eventually acquitted; in 1901, the true treason was revealed to be that of the French military establishment and, the following year, Zola died, mysteriously asphyxiated by his heating. The question of his murder has never been resolved.

The Dreyfus affair stirred strong emotions and opinions about what it meant to be French. The argument was perhaps not really about absolutes, but about relative values, especially where morality was concerned. It was Esterhazy, a mythomaniac to boot, who had sold the secrets; in an extra twist, it has been suggested that these 'secrets' were actually decoys planted by the top brass that was so anxious to defend him. Yet morality was neither here nor there: what mattered was being on the right side. The 'absolutes' were nonsense, as Jarry's sketch *L'Île au diable* (1899) shows:

Père Ubu: Notre fils Malsain-Athalie-Afrique est le vrai coupable, mais il est l'héritier de notre savoir théologique et de nos études au séminaire de Saint-Sulpice; il s'est confessé de son crime à notre Chanoine, il en a été absous, il n'est plus coupable, il ne l'a jamais commis.

Mère Ubu: Oui, père Ubu; tandis que Bordure, depuis que tu l'as fait jeter en prison, ne cesse de crier son innocence.

Père Ubu: D'ailleurs le capitaine Bordure est un dissident.

(Père Ubu: Our son Malsain-Athalie-Afrique is the real culprit, but he is heir to our theological knowledge and our studies at the seminary

of Saint-Sulpice; he has confessed his crime to our Canon, he has
been absolved, he is no longer guilty, he never committed it./Mère
Ubu: Yes, father Ubu; while Bordure has not stopped claiming his
innocence since you had him thrown into prison./Père Ubu: Besides,
Captain Bordure is a dissident.)

As often, the view from the margins reveals a central truth.

## 7.5. Coda: two telling texts

We shall close by looking at two works that exemplify many of the
paradoxes of nineteenth-century France: Rostand's *Cyrano de
Bergerac* (1897) and Mirbeau's *Le Journal d'une femme de chambre*
(1900).

Rostand's *Cyrano de Bergerac*, a play about the real seventeenth-
century poet, swordsman and adventurer, is full of exciting exploits
and derring-do. The title role is one of the great roles of French
theatre, immortalised by its first performer, Coquelin; Cyrano himself
can be – and was – seen as representing the true, unquenchable spirit
of France, a poet-hero whose wit and vigour triumph over any adver-
sity, who fears no one and who is an absolute model of integrity.

Yet there are several paradoxes in this portrait of the hero. First
is the fact that Cyrano is not a Parisian, but a Gascon – thus not from
the centre, but from the periphery, from the province whose inhabitants are known for their roughness and unreliability. Salvation, it
seems to imply, comes not from the old core of France, from the *Ile
de France*, but from its outer reaches – not from the tired conventions
represented by Montfleury, or the superannuated aristocrat the Duc
de Guiche, who treats his men with contempt, and earnestly,
witlessly, and thus ultimately unsuccessfully, pursues the heroine,
the beautiful Roxanne, but from the earthier world of Cyrano and
his friend, the pastry cook-poet Raguneau. Then there is the more
famous fact of Cyrano's grotesquely oversized nose – a source of
phallic pride yet also insecurity, the subject both of crowing
speeches by its owner, but also mockery from others that gets him

into fights. It is the subject, and the symbol, of great prowess, but also a fatal flaw; for although Cyrano has the wit, and swordsmanship, to take on any man, his ugliness debars him from success in the only way that really matters, in love.

It is thus that Cyrano finds himself standing in for the handsome but tongue-tied Christian in his seduction of Roxanne in the famous balcony scene in Act II, ghosting the words that Christian cannot think of for himself, and which lead to Christian's successful seduction of her. The moment when the two kiss, her subsequent arrival on the field of battle, and inconsolable grief when Christian is killed, leading to her withdrawal to a convent, are some of the most moving in French theatre. For Cyrano has been deeply in love with her all along, and it is this that has enabled him so successfully to express what is supposedly Christian's affection, which allows Cyrano to write Roxanne more letters from the front, in Christian's name but giving voice to his own feelings, than Christian realises he has ever sent; and it is this love for Roxanne that allows Cyrano to keep his love for her silent even years after Christian's death, so as not to destroy her illusions or taint her grief.

This phenomenal act of will apparently attests Cyrano's integrity, his placing of his own feelings after those of Roxanne. Yet he has been less than honest with himself, or with her, in ghosting Christian's declarations, as a way of assuaging, or inflaming, his own unrequited feelings; his wish to leave her illusions undisturbed raises deeper questions about identity, about precisely with whom, or what, lovers fall in love. Christian is mortified when she says she would love him even if he were ugly, that she loves his soul, and his wit, apologising for falling only for his looks; for his wit comes entirely from Cyrano, who is simultaneously encouraged and appalled. Christian thus represents the body, and Cyrano the soul with which she has fallen in love; if the blood on his last letter to Roxanne was Christian's, the tears, and the words, were Cyrano's. When the secret is finally revealed as Cyrano is dying, Roxanne declares her love – a love not negating her feeling for Christian – whatsoever that may have been.

The ending's audacious uneasiness throws into stark relief the paradoxes of identity and integrity that lie at the drama's heart. Cyrano's denial of his love has actually been a way of assuaging it, of turning it into a kind of fiction through ghosting Christian's letters. Christian's handsome externals have concealed a void, while Cyrano's ugliness has been redeemed by wit. While Cyrano represents authenticity, he is, inescapably, a Gascon, and in his conduct of his personal life and of Christian's, has been guilty of disingenuousness in the extreme. The drama's moving ending can thus obscure its paradoxes, no doubt helping to explain its astonishingly consistent success since its launch in 1897. Rostand seemed to initiate a new national school of drama, a reworking of Hugolian sublime and grotesque, a return both to the high days of Romanticism where the poet, like Cyrano, would be a saviour (it is significant that, at the opening, we approach the fictional 'reality' through a play), but also to the seventeenth century, to the heroism of Corneille's *Le Cid*. The play is certainly a remarkable achievement, probably the greatest French verse drama since *Hernani* or *Ruy Blas*, and arguably a better play than either. Yet its need to call on history, the problematic integrity of its heroes, its questioning of identity (Cyrano or Christian? Soul or Body? French or Gascon? Past or Present?) sets in stark perspective some of the bravado insecurities of *fin de siècle* France. Cyrano dies with his panache; but nonetheless, he dies. Cyrano was successful because it gave its audiences exactly what they wanted, as Rostand tried to do with his subsequent plays *L'Aiglon* (1900) and *Chantecler* (1910), both nationalistic celebrations of the past. But this pinnacle of his career, and of nineteenth-century French drama, is shadowed both by the past, and by the contradictions at its heart.

*Le Journal d'une femme de chambre* explores similar and equally important contradictions in a more direct and overtly modern way. Although neither subtle nor stylistically innovative, its very crassness mirrors and exposes the brutality at the heart of *fin de siècle* France. Through the chambermaid, Célestine's, diary we follow her string of masters, liaisons and one-night stands, and a repertory of avarice, vices and perversions – from the fetishism of the first employer, to another stopped by customs with a dildo in her bag, to lesbianism, to the sexual decadence of artists, to Célestine's affair with the dying, consumptive Georges, or the cook's infatuation with the neighbouring concierge's effeminate son, to a range of other assignations. On one level, sex is the *Journal's raison d'être*, and it is unsurprising that Célestine, sacked from nearly every job for speaking her mind, almost ends up as a whore.

But although, in technical terms, the work can seem sometimes too contrived to be totally believable as a diary, in terms of content and conviction, it convinces utterly. Célestine's outrage gradually builds throughout, from protest at her master's avarice (a recurrent theme) to invective against men's infidelity, writing in Chapter 16, when William, the last of her exploitative suitors, leaves her:

> Ah! oui! les hommes! ... Qu'ils soient cochers, valets de chambre, gommeux, curés ou poètes, ils sont tous les mêmes ... Des crapules!

> (Ah! Yes! Men! – Whether coachmen, manservants, coxcombs, vicars, or poets, they're all the same – all scum!)

Mirbeau's novel is a triumph of transcendence, of writing from the margins to show the canker at the centre. It is as striking a piece of psychological 'ventriloquising' as any by a nineteenth-century writer. Célestine's position on the margins, or in the dregs of society, as a *bohème*, as she puts it, yet also at its centre, at the heart of the homes and lives, of the bourgeoisie, gives her an identification with the underdog, with the servant, with the white slave trade, with the dealer in human flesh who is the brothel-keeper, yet also a deep insight into the lives and mindsets of the masters. Her affairs transcend class and reverse conventional social and moral boundaries, more than once revealing parallels between upper and lower orders, usually to the advantage of the latter.

Yet the *Journal's* fundamental import is as a critique of contemporary France, an indictment of money's omnipotence and of the bourgeois who exploits. The nineteenth-century apotheosis of money finds its fictional consummation in this novel, where, beneath its panoply of hypocrisies, Catholicism, Nationalism, anti-Semitism, *dreyfusards* and *anti-dreyfusards*, there is only one sincere desire, for money. Even desire itself is deviant, lust hiding behind the respectabilities of rank or religion, self-interest masquerading as love. What saves the *Journal* from being a one-sided diatribe, however, is Célestine's own self-interest: she ends up marrying Joseph, a fellow servant, anti-Semite, and suspected child murderer, who uses the proceeds of stealing his master's silver, together with that of many earlier thefts, to set up a bar in Cherbourg with Célestine as its mistress. Her decision is rationally perfectly well motivated: it saves her from a continuing life of exploitation and poverty, and probably inevitable descent into the gutter; and, as the proceeds of a theft, it is a triumphant act of revenge against – but also emulation of – the bourgeois. For, as Célestine asks in the final chapter, echoing Proudhon's famous assertion that property is theft, is there any kind of money that is not stolen? She is as morally bankrupt as everyone else in the *Journal*, a mere vessel for others' desires, and ultimately, a void – one of the many people who, in her words (Chapter 16), seem not to be totally alive.

This emptiness comes to a head at the very end when, having initially rejected the notion, Célestine, a Breton, agrees to dress as an Alsatian girl (Alsace-Lorraine, lost to Germany in 1871, was a focus of nationalist feeling) in order to entice anti-dreyfusard clients to Joseph's bar (she has already half-sold herself by dressing provocatively to do so). The instance shows how totally even she has been brutalised by cupidity, by self-interest, by the need to save her skin. For Joseph is a brute, a virulent Catholic Boulangist anti-Semite, subscribing only to extreme and reactionary 'ideas'. His brutality is evident in his shockingly bigoted conversations with the sacristan, a seminary reject, and in a rabble-raising scene at the end when, as Dreyfus returns to Cherbourg, Joseph declares, to his approving, table-thumping audience of servicemen, 'Si le traître est coupable, qu'on le rembarque ... S'il est innocent, qu'on le fusille' ('If the traitor is guilty, they should re-embark him.... If he is innocent, they should shoot him'). This is the summit, but only the tip, of the iceberg of hatred in the novel: the hatred that leads the captain, who lives next to Célestine's first masters, to throw stones and rubbish over his neighbour's wall, which leads Joseph to hate all Jews (although, or perhaps because, as far as we know, he knows none) or Célestine to hate all bourgeois. 'Je ne suis pas méchante' ('I am not bad') she says; but, like the gardener who is refused a job, bourgeois meanness moves her to murder. Through his feisty protagonist, Mirbeau, a Catholic turned anarchist, forcefully suggests that the fault is with the system; writing from the margins (of femininity, the underclass, of crime) he sheds light on the canker at the core.

In their different ways, *Le Journal d'une femme de chambre* and *Cyrano* explore the ferment and contradictions of late nineteenth-century France. Yet they have also prompted major film adaptations in the twentieth: Buñuel's *Journal d'une femme de chambre* (1964), Jean-Paul Rappeneau's *Cyrano*, with Gérard Dépardieu in the title role (1990); *Roxanne*, Fred Schepisi's updating with Darryl Hannah as the Roxanne character and Steve Martin in the Cyrano role. Indeed, Rostand's play seems to be undergoing something of a revival, with a recent (2004) version by the Irish poet Derek Mahon at the London National Theatre, turning Cyrano and his gang into republican rebels.

As these modern versions show, such nineteenth-century texts are always relevant. But they do not need revamping to be so. The transcendence of barriers – of gender, race, class, place, status, of conformity and difference, periphery and centre, past and present – is already there, in potential, in the text, waiting only for imagination, Baudelaire's queen of the faculties, to call.

## Selected reading

Michel Crouzet, *Stendhal et l'Italianité* (Paris: José Corti, 1982). Dynamic, intelligent exploration of the Italian myth in Stendhal's work.

Patrick Favardin and Laurent Boüexière, *Le Dandysme* (Lyon: La Manufacture, 1988). Readable account of the phenomenon from the Restoration to the *fin de siècle*.

Alison Finch, *Women's Writing in Nineteenth-Century France* (Cambridge: Cambridge University Press, 2000). A comprehensive and accessible study.

Mary Gluck, *Popular Bohemia: Modernism and Urban Culture in Nineteenth-Century Paris* (Cambridge, MA and London: Harvard University Press, 2005). In-depth investigation of Bohemianism's literary and cultural manifestations.

Alain Guyot and Chantal Massol, *Voyager en France au temps du romantisme: Poétique, esthétique, idéologie* (Grenoble: ELLUG, 2003). Diverse essays covering the historical, ideological and literary implications of the provincial journey.

Léon-François Hofmann, *Le Nègre romantique: Personnage littéraire et obsession collective* (Paris: Payot, 1973). Thorough historical and literary study, ranging from the Middle Ages to 1848, and touching on Dumas, Duras and Lamartine.

Diana Holmes, *French Women's Writing: 1848-1994* (London: Athlone 1996). An excellent overview.

—— *Rachilde* (Oxford: Berg, 2001): Insightful critical biography of the most shocking nineteenth-century woman writer.

Daniel Sangsue, *Le Récit excentrique: Gautier, De Maistre, Nerval, Nodier* (Paris: José Corti, 1987). Illuminating excursus on Romantic 'anti-novels'.

Laurence Schehr, *Figures of Alterity: French Realism and its Others* (Stanford, CA: Stanford University Press, 2003). Ambitious, thought-provoking exploration of how French novelists in the century from 1830 negotiate the representation of sexual and cultural otherness.

Margaret Topping (ed.), *Eastern Voyages, Western Visions: French Writing and Painting of the Orient* (Oxford: Peter Lang, 2004). Conference proceedings on various sixteenth to twentieth-century topics including Nerval, Flaubert and Loti.

Nathaniel Wing, *Between Genders: Narrating Difference in Early French Modernism* (Newark, DE and London: University of Delaware Press, 2004). Accessible study of authors including Balzac, Baudelaire, Duras and Gautier.

Michel Winock (ed.), *L'Affaire Dreyfus* (Paris: Seuil, 1998). Informative casebook covering various aspects of *L'Affaire*.

# Glossary of Literary Figures

**Agoult, Marie d'** (Marie de Flavigny, comtesse d') (1805-76). Journalist, novelist and art-critic, writing under the pen-name Daniel Stern (*Nélida*, 1845).

**Alexis, Paul** (1847-1901). Naturalist novelist and playwright, most faithful of Zola's disciples, author of *La Fin de Lucie Pellegrin* (1880) and *Celle qu'on n'épouse pas* (1879).

**Allais, Alphonse** (1854-1905). Humorist and short-story writer (*On n'est pas des boeufs*, 1896, *L'Affaire Blaireau*, 1899, *Captain Cap*, 1902), exploiting the logic of the absurd.

**Amiel, Henri-Frédéric** (1821-81). Professor of aesthetics and philosophy at Geneva, author of a lifelong *Journal* (1839-81), the most sustained example of Romantic self-analysis.

**Arlincourt, Charles-Victor-Prévôt, vicomte d'** (1789-1856). Historical epic poet (*Charlemagne ou la Caroléide*, 1818) and popular novelist (*Le Solitaire*, 1821).

**Augier, Émile** (1820-89). Writer of Second-Empire social comedies, notably *Le Gendre de M. Poirier* (1854), *Le Mariage d'Olympe* (1855) and *Les Effrontés* (1861).

**Balzac, Honoré de** (1799-1850). The most influential novelist of nineteenth-century France, author of early Gothic novels (*Annette et le criminal*, 1824) and the 95-fiction cycle *La Comédie humaine* (1828-47), including *La Peau de chagrin* (1831), *Eugénie Grandet* (1833), *Le Père Goriot* (1834), *La Vielle fille* (1836), *Illusions perdues* (1837-43), *La Cousine Bette* (1846) and *Splendeurs et misères des courtisanes* (1837-47).

**Banville, Théodore de** (1823-91). Proto-Parnassian poet, highly esteemed by contemporaries, author of *Les Caratides* (1842) and *Les Stalactites* (1846) and a *Petit traité du vers français* (1872).

**Barante, Amable-Guillaume-Prosper Brugière, baron de** (1782-1866). Diplomat and historian, author of *Histoire des ducs de Bourgogne, de la Maison de Valois, 1364-1477* (1824-6).

**Barbey d'Aurevilly, Jules-Amédée** (1808-89). Reactionary Norman aristocratic essayist, critic and novelist, author of *Du dandysme et de George*

*Brummell* (1844), of novels on his native Cotentin (*L'Ensorcelée*, 1854, *Le Chevalier des Touches*, 1864) and of a scandalous story-collection, *Les Diaboliques* (1874).

**Barrès, Maurice** (1862-1923). Author of novel-trilogies *Le Culte du moi* (1888-91: *Sous l'œil des barbares*, 1888, *Un homme libre*, 1889, *Le Jardin de Bérénice*, 1889) exploring sensations and the intuitive, and *Le Roman de l'énergie nationale: Les Déracinés* (1897), *L'Appel au soldat* (1900) and *Leurs figures* (1902); in the twentieth century, a prominent reactionary Nationalist.

**Baudelaire, Charles-Pierre** (1821-67). The greatest poet and most influential art-critic of the century, author of *Les Fleurs du mal* (1857, revised 1861, 1868), *Petits poèmes en Prose* (*Le Spleen de Paris*, 1869), stories and essays (*La Fanfarlo*, 1847, *Les Paradis artificiels*, 1860, *L'Art romantique*, 1869) and artistic *Salons* (1846, 1856, 1859).

**Becque, Henry** (1837-99). Third Republic dramatist, rigorous realist observer of social mores (*Les Corbeaux*, 1882, *La Parisienne*, 1885).

**Béranger, Pierre-Jean de** (1780-1857). Popular Republican poet and song-writer, author of patriotic and anti-clerical, anti-Royalist songs instrumental in the July Revolution, admired by Goethe and Stendhal, despised by Baudelaire and Flaubert, honoured as a national poet at his death.

**Bernard, Claude** (1813-78). Physiologist, professor at the Collège de France, major proponent of systematic scientific method in *Introduction à la médecine expérimentale* (1865) and *La Science expérimentale* (1878), a significant point of reference for Zola and other Naturalists.

**Bernardin de Saint-Pierre, Jacques-Henri** (1737-1814). Utopian and exotic traveller and writer (*L'Arcadie*, 1781, *Paul et Virginie*, 1788, *La Chaumière indienne*, 1790), in his praise of nature and melancholy sensibility an important precursor of Romanticism.

**Bertrand, Louis** (known as Aloysius) (1807-41). Author of the canonical first collection of French prose poetry, *Gaspard de la nuit, fantaisies à la manière de Rembrandt et de Callot* (1842).

**Bloy, Léon** (1846-1917). Reactionary visionary Catholic journalist and novelist, adversary of Naturalism, author of *Le Désespéré* (1886) and *La Femme pauvre* (1897).

**Borel, Petrus** (Petrus Borel d'Hauterive, 'le Lycanthrope') (1809-59). Anti-social republican poet, storyteller and novelist, author of *Rhapsodies* (1832), *Champavert, contes immoraux* (1833) and *Madame Putiphar* (1839).

**Boulanger, Georges** (1837-91). General and politician, Minister of War (1886), leader of opposition to the parliamentary regime (1886-9).

**Bourget, Paul** (1852-1935). Critic and psychological novelist (*Essais de* *psychologie contemporaine*, 1883, *Cruelle énigme*, 1885, *Un crime d'amour*, 1886, *André Cornélis*, 1887, and *Le Disciple*, 1889), who turned to reactionary Catholicism after 1900.

**Brachet, Jean-Louis** (1789-1858). Physiologist and neurologist, author of a *Traité de l'hystérie* (1847) used by the Goncourts for *Germinie Lacerteux*.

**Céard, Henry** (1851-1924), Journalist and critic, member of the Groupe de Médan, author of *Une belle journée* (1881), usually regarded as an exemplary Naturalist novel.

**Champfleury** (pseud. of Jules Husson) (1821-69). Novelist and art historian, with Duranty the principal advocate of realism (*Chien-Caillou*, 1847, *Les Bourgeois de Molinchart*, 1855, and the manifesto-collection *Le Réalisme*, 1855).

**Charles X** (1757-1836). The second Restoration monarch (1824-30), brother of Louis XVIII.

**Chateaubriand, François-René, vicomte de** (1768-1848). Writer, diplomat and statesman, author of *Génie du Christianisme* (1802), two monographs on Napoleon (*De Buonaparte et des Bourbons*, 1814, and *Vie de Napoléon*, 1834), along with the first-person narratives *Atala* (1801) and *René* (1802) and the autobiographical *Mémoires de ma vie* (1803-32) and *Mémoires d'outre-tombe* (1847).

**Chênedollé, Charles Lioult de** (1769-1833). Pre-Romantic poet, friend of Staël and Constant, author of *Le Génie de l'homme* (1807) and *Études poétiques* (1820).

**Comte, Auguste** (1798-1857). Philosopher and collaborator of Saint-Simon, father of positivism outlining the progress of humanity through science, author of *Cours de philosophie positive* (1830-2), *Système de politique positiviste* (1851-4) and *Catéchisme positiviste* (1852), a pioneer of sociology.

**Constant, Benjamin** (1767-1830). Liberal political theorist, intellectual and novelist, leading light of Staël's *Groupe de Coppet*, author of the first-person narrative *Adolphe* (1816) and of the autobiographical *Cécile* (c. 1810) and *Le Cahier rouge* (1811).

**Coppée, François** (1842-1908). Popular intimist dramatist (*Le Passant*, 1869), poet (*Les Humbles*, 1872), novelist (*La Bonne souffrance*, 1898) and *anti-dreyfusard*, much mocked by Rimbaud.

**Corbière, Édouard-Joachim** (known as Tristan) (1845-75). Radically innovative poet, tormented by his own inadequacies and the difficulties of writing after 1870, author of *Les Amours jaunes* (1873).

**Cottin, Mme Sophie** (née Marie Rusteau) (1773-1807). Popular sentimental novelist, author of *Claire d'Albe* (1799), *Amélie Mansfield* (1803) and *Élisabeth ou les exilés de Sibérie* (1806).

**Courbet, Gustave** (1819-77). Anti-classical and anti-Romantic socialist artist, portrait, genre and landscape painter, a prime mover, with Champfleury, in the Realist movement (*Les Casseurs de pierres*, *Un Enterrement à Ornans* (1850 Salon, now in the Musée d'Orsay), admired by Proudhon and Zola.

**Courteline, Georges** (pseud. of Georges-Victor-Marcel Moineaux) (1858-1929). Humorous novelist (*Messieurs les ronds-de-cuir*, 1893), storywriter and dramatist, author of over one hundred satirical farces including *La Paix chez soi* (1893), *Un Client sérieux* (1896) and *L'Article 300* (1900).

**Cousin, Victor** (1792-1867). Philosopher, apostle of eclecticism, and Minister of Public Instruction (1840), responsible for introducing German philosophical ideas into France and for the reform of elementary education.

**Cros, Charles** (1842-88). Inventor, Bohemian poet (*Le Coffret de Santal*, 1873, *Le Collier de griffes*, 1908), and precursor of Surrealism.

**Daudet, Alphonse** (1840-97). Author of popular autobiographical and regionalist novels and stories (*Lettres de mon Moulin*, 1869, *Tartartin de Tarascon*, 1872, *Contes du lundi*, 1873), later a tardy but never doctrinaire follower of Zola.

**Debussy, Achille-Claude** (1862-1918). Composer, friend of Mallarmé and the Symbolists, who departed from German Romanticism, introducing oriental harmonies and colour into his work (*Prélude à l'après-midi d'un faune*, 1894, *La Mer*, 1903-5) and his Maeterlinck opera *Pelléas et Mélissande* (1902).

**Delacroix, Ferdinand-Victor-Eugène** (1798-1863). Leader of the French Romantic school in painting, master of Classical and modern literary subjects (*Dante et Virgile aux enfers*, 1822, but also Shakespeare, Goethe and Byron), as well as political, oriental and monumental works: *La Liberté guidant le peuple*, 1830, *Les Femmes d'Alger*, 1834, the *Chapelle des anges* of Saint-Sulpice, and the Chamber of deputies, admired by Balzac and Baudelaire.

**Delille, abbé Jacques** (1738-1813). Poet and advocate of liberation from the Classical aesthetic via new subjects, language and verse forms (*Les Jardins*, 1772), author of philosophical works such as *L'Imagination* (1806), *Les Trois règnes* (1808).

**Desbordes-Valmore, Marceline** (1789-1859). Actress, greatest woman poet of the century, author of its first Romantic collection (*Élégies*, 1819), as of *Poésies* (1842) and *Poésies inédites* (1866), admired by Baudelaire and Verlaine, an innovator in *vers impair*.

**Dreyfus, Captain Alfred** (1859-1935). French-Jewish Solider at the centre of the Dreyfus Affair that polarised progressives and reactionaries as his supporters or opponents (*dreyfusards* or *anti-dreyfusards*).

**Drumont, Édouard** (1844-1917). Journalist, politician, prominent *anti-drey-fusard* and anti-Semite, author of *La France juive: Essai d'histoire contemporaine* (1866), and of *De l'or, de la boue et du sang* (1896); founder of the newspaper *La Libre Parole* (1892).

**Du Camp, Maxime** (1822-94). Novelist, poet, art-critic, friend and travel companion of Flaubert, co-author of *Par les champs et par les grèves* (1847).

**Ducray-Duminil, François-Guillaume** (1761-1819). Popular novelist, author of *Victor ou l'enfant de la forêt* (1796) and *Coelina ou l'Enfant du mystère* (1798).

**Dumas, Alexandre** (Dumas *père*) (1802-70). The most successful serial-novelist of nineteenth-century France, still her most widely-read author, creator of the first successful Romantic drama, *Henri III et sa cour* (1829), of the race novel *Georges* (1843), as well as countless serialised master-pieces (*La Reine Margot, Le Comte de Monte-Cristo*, both 1844, *Les Trois Mousquetaires*, 1844-5), and voluminous memoirs.

**Dumas, Alexandre** (Dumas *fils*) (1824-95). Novelist, dramatist and social campaigner, author of *La Dame aux camélias* (novel, 1848, stage version 1852), as well as of numerous plays and essays on social and moral ques-tions (*Le Demi-monde*, 1855, *Le Fils naturel*, 1858, *Un père prodigue*, 1859, *La Question du divorce*, 1880).

**Duranty, Louis-Édmond** (1833-80). With Champfleury, the chief expo-nent of realism (*Le Malheur d'Henriette Gérard*, 1860, *La Cause du beau Guillaume*, 1862), friend of Courbet, Manet and Degas, defender of Impressionism (*La Nouvelle peinture*, 1876).

**Duras, Claire Lechat de Kersaint, duchesse de** (1778-1828). Novelist and society hostess, author of *Ourika* (1824) and, erroneously, of Latouche's *Olivier ou le secret* (1827), friend of Chateaubriand and Mme de Staël.

**Ferry, Jules-François-Camille** (1832-93). Lawyer and politician. As Minister of Public Instruction and Prime Minister, responsible notably for the *Loi Ferry* introducing free compulsory primary education, for establishing numerous civil liberties, and for colonial expansions in Africa and Asia.

**Féval, Paul** (1817-87). Highly successful serial-novelist, Dumas's mid-century rival (*Les Mystères de Londres*, 1844, *Le Bossu*, 1858).

**Feydeau, Georges** (1862-1921). The most successful vaudeville writer of the *belle époque*, author of comic farces such as *Le Fil à la patte* (1892), *Le Dindon* (1896), and *Occupe-toi d'Amélie* (1908).

**Flahaut, Adélaïde-Marie-Émilie Filleul, comtesse de** (later Marquise de Souza) (1761-1836). Popular novelist, alleged creator of the term *roman sentimental* (*Adèle de Sénange*, 1794).

**Flaubert, Gustave** (1821-80). The great proto-modernist and (although he

denied it) Realist novelist of nineteenth-century France, 'vieux roman-
tique enragé', author of *Madame Bovary* (1857), *Salammbô* (1862),
*L'Éducation sentimentale* (1869), *La Tentation de Saint-Antoine* (1874) and
*Trois contes* (1877), as well as of travel-journals on Brittany, Egypt and the
Orient.

**Fort, Paul** (1872-1960). Symbolist poet, founder of the anti-Naturalist *théâtre
d'art* (1890-3), author, from 1896, of the monumental *Ballades françaises*
(1922-51).

**Fourier, François-Charles-Marie** (1772-1837). Radical precursor of
French socialism, attacking the anarchy of free-market mechanisms in *Le
Nouveau Monde industriel et sociétaire* (1829) and *La Fausse industrie* (1835-
6) and envisaging their replacement by self-sufficient communitarian
units.

**France, Anatole** (pseud. of Jacques-Antoine Thibault) (1844-1924).
Parnassian poet, critic, satirist and novelist, author of novels of passion
(*Thaïs*, 1890, *Le Lys rouge*, 1894), *L'Anneau d'Améthyste* (1899), and his
masterpiece on the Revolution, *Les Dieux ont soif* (1912).

**Fromentin, Eugène-Samuel-Auguste** (1820-76). Orientalist artist, travel
writer and art-critic, author of *Les Maîtres d'autrefois* (1876) and the autobiographical novel *Dominique* (1862).

**Fustel de Coulanges, Numa-Denis** (1830-89). Historian, founder of
French academic history, stressing objectivity, austerity and rigorous
documentation, author of *La Cité antique* (1864), *Histoire des institutions
politiques de l'ancienne France* (1875-91), and *Questions historiques* (1892),
mentor of Durkheim and, in his insistence on the primacy of beliefs in
social identity, an influence on Barrès and forerunner of twentieth-
century historiography and sociology.

**Gaboriau, Émile** (1832-73). Poe-inspired French pioneer of the detective
novel based around the logical solution to a crime, in serialised novels
such as *L'Affaire Lerouge* (1866), *Le Crime d'Orcival*, *Le Dossier 113* (1867),
*La Vie infernale* (1870) and *La Corde au cou* (1873).

**Gautier, Théophile** (1811-72). Poet, short-story writer, novelist, art-critic
and essayist, one of the pivotal figures of French Romanticism and
author of *Mademoiselle de Maupin* (1835-6), numerous fantastic stories and
novels, the emblematic poetry collection of *L'Art pour l'art*, *Émaux et
camées* (1852), and a valuable *Histoire du romantisme* (1874).

**Genlis, Stéphanie-Félicité du Crest, Madame de** (1746-1830). Prolific
and influential educationalist, storyteller and novelist (*Mademoiselle de La
Fayette*, 1813, *Six nouvelles morales et religieuses*, 1819, *Mémoires inédits sur le
XVIIIᵉ siècle et la révolution française*, 1825-8).

**Gide, André-Paul-Guillaume** (1869-1951). Prominent twentieth-century novelist whose work owes much to the nineteenth in which he matured, indebted in particular in *Les Cahiers d'André Walter* (1891), *Les Nourritures terrestres* (1897), *L'Immoraliste* (1902) and *Les Faux-Monnayeurs* (1926) to the moral dilemmas, individualism and experiment represented by Bourget and Barrès.

**Girardin, Émile de** (1806-81). The most significant press-magnate of the century, tapping a new bourgeois market with *Le Musée des familles* (1833), pioneer of the serialised novel from his launch of *La Presse* in 1836.

**Gobineau, Joseph-Arthur, comte de** (1816-82). Diplomat, novelist (*Ternove, Le Prisonnier chanceux*, both 1847) and storywriter (*Madame Irnois*, 1847, *Adélaïde*, 1869), author of *Essai sur l'inégalité des races humaines* (1853-5) exploited by the Nazis.

**Goncourt, Edmond and Jules de** ('the Goncourt brothers') (1822-96, 1830-70). Art-critics, collectors and novelists (*Soeur Philomène*, 1861, *René Mauperin, 1864, Germinie Lacerteux*, 1865), whose interest in art and art history (*L'Art du XVIIIe siècle*, 1859-75) gave rise to an *écriture artiste* combining aestheticised notation with a pathologised, proto-Naturalist attention to the real.

**Groupe de Coppet**. Clutch of writers and intellectuals opposed to Napoleon, grouped around Constant and Staël, and including Barante, Kant and August Wilhelm von Schlegel, who gathered at Staël's château at Coppet on the shores of Lake Geneva during the first decade of the nineteenth century.

**Groupe de Médan**. Naturalist caucus centred on Zola's house at Médan outside Paris around 1880, consisting of Alexis, Céard, Huysmans and Maupassant, the contributors, with Zola, to the story-collection *Les Soirées de Médan* (1880).

**Guizot, François-Pierre-Guillaume** (1787-1874). Politician and historian, successively Minister of the Interior (1830), of Public Instruction (1832-7), of Foreign Affairs and effective head of government from 1840, author of an *Histoire des origines du gouvernement représentatif* (1821-2).

**Halévy, Ludovic** (1834-1908). Light comic dramatist and opera librettist, above all with Meilhac and Offenbach, responsible for such successes as *La Belle Hélène* (1865), *La Vie Parisienne* (1866), and *La Grande Duchesse de Gérolstein* (1867).

**Heredia, José-Maria de** (1842-1905). Parnassian poet, follower of Leconte de Lisle, Sully-Prudhomme and Mendès, author of *Les Trophées* (1893), a collection of 118 sonnets combining striking evocation with tight formal control.

**Hugo, Victor** (1802-85). Most enduringly prominent writer of nineteenth-century France, author of, notably, the Romantic manifesto *Préface de*

*Cromwell* (1827), the dramas *Hernani* (1830) and *Ruy Blas* (1838), the novels *Notre-Dame de Paris* (1832), *Les Misérables* (1862), and *Quatre-vingt-treize* (1874), and the poetry collections *Les Châtiments* (1853) and *Les Contemplations* (1856).

**Huysmans, Joris-Karl** (1848-1907). Initially a Naturalist novelist (*En Ménage*, 1881, *A vau-l'eau*, 1882), collaborating with Zola and others in the story-collection *Les Soirées de Médan* (1880), becoming the archetypal Decadent writer in *A rebours* (1884) and *Là-bas* (1891), preludes to Catholic conversion: *La Cathédrale* (1898), *L'Oblat* (1903).

**Jammes, Francis** (1868-1939). Popular Regionalist and in due course Catholic poet exploiting *vers libre* to transmit the simplicity of his vision (*De l'angélus de l'aube à l'angélus du soir*, 1898).

**Jarry, Alfred** (1873-1907). Radical, proto-absurdist playwright and novelist, creator of the Ubu plays (*Ubu roi*, 1896, *Ubu enchaîné*, 1900, *Ubu sur la butte*, 1901, two-act puppet-theatre version of *Ubu roi*); *Ubu cocu* (published posthumously 1944) and the articles *De l'inutilité du théâtre au théâtre* (1896) and *Questions de théâtre* (1897).

**Kock, Charles-Paul de** (1793-1871). Popular novelist and comic dramatist, chief exponent of the Restoration and July Monarchy *roman gai* exemplified by *Gustave ou le Mauvais Sujet* (1821) and *Le Cocu* (1831).

**Labiche, Ernest** (1815-88). Second Empire vaudevilliste, author of *Un Chapeau de paille d'Italie* (1851), *Le Voyage de M. Perrichon* (1860) and *La Cagnotte* (1864).

**Lacenaire, Pierre-François** (1800-36). Celebrity murderer, author of famous *Mémoires*, a subject of fascination and inspiration for artists as varied as Balzac, Doestoevsky and Marcel Carné.

**Lacordaire, Henri** (1802-11). Priest and dominican, with Montalembert and Lamennais one of the leaders of liberal Catholicism from which he parted company in1832.

**Laforgue, Jules** (1860-87). Decadent poet, friend of Cros and Bourget, inspired by Corbière, author of *Complaintes* (1885), *L'Imitation de Notre-Dame la Lune* (1886) and *Derniers vers* (1887, published in 1890) and a collection of *nouvelles*, the *Moralités légendaires* (1885-6, published in 1887).

**Lamartine, Alphonse de** (1790-1869). Poet and politician, with *Méditations poétiques* (1820) the first great French Romantic poet. Author also of other lyric collections (*Harmonies poétiques et religieuses*, 1829, *Recueillements*, 1839) and of visionary epics (*Jocelyn*, 1836, *La Chute d'un ange*, 1839); a deputy from 1832, Minister of Foreign Affairs and presidential candidate in 1848.

**Lamennais, Félicité-Robert de** (1782-1854). Initially Royalist, later liberal Catholic cleric and thinker, founder with Lacordaire and Montalembert of *L'Avenir* (1830), author of *Paroles d'un croyant* (1834), *Le Livre du peuple* (1837) and *Esquisse d'une philosophie* (1840-6); elected a deputy in 1848.

**Las Cases, Emmanuel, comte de** (1766-1842). Historian, Napoleon's secretary on St Helena, amanuensis of the *Mémorial de Sainte-Hélène* (1822-3).

**Latouche, Henri de** (pseud. of Hyacinthe-Joseph-Alexandre Thabaud de Latouche) (1785-1853). Poet, playwright and novelist, publisher of Chénier's *Élégies*, 1819, of *Olivier ou le secret* (mischievously ascribed to Mme de Duras) and *Fragoletta, ou Rome, Naples et Paris en 1799* (1829).

**Lautréamont, comte de** (pseud. of Isidore Ducasse) (1846-70). Author of the *Chants de Maldoror* (1874) and *Poésies* (published in 1920), whose aggressively radical proto-modernist subversion of conventional plot and morality was an inspiration to twentieth-century Surrealism.

**Leconte de Lisle** (pseud. of Charles-Maurice Leconte) (1811-94). Poet, leader of the Parnassian school dominant under the Second Empire, author of *Poèmes antiques* (1852), *Poèmes barbares* (1862) and *Poèmes tragiques* (1884).

**Leroux, Pierre** (1797-1871). Socialist thinker, founder of the Saint-Simonian newspaper *Le Globe* (1824), author of *De l'humanité* (1840) and *De l'égalité* (1848), influential on Hugo, Sand and Sue.

**Loti, Pierre** (pseud. of Julien Viaud) (1850-1923). Sailor, exotic novelist and travel writer, author of *Aziyadé* (1879), *Madame Chrysanthème, Pêcheur d'Islande* (1886) and *Ramuntcho* (1897).

**Louis XVI** (Louis-Auguste) (1754-93). The final monarch of *ancien régime* France, executed for conspiring against the liberty of the nation.

**Louis XVII** (Louis-Charles de France) (1785-95). Second son of Louis XVI, acclaimed monarch after his father's execution, imprisoned in 1792, presumed dead 1795.

**Louis XVIII** (Louis-Stanislas-Auguste) (1755-1824). Brother of Louis XVI, first Restoration monarch (1814-24).

**Louis-Philippe I** (Louis-Philippe d'Orléans) (1773-1850). Son of Louis-Philippe Joseph d'Orléans, known as Philippe Égalité (1747-93). King of France 1830-40, the *roi bourgeois* of the July Monarchy.

**Louÿs, Pierre** (pseud. of Pierre Louis) (1870-1925). Symbolist and Hellenist, friend of Gide, associate of Leconte de Lisle and Heredia (whose daughter he married). Author of the suggestively erotic *Les Chansons de Bilitis* (1894), and the novels *Aphrodite* (1896) and *La Femme et le pantin* (1898).

**Lucas, Prosper** (1805-85). Physiologist, author of a *Traité philosophique et physiologique de l'hérédité naturelle* (1847-50), influential on Zola.

**Maeterlinck, Maurice** (1862-1949). Belgian Symbolist poet and dramatist, author of the poetry collections *Serres chaudes* (1889) and *Quinze chansons* (1896), dramas such as *La Princesse Maleine* (1889), *Pelléas et Mélisande* (1892), and *Intérieur*, and metaphysical meditations such as *La Sagesse et la Destinée* (1898) and *L'Intelligence des fleurs* (1907).

**Mallarmé, Étienne** (known as Stéphane) (1842-98). The pre-eminent poet of French Symbolism, but also a precursor of modernists from Valéry to Bonnefoy, seeking metaphysical transcendence within language itself, in works from *L'Azur* (1862) and *Brise marine* (1864) to *L'Après-midi d'un faune* (1876; the inspiration for Debussy's 1894 composition) and *Un coup de dés* (1897).

**Manet, Édouard** (1832-83). Artist admired especially by Mallarmé and Zola (both of whom he painted). His masterworks *Le Déjeuner sur l'herbe* and *Olympia* (both 1863) provoked violent conservative criticism, but along with *Nana* (1877) and *Un Bar aux Folies-bergère* (1881-2) heralded Impressionism.

**Maupassant, Guy de** (1854-93). Prolific and widely-read storywriter, disciple of Flaubert and Zola, author of over 300 tales including many classics (*Boule de suif,* 1880, *Le Horla,* 1887, *Sur l'eau,* 1888) and also of Naturalist novels such as *Bel-Ami* (1885) and *Pierre et Jean* (1888).

**Maurras, Charles** (1868-1952). Critic and journalist, virulent Royalist anti-Semite and *anti-dreyfusard,* founder (1899) of *Action Française.*

**Meilhac, Henri** (1831-87). Writer of comedies and librettist with Halévy and others of Offenbach operas and Massenet's *Manon* (1884).

**Mendès, Catulle** (1841-1909). Parnassian poet, novelist and essayist (*La Légende du Parnasse contemporain,* 1884, *L'Oeuvre wagnérienne en France,* 1899).

**Mérimée, Prosper** (1803-70). Novelist, storywriter, and art historian, author of *Chronique du règne de Charles IX* (1829), *Mosaïque* (1833, including *Mateo Falcone* and *Tamango*), *La Vénus d'Ille* (1837) and *Carmen* (1847); Inspector-General of Historical Monuments for three decades from 1834.

**Michelet, Jules,** (1798-1874). The greatest French Romantic historian, dedicated, in works such as *Histoire de France* (1833-44, 1855-67) and *Histoire de la Révolution française* (1847-53) to the complete and vivid resurrection of the nation.

**Mignet, Auguste** (1796-1884). Historian, author of an *Histoire de la Révolution française* (1824), Thiers's collaborator on the late Restoration opposition newspaper *Le National* (1830).

**Millevoye, Charles-Hubert** (1782-1816): Imperial poet, proto-Romantic in sentiment but Classical in expression, author of *Élégies* (1812).

**Mirbeau, Octave** (1848-1917). Journalist, novelist, and political activist, moving from Royalist Catholicism and anti-Semitism to anarchism, author of *L'Abbé Jules* (1888), *Sébastien Roch* (1890) and *Le Journal d'une femme de chambre* (1900).

**Mistral, Frédéric** (1830-1914). Provençal Occitan language poet, one of the founders, in 1854, of *Le Félibrige*, a movement dedicated to the renovation of Provençal traditions and language, author of the epic poem *Mireille* (*Mirèio*, 1859), of numerous other poems and a dictionary, the *Trésor du Félibrige* (1876-86).

**Montalembert, Charles Forbes, comte de** (1810-70). Liberal Catholic, Lamennais's collaborator on *L'Avenir* (1830), subsequently a peer, member of the *Corps législatif* and director of the Catholic liberal newspaper *Le Correspondant.*

**Montolieu, Élisabeth-Jeanne-Pauline Polier de Bottens, baronne de** (known as Isabelle) (1751-1832). Sentimental novelist, author of *Caroline de Lichtfield* (1781), of *contes moraux*, translator of Jane Austen and of Wyss's *The Swiss Family Robinson.*

**Murger, Henry** (1822-61). Journalist, creator of the Bohemianism immortalised in *Scènes de la vie de Bohème* (1851), and of similar lesser works.

**Musset, Alfred de** (1810-57). Quintessential if under-read Romantic poet (*Contes d'Espagne et d'Italie*, 1829), dramatist (*Lorenzaccio*, 1834, arguably the greatest Romantic drama), novelist (*Confession d'un enfant du siècle*, 1836) and storywriter.

**Napoleon I** (known as Napoleon Bonaparte) (1769-1821). Soldier, First Consul (1799), Consul for life (1802), Emperor (1804-15). Despite post-revolutionary consolidation and radical and enduringly successful reorganisation of almost every national structure (legal, military, educational, financial) and restoring national prestige, Napoleon's dictatorship abolished democracy, destroyed opponents and wrecked France and Europe in a succession of futile wars. Yet his relentless energy, enterprise and vision made him an inspiration for future generations, the very embodiment of the paradoxes of the nineteenth-century sublime.

**Napoleon II** (later duc de Reichstadt) (1811-32). Son of Napoleon I and Marie-Louise de Beauharnais, given the title *roi de Rome* at his birth but destined never to reign.

**Napoleon III** (Louis-Napoléon Bonaparte) (1808-73). Nephew of Napoleon I, a centre of opposition during the July Monarchy, elected President of the Second Republic 1848-51, seizing power as Emperor 1851-70. Manoeuvred into war with Prussia by Bismarck 1870, leading to the catastrophic national defeat at Sedan.

**Nerval, Gérard de** (pseud. of Gérard Labrunie) (1808-55). Translator (Goethe, *Faust*, 1827), storywriter and poet, author of anecdotes such as

*Petits châteaux de Bohème* (1852), stories (*Sylvie*, 1853, *Aurélia*, 1855), and the enigmatic sonnet-cycle *Les Chimères* (1854); his fascination with the world of dreams was an inspiration to the twentieth-century Surrealists.

**Nodier, Charles** (1780-1844). Novelist and bibliophile, 'pilot of Romanticism', author of the Wertheresque *Le Peintre de Salzbourg* (1803), the bandit novel *Jean Sbogar* (1818), the experimental *Histoire du roi de Bohème et de ses sept châteaux* (1830), of fantastic tales such as *Smarra ou les demons de la nuit* (1821) or *Inès de las Sierras* (1837), exploring madness in *La Fée aux miettes* (1832) and *Jean-François les bas-bleus* (1833).

**Parny, Évariste-Désiré de Forges, vicomte de** (1753-1814). Author of *Poésies érotiques* (1778-84), timidly pre-Romantic in the nostalgia and lyricism of certain works ('Enfin ma chère Eléonore', 'Projet de solitude'), and in the descriptive luxuriance and supposed ethnological authenticity of the *Chansons madécasses* (1787), set to music by Ravel.

**Péguy, Charles** (1873-1914). Socialist and fervent *dreyfusard*, who would turn, in the twentieth century, to a Catholic socialism foreshadowed by his 1897 drama *Jeanne d'Arc*, partly reworked in 1910.

**Pigault-Lebrun** (pseud. of Charles-Antoine-Guillaume-Pigault de l'Épinoy) (1753-1835). Popular comic dramatist and libertine novelist, influential on Balzac and Dumas, author of *L'Enfant du carnaval* (1792), *Les Barons de Felsheim* (1798) and *Monsieur Botte* (1802).

**Pixérécourt, Guilbert de** (1773-1844). The most successful writer of melodramas under the Empire, including *Victor ou l'enfant de la forêt* (1797), *Coelina ou l'Enfant du mystère* (1800) and *L'Homme à trois visages* (1801).

**Ponson du Terrail, Pierre-Alexis, vicomte** (1829-71). Second Empire serial-novelist, author of *Les Coulisses du monde* (1853) and the 30-fiction *Les Drames de Paris* (1859-84) featuring his adventurer hero Rocambole.

**Proudhon, Pierre-Joseph** (1809-65). Anarchist social theorist, author of *Qu'est-ce que la propriété?* (1840). His *La Guerre et la paix* (1861) inspired Tolstoy's novel.

**Proust, Marcel** (1871-1922). Author of novels of self-exploration, *Jean Santeuil* (published posthumously in 1952) and above all *A la recherche du temps perdu* (1913-27), foreshadowed by, but vastly surpassing, the Barrès of *Le Culte du moi.*

**Quinet, Edgar** (1803-75). Freethinking anti-clerical historian, poet, dramatist and politician, a significant conduit for German ideas in France and an inspiration for contemporaries, twice deputy (1848, 1871), exiled during the Second Empire, author of works including the epic poems *Ahasvérus* (1833) and *Napoléon* (1836), *La Révolution* (1865), *L'Enseignement du peuple* (1850), *La République* (1872) and *L'Esprit nouveau* (1875).

**Rachilde** (pseud. of Marguérite Eymery) (1860-1953). Anarchist and radical feminist writer, author of provocative decadent novels such as *Monsieur Vénus* (1884) and *La Marquise de Sade* (1887), dramas (*Madame la mort*, 1891), and short stories, through the review *Le Mercure de France* and its publications a significant figure in the later nineteenth and early twentieth-century literary world.

**Redon, Odilon** (1840-1916). Decadent artist and illustrator (1890) of *Les Fleurs du mal*, as also of Flaubert and Poe, author of the autobiographical *A soi-même* (1922).

**Renan, Ernest** (1823-92). Positivist philosopher of history and historian of religion, author notably of the controversial *Vie de Jésus* (1863) and *L'Avenir de la science* (1849, published in 1890), assigning to science the status of a new religion of humanity.

**Renard, Jules** (1864-1910). Storywriter, popular dramatist and novelist of everyday life, author of *L'Écornifleur* (1892) and *Poil de carotte* (1900).

**Rimbaud, Arthur** (1854-91). The century's most iconoclastic poet, *voyant* and *voyou*, his whole output crammed into three teenage years and two collections, *Illuminations* (1872-4, published in 1886), *Une Saison en enfer* (c. 1873), plus earlier poems foreshadowing his violence of revolt: *Vénus anadyomène* (1870), *Les Assis* and *Les Premières Communions* (both 1871).

**Rostand, Edmond de** (1869-1918). Poet and dramatist, author of an enduring masterpiece, *Cyrano de Bergerac* (1897), and of *L'Aiglon* (1900) and *Chantecler* (1910).

**Sainte-Beuve, Charles-Augustin** (1804-69). Poet (*Les Consolations*, 1830), autobiographical novelist (*Volupté*, 1834), and one of the century's most influential critics (*Port-Royal*, 1840-59), *Critiques et portraits* (1836-46), *Causeries du Lundi* (1851-62) and *Nouveaux Lundis* (1863-9).

**Sand, George** (pseud. of Aurore Dupin, baronne Dudevant) (1804-76). Progressive storyteller, political and travel-writer and novelist, author of *Indiana* (1832), *Mauprat* (1837), *Consuelo* (1842-3), *La Mare au diable* (1846), *François le Champi* (1847-8), *La Petite Fadette* (1849) and an autobiography, *Histoire de ma vie* (1854). With Staël, the century's greatest woman writer.

**Sanson, Henri** (1767-1840). Last but one of a long dynasty of executioners, and that of Marie-Antoinette; subject of Balzac's *Mémoires de Sanson* (1829).

**Sardou, Victorien** (1831-1908). Dramatist, master of the well-made play: bourgeois drama (*La Famille Benoîton*, 1865), melodrama (*Tosca*, 1887) and historical drama (*Madame Sans-Gêne*, 1893).

**Schwob, Marcel** (1867-1905). Proto-modernist formal and generic experimenter, author of fictional biographies, journalism, essays, melding fiction and reality, poetry, short story and novel (*Le Livre de Monelle*, 1894, *Vies imaginaires*, 1896).

**Scribe, Eugène** (1791-1861). Comic dramatist of the Restauration and July Monarchy, author of over 350 comedies including *Bertrand et Raton* (1833), *Une Chaîne* (1841), and *Bataille de Dames* (1851).

**Senancour, Étienne Pivert de** (1770-1846). Introspective Swiss essayist and novelist, author of *Rêveries sur la nature primitive de l'homme* (1799) and the epistolary *Obermann* (1804).

**Staël, Anne-Louise-Germaine Necker, Mme de** (1766-1817). Leading intellectual, critic and novelist, cynosure, with Constant, of the *Groupe de Coppet* and a major conduit for German ideas in France in her period, author of an *Essai sur les fictions* (1795), *De la littérature considérée dans ses rapports avec les institutions sociales* (1800), *Delphine* (1802), *Corinne ou l'Italie* (1807) and *De l'Allemagne* (1807).

**Stendhal** (pseud. of Henri Beyle) (1783-1842). Soldier, diplomat and writer, author of essays on travel and art (*Rome, Naples et Florence*, 1817, *Promenades dans Rome*, 1838, and *Mémoires d'un touriste*, 1838), four novels (*Armance*, 1827, *Le Rouge et le noir*, 1830, *Lucien Leuwen*, 1834-6 and *La Chartreuse de Parme*, 1839), as well as an autobiography, *Vie de Henry Brulard* (1835) and the treatise *De l'amour* (1822).

**Sue, Eugène** (1804-17). Popular serialised novelist, author of *Les Mystères de Paris* (1842-3), *Le Juif errant* (1844-5) and *Les Sept Péchés capitaux* (1849-50).

**Sully-Prudhomme** (pseud. of René-François-Armand Prudhomme) (1839-1907). Engineer and Parnassian poet, author of *Stances et poèmes* (1865), whose work moved from the impersonal towards the personal (*Les Solitudes*, 1869), seeking to reconcile subjectivity and science in later epics (*La Justice*, 1878, *Le Bonheur*, 1882).

**Taine, Hippolyte** (1828-93). Critic and historian, author of the *Essais de critique et d'histoire* (1858), *Nouveaux essais de critique et d'histoire* (1865) and *Histoire de la littérature anglaise* (1864), champion of anti-Romantic positivism and determinism that influenced Zola.

**Talleyrand, Charles-Maurice de Talleyrand-Périgord** (1754-1838). Cleric and Politician, moderate Revolutionary reformer, foreign minister under the Directory and Napoleon (1797-9, 1799-1807) and at the Congress of Vienna (1814-15), Ambassador to Britain (1830-4), author of possibly apocryphal *Mémoires* (1891-2).

**Taylor, Isidore-Justin-Séverin, Baron** (1789-1879). Influential soldier, playwright, antiquarian, director of the Comédie Française and philanthropist, with Nodier co-author of *Voyages pittoresques et romantiques dans l'ancienne France* (1820-80), enabler of the first performance of *Hernani* (1830).

**Thierry, Augustin** (1795-1856). Historian, author of *Histoire de la Conquête de l'Angleterre par les Normands* (1825), *Récits des temps mérovingiens* (1840) and *Histoire de la formation et des progrès du Tiers État* (1850), combining local colour and accuracy.

**Thiers, Louis-Adolphe** (1797-1877). Historian, journalist and politician, author of *Histoire de la Révolution française* (1823-7), co-founder of *Le National* (1830), one of the most enduring political operators of the century: holder of numerous cabinet posts under Louis-Philippe, leader of parliamentary opposition to Napoleon III from 1863, first President of the Third Republic.

**Tristan, Flora** (1803-44). Socialist woman writer, author of *Promenades dans Londres* (1840) and the utopian *L'Union ouvrière* (1843).

**Vallez, Jules** (known as Jules Vallès) (1832-85). Radical journalist and novelist, author of the *Jacques Vingtras* trilogy (*L'Enfant*, 1879, *Le Bachelier*, 1881, *L'Insurgé*, 1886).

**Verhaeren, Émile** (1855-1916). Wide-ranging Belgian poet, author of over thirty collections touching on Romantic socialism (*Les Flamandes*, 1883), mysticism (*Les Moines*, 1886), madness and death (*Les Flambeaux noirs*, 1890), and the changing modern world (*Les Campagnes hallucinés*, 1893, *Les Villes tentaculaires*, 1895).

**Verlaine, Paul** (1844-96). One of the most important poetic innovators, in both versification and expression, of nineteenth-century France, mentor of Rimbaud, moving from post-Romantic Parnassianism (*Poèmes saturniens*, 1866) to subjective reverie in later collections such as *Fêtes galantes* (1869) and *Romances sans paroles* (1874); also author of a breviary of Decadence, *Les Poètes maudits* (1884).

**Verne, Jules** (1828-1905). Still France's most translated novelist, author of classic science fiction and adventure novels, including *De la terre à la lune* (1865), *Vingt mille lieues sous les mers* (1870), *Autour de la lune* (1871), *Le Tour du monde en quatre-vingts jours* (1873), and the futuristic *Paris au XX$^e$ siècle* (1994).

**Vidocq, Eugène-François** (1775-1857). Soldier of fortune, convict and supergrass, creator of a *brigade de sûreté* (essentially, protection racket) legalised under the Restoration; a model for Balzac's Vautrin in *Le Père Goriot* and elsewhere.

**Vigny, Alfred de** (1797-1863). Soldier, novelist, poet and dramatist, author of the novels *Cinq Mars* (1826) and *Stello* (1833), the dramas *Quitte pour la peur* and *Chatterton* (1833, 1835) and the *Poèmes antiques et modernes* (1837).

**Villiers de L'Isle-Adam** (Jean-Marie-Mathias-Philippe-Auguste, comte de) (1838-89). Reactionary Symbolist playwright, novelist and storyteller, author of *Axël* (1872-90), *Contes cruels* (1883), *L'Eve future* (1886) and *Tribulat Bonhommet* (1887).

**Zola, Émile** (1840-1902). Principal exponent of Naturalism, author of *Thérèse Raquin* (1867), and the 20-novel *Les Rougon-Macquart: Histoire naturelle et sociale d'une famille sous le Second Empire* (1871-93), including *L'Assommoir* (1877), *Nana* (1880), *Germinal* (1885), *La Bête humaine* (1890) and the manifesto collections *Les Soirées de Médan* and *Le Roman expéri-mental* (1880). The political engagement implicit in Zola's Naturalism reached a climax in the Dreyfus affair, and in Zola's polemic *J'accuse* (1898).

# Index

Absurd, Theatre of the 165;
absurdism 160; absurdist
drama 159
*Action Française* 146, 172
Agoult, d' 35
Alexis 129
Allais 49
Amiel 44-5
*Ancien régime* 13, 21
androgynes 139, 178
*anti-dreyfusards* 187, 192
anti-Semitism 146, 186, 192
Aristotle 45
*arrivisme* 16; *arriviste,* 20, 23, 116,
169
art 21, 65, 79, 91, 130, 157; art-
establishment 23; artists 90-1,
124, 125, 126, 172
Attenborough 142
Augier 93, 101
*L'Art pour l'art* 66-8

Balzac 19-20, 20, 21, 22, 23, 24, 25,
26, 28, 29, 30, 37, 46-8, 101,
102, 109-10, 112-13, 117, 118,
119, 120-1, 122, 123-4, 124, 125,
127, 129, 157, 168, 169-70, 171,
173, 177, 178, 179, 180, 186
Banville 66
Barante 25
Barbey d'Aurevilly 25, 26, 154,
172, 173, 174
Barrès 13, 16, 80, 145-6, 172
Barthes 154
Bataille 154

Baudelaire 20, 55, 59-66, 70, 72,
73, 75, 78, 79, 82, 123, 124, 135,
149-52, 153, 154, 171, 173-4, 183,
186, 193
Beaumarchais 88, 97
Beauvoir 157
Beckett 160, 161, 165
Becque 101-3
Béranger 15
Bernard 130
Bernardin de Saint-Pierre 183
Bernhardt 91
Bertrand 149
Bible 15, 28, 106, 153, 164
Bloy 172
Bluebeard 117
Boccacio 48
Bohemians 172-6, 179, 191
Bonaparte, Louis-Napoleon, see
Louis-Napoleon Bonaparte;
Napoleon III
Bonaparte, Napoleon (Napoleon I)
16, 119; see also Napoleon
Bonaparte
Bond 143
Bontoux 170, 171
Borel 174
Boulanger 14, 16; Boulangist 192
bourgeois 95, 172-3, 174, 175, 177,
182, 191, 192, 193; ideas 20;
objects 69; pretension 139;
ugliness 66; readers 123; *roi
bourgeois* 17, 177; bourgeoisie 17
Bourget 144-5, 146, 155
Brachet 125

Brummel 173
Brunschvicg 160
Buddhism 144
Buñuel 192
Byron 53

*cabinets de lecture* 112
Camus 161
Carlyle 33
Catholic 171, 172, 186, 192, 193;
    Catholicism 146, 172, 192;
    Catholics 187
Cazalis 52, 82, 83
Céard 129
censorship 107, 110, 117, 128
Cervantes 22
Champfleury 23, 24, 101, 124
Charte 113
Chateaubriand 14, 15, 18, 33, 34,
    36, 38-41, 138, 180
Chatterton 90
Chênedollé 53
Christ 78, 106, 122, 164;
    Christianity 148; Christian self-
    abnegation 179; Christian
    civilisation 186
Church 13, 19, 170
classical constraints 157; drama 87,
    102; models 57; references 148;
    rules 87, 88; tragedy 125; unities
    87-8
Classicism 53, 56, 58, 126
*Code civil* 13, 117, 118
Colet 35
*Collège de 'Pataphysique* 166
Comédie française 87
comedy 87, 89, 97, 100, 111
Constant 34, 35, 36, 40, 114, 145
*conte* 45, 48; *conte fantastique* 47
Coquelin 188
Corbière 138, 157
Corneille 53, 87, 190; *Le Cid* 190
Cottin, Mme 115, 176

*coup d'état* (Louis-Napoleon) 14, 170
Courbet 23, 24, 125
Courteline 101
Cousteau 142
Cros 157
Cubist painting 155

Dandies, dandyism 172-4, 178
Dante 122
Danton 28
Darwin 102, 155
Daudet, Alphonse 172
Daudet, Léon 172
De Gaulle 14
Debussy 159
Decadence 138, 139, 191
*Déclaration des droits de l'homme et du
    citoyen* 113
Deconstruction 166, deconstruc-
    tionist 148
Delacroix 20
Delille 53
Demeny 76
Dépardieu 193
Derrida 166
Desbordes-Valmore 55, 58-9, 176,
*désenchantement* 16
Diderot 175
dilettantism 144
Don Carlos 88
dramatic rules 86-7
*drame* 88
dream 21, 146-8
Dreyfus 186-7, 170, 192
*dreyfusard* 146, 187
Drumont 186
Du Camp 180
Ducange 87
Ducray-Duminil 87, 111
Dumas 20, 37, 120, 121-2 184-6
Dumas *fils* 22, 93-5, 101, 103, 157,
    177
Duranty 124

Duras, Mme de 115, 176, 183, 184

*écriture artiste* 125
Edison 139, 140, 141
Empedocles 45
Empire (First) 13, 46; (Second) 11, 87, 146, 169
Enlightenment 13, 33, 124
Esterhazy 187
Existentialism 160
exotic 21, 68, 69, 94, 114, 125, 127, 138, 139, 180, 182, 185, 186
Eylau 13, 46

fairy tale 45, 186
fantastic 47, 49
farce 96-101
Fauré 159
*Félibrige, Le* 172
Fenimore-Cooper 25
Ferry 199
Féval 120
Feydeau 9, 93, 96, 99-101
*fin de siècle* 138, 179, 187, 190
Flahaut, Mme de 117
Flaubert 18, 22, 23, 34, 37, 109, 117, 118, 126-8, 129, 132, 144, 164, 168, 169, 171, 174, 177, 178, 180, 182, 183
Fort 161
France, Anatole 22, 182
François I 88
Franco-Prussian war 50, 171
*frénétique* 111, 113
Freud 144, 147, 154
Fromentin 36-7
Fumaroli 14
Fustel de Coulanges 25

Gaboriau 123
Gautier, Judith 35
Gautier, Théophile 47, 66-8, 123, 173, 174, 175, 177, 178, 179, 182

Genettes, Mme des 177
Genlis, Mme de 117, 176
*Gesamtkunstwerk* 164
Gide 45, 145
Giorgione 126
Girardin, Delphine de 176
Girardin, Émile de 120
Gobineau 186
Goethe 22, 33-4
Goncourt brothers 102, 109, 125, 126, 129, 142
Gothic 48, 118, 119
Gothic novel 110-12, 143, 152
Gros 43
Groupe de Médan 129
Guys 173

Halévy 101
Hamlet 154, 155
Hannah 193
Hartmann 144, 155
Hennique 168
Heredia 67
Hobbes 28, 45
Hoffmann, E.T.A. 47
Hoffmann, L.-F. 186
Hugo, François-Victor 158
Hugo, Léopoldine 60
Hugo, Victor 15, 16, 20, 24, 26, 27, 52, 53, 54, 55, 60-4, 65, 68, 73, 86-8, 89, 90, 92, 93, 112-13, 122, 123, 135, 143, 153, 157-61, 166, 174, 182, 183-4, 190
Huret 82
Huysmans 129, 135, 137-9, 171, 174

Icarus 79
ideal 20, 41, 53, 60, 66, 67, 68, 95, 115, 119, 139, 140, 141, 146, 147, 151, 157, 158, 173, 177, 178, 179, 182; idealism 84
individual 16, 20, 21, 22, 23, 33, 34, 35, 36, 37, 52, 53, 104, 105, 106,

107, 113, 114 115, 116, 119, 120,
121, 135, 136, 137, 144, 145, 146,
154, 155, 156, 164; individualism
21, 33, 92, 103, 146; individuality 173
Ingres 43
Ionesco 159, 166
Iraq 187
Islam 181

Jarry 163-6, 187
Jews 186, 192
July Monarchy 14, 15, 17, 116, 169
July Revolution 11, 20, 89

Kock, Paul de 111

Labiche 93, 96-9, 101
Lacenaire 37
Laforgue 154-7
Lamartine 52, 53, 55, 56-8, 59, 60,
72, 74
Las Cases 37
Latouche 115, 116, 177
Lautréamont 149, 152-4, 157
Leconte de Lisle 66, 68-9
Legouvé 53
Lemaître 136
Lemercier 53
Lesage 111
Lewis 110, 111
local colour 21, 182
Louis XVI 21
Louis XVII 21
Louis XVIII 21
Louis-Napoleon Bonaparte 14, 121
Louis-Philippe 17, 177
Lucas 130
Lucretius 45
lyric 56; lyricism 55, 56, 60, 61

Maeterlinck 86, 103-7, 161-3
Magnat 94

Magritte 153
Mahon 193
Maistre 113
*mal du siècle* 17
Mallarmé 52, 55, 66, 69, 78-84, 138
Manet 125, 126, 127
Martin 193
Marx 170
Maturin 110-11
Maupassant 48, 50, 129
Mauritius 184, 185
Maurras 172
melodrama 87, 88, 89, 111 112, 152
Mendès 68
Mérimée 25, 26, 27, 29, 37, 47-8
Michelet 25
Mignet 20
Millevoye 53
Milton 15
Mirbeau 188, 190-3
Missolonghi 181
Mistral 172
Molière 87
Montolieu, Mme de 117
moral tale 45
Murger 174, 175
Muslim 182
Musset 17, 18, 22, 33, 34, 35, 36,
37, 53, 54, 55, 59, 90-2, 158,
173, 182-3

Napoleon Bonaparte (Napoleon I)
13, 14, 15, 16, 18, 37, 46, 87,
110, 115, 118, 119, 146
Napoleon III 11, 14, 15, 16, 18, 19,
128, 158, 170, 174
National Theatre (London) 193
Nationalism 146, 172
Naturalism 102, 119, 129-33, 136-7,
138, 139, 145, 146
Nature 21, 61, 64, 66, 72, 87, 110,
139, 135, 143, 156, 158, 160, 174
Navarre, Marguerite de 48

Nerval 60, 135, 146-8, 149, 153, 174, 175, 182
newspapers 112, 120-3
Nietzsche 145
Nodier 46, 112, 113, 168
*nouvelle* 45, 48

Occitan 172
opera 92-3, 164
Orient 182; oriental 68; *Les Orientales* 15, 54
Ottoman Empire 181
Ovid 178

pantheism 60, 159
Paris Commune 171, 172
Parnassianism 66, 68-9, 78
Parny 53
Pascal 160
Péguy 172
Pétain 14
Pierrot 154, 155
Pigault-Lebrun 111
Pinter 162, 163
Pixérécourt 87
Poe 142
*poètes maudits* 66
Ponson du Terrail 123
positivism 164
Prometheus 141
Proteus 163
Proudhon 192
Proust 45, 145, 146
Puccini 175
Pygmalion 179

Quinet 25, 44

Rabelais 164
race 180, 183-6, 193
Rachilde 176, 177, 178
Racine 53, 87, 88
Radcliffe 110

Raphael 126
Rappenau 193
Ravel 159
Realism 20, 21, 23-4, 103, 109, 110, 123-8, 129, 153, 159, 176; realist 102, 109-10, 129, 133; realist drama 102; writing 138-9
Redon 44
Reformation 25
Renaissance 174, 177
Renan 44
Restoration 14, 15, 19, 21, 46, 53, 87, 122, 135
Revolution (1789) 46, 87, 184; (1830) 173; (1848) 23; see also July Revolution
Rimbaud 57, 59, 66, 69, 70, 71-8, 82, 138, 153, 157
*roman gai* 111; *roman-feuilleton* 120-3; *roman noir* 111, 118 (see also Gothic novel); *roman populaire* 111; *roman sentimental* 117; *roman social* 122
Romantic agony 183; *arriviste* novel 16; artist 124; drama 87-93, 112, 157; ego 36; experience 37; generation 107; hero 36; poetry 55; poets 154, 159; self 58; sensibility 34; stirrings 53; travel writing 180-2; vision 124; writer 178
Romanticism 20-1, 135
Romantics 66, 138
Rostand 188-93
Rousseau 37, 38
Royalist 15, 25, 171, 172

Sade 154
Saint Augustine 37
Saint Louis 21
Sainte-Beuve 33, 34, 35, 36, 37
Sand 18, 25, 44, 59, 116-20, 124-5, 174, 176

Sanson 37
Scarron 111
Schepisi 193
Schopenhauer 138, 139, 141, 144,
    155
Schwob 45
science fiction 141, 142
Scott 25, 26, 27, 112
Scribe 93, 101
Second Empire see Empire
Senancour 34
serialisation 116, 120-3; see also
    *roman-feuilleton*
Shakespeare 53, 87, 90, 91, 154,
    155, 159
slavery 184
soap opera 121
*spleen* 60, 151, 152
Staël, Mme de 113-16, 176
Stendhal 15, 18-19, 20-1, 23, 24,
    26-9, 30, 37, 38, 41-4, 88, 109,
    115-16, 127, 144, 145, 169, 177,
    180, 181
Sterne 168, 175
*style indirect libre* 128
Sue 112, 120, 121, 122, 123
Surrealism 153, 154, 165
Swedenborg 65, 124
Symbolism 83, 103-7; Symbolist
    drama 103-7, 161-3; Symbolist
    movement 161
synaesthesia 64-5, 75, 82

Taine 129, 145
Talleyrand 37
Taylor, Baron 180-1
television 103, 121
Terror, The 183

Thierry 25
Thiers 20
Third Republic 169
Tocqueville 25
tragedy 53, 87, 89, 106, 125
Tristan, Flora 176

Uccello 45
Unconscious, the 144, 155, 157
*Union générale* 170

Vallès 172
Vauvenargues 151
Venus 47
Verdi 92, 93
Verlaine 54, 59, 66, 69-71, 76, 138
Verne 135, 141-4
Versailles, *Versaillais*, 171
verse: alexandrines 53, 54, 56, 57,
    68; *enjambement* 89; octosylla-
    bles 56; pentasyllables 69;
    periphrasis 53, 89; rules 89
Vidocq 37
Vigny 25, 29, 60, 90-2, 93, 173, 175
Villiers de l'Isle-Adam 49, 103,
    135, 138, 139-41, 142, 144, 147,
    179
Voltaire 53, 87

Wagner 164
Waterloo 13, 115
Wilde 94, 174

Zola 102, 110, 119, 129-32, 135,
    136-7, 144, 145, 146, 170, 171,
    177, 186, 187
Zoppini 142